Great Bread Machine Baking

Great Bread Machine Baking

Over 250 Recipes for Breads From A to Z

Marlene Brown

Produced by
The Philip Lief Group, Inc.

This book is dedicated to my husband, John Oliphant,
my right hand man in the kitchen and in life,
and to my gift children, Heather and Dan, who are
always willing to loan me their taste buds,
and never fail to light up my life.

This edition published by Barnes & Noble, Inc.,
by arrangement with The Philip Lief Group, Inc.

1999 Barnes & Noble Books

ISBN 0-7607-1353-7

Book design by Kathryn Plosica

Printed and bound in the United States of America

01 02 03 MC 9 8 7 6 5 4

FG

Acknowledgments

This book represents the 25th cookbook project I have worked on, either on my own or for food industry clients. My experience with bread machines goes back a decade, when I wrote the first use and care/cookbooklet for Zojirushi's original American bread machine model.

Knowing that I'd have to convert my kitchen into a testing "lab," I called not only on Zojirushi, but also six other top bread machine manufacturers to share their latest machines with me for testing the 200-plus recipes needed for this book. Special thanks go to the following people and manufacturers: Jeff Hamano of Zojirushi America Corporation (who sent two different machines: Zojirushi models BBCC-V20, and BBCC-S15A), Pat Boehm of Appliance Corporation of America (who sent Welbilt model ABM6000), Marilyn Wise of Toastmaster (who sent Toastmaster Corner Bakery Bread & Dessert Maker), Barbara Westfield of Salton Maxim Housewares, Inc. (who sent Breadman Ultimate model TR2200 '97), Susan Anderson of Regal Ware, Inc. (who sent Regal K6745S Super Rapid Breadmaker), and Ann Knutson of West Bend (who sent West Bend Baker's Choice Plus Bread Machine and Dough Maker).

Just for fun, I kept a running tally of the amount of flour used during my frequent bread-baking marathons, and the number of recipe tests I did to finalize the recipes. Here are the results: 475 pounds of bread flour were used, and 529 recipe tests were done to insure the success of all of the recipes in this book!

My longtime friend and colleague, Mary Bartz at General Mills Inc., was a great catalyst, and she supplied me with enough Gold Medal Bread Flour for all of my recipe testing. Glenna Vance of Universal Foods likewise provided plenty of Red Star Yeast, and offered sage advice along the way, being a bread machine expert herself.

Love and gratitude to my husband John, who put up with my constantly-running bread machine factory for months on end, tasted many samples of bread, and efficiently typed up several chapters of recipes. Thanks to my parents, Lorraine and Bill Brown, who called me frequently with their recipe ideas and encouragement. Thank you to Heather and Dan, as well as my friends and neighbors, and my husband's coworkers, who cheerfully took all of the excess loaves off my hands, became expert tasters, and passed on their constructive comments!

Hugs and gratitude go to my friend and client Jamie Saxon of The Philip Lief Group, who brought this project to me, and guided it carefully along the way; to Jim Pomager, Associate Editor, for his patient efforts, and to the excellent staff of The Philip Lief Group. Last but not least, thank you, Carol Kelly-Gangi of Barnes and Noble Books, for your support in making this project possible.

Marlene Brown

Contents

CHAPTER 4: Sweet Breads for the Sweet • 70

CHAPTER 5: Vegetable, Cheese, and Herb Breads • 96

CHAPTER 6: Sourdough Breads • 122

CHAPTER 9: Glazes, Butters, and Spreads for Breads • 202

CHAPTER 10: Quick Breads, Jams, and Easy Treats • 216

CHAPTER 11: Delectable Uses for Day-Old Bread • 242

CHAPTER

1

Savvy Baking with Your Bread Machine

Once an occasional treat, fresh homemade bread is now an everyday pleasure that can be had by anyone who owns a bread machine. Even if you've never baked your own bread before, you will be able to experience the satisfaction of producing your own loaves—and the wonderful aroma that accompanies them—by investing just five or ten minutes of your time.

Whether you are a complete bread-baking novice, a scratch bread baker, or a bread machine enthusiast, you'll find all of the tips and tricks you need to know in this book, along with over 250 interesting and fun new recipes to try. Let's get started!

A Simple Learning Curve

If you start by following these five golden rules for success, you're guaranteed to get the best use from your bread machine.

1. **Read your bread machine manual.** Take a few minutes to learn what each feature does, how to properly install the bread pan and the kneading paddle, and the recommended ingredient order for your machine. Do the liquids go in first or on top? The recipes in this book list liquids first, and flours and yeast last. Follow your manufacturer's tips on which ingredients to measure into the machine first.
2. **Choose the right recipe.** Know the capacity of your machine and which size loaf fits best in your bread pan. Check any variations ahead of time if you plan to use them.
3. **Use only the freshest ingredients—and use them at the proper temperature.** Warm a cup of milk from the refrigerator by microwaving it for just a few seconds. Rinse eggs under warm water to remove the chill. Cut up butter or margarine so it mixes well into the dough. Give your loaf-to-be every advantage!
4. **Measure ingredients like a scientist.** It's not difficult, and proper measuring will pay wonderful dividends—with consistently great results, no matter what you are baking. (See the section called "How to Measure Ingredients Accurately" on page 12).

5. **Get organized before you begin.** Assemble all of your ingredients before you begin. Measure them into the machine in the order recommended by your machine's manufacturer. Better yet, store all of your bread-making dry ingredients in canisters near your machine, so they will always be handy and you can keep track of anything that needs to be replenished.

Baking Tips

How Many Slices Are in a Loaf?

The recipes in this book allow you to choose to make either a 1½- or 2-pound recipe. If you're not sure about which size loaf to make, here's a good guide for the number of slices you can count on:

1½-pound loaf–12 slices per loaf

2-pound loaf–16 slices per loaf

Bread Machine Cycles

Here are the typical cycles found on most bread machines:

- **Basic or White Bread Cycle.** Averaging 3 to 4 hours and intended for use with many simple bread recipes, you'll use this all-purpose setting most often.
- **Whole Wheat or Whole-Grain Cycle.** With the longer kneading and rising times characteristic of this cycle, you can produce whole-grain loaves that have good texture and good height. Choose this cycle for recipes that call for whole-grain flours, or cereals.
- **French Bread Cycle.** Because they have little or no sugar, French breads require longer rising times and a higher baking temperature. Use this cycle for breads that have little or no fat or sugar.
- **Sweet Bread Cycle.** This cycle is intended for breads that have a higher fat or sugar content, or recipes that call for eggs or cheese. The baking temperature is lower to prevent a burned or dark crust, which can be caused by these ingredients.
- **Raisin/Nut Cycle.** During kneading, some machines can grind dried fruits or nuts too finely. This cycle alerts you with a signal, such as a beep, late in the kneading process so you can add these ingredients just in time to have them mixed lightly into the dough.

- **Dough Cycle.** This function allows you to remove the dough just before the baking cycle, so you can add fillings and/or shape the dough into rolls, pizza crusts, breadsticks, flatbreads, or anything else you like. You bake these breads in your conventional oven.
- **Rapid-Bake Cycle.** If you like to use quick-rise yeast, select this cycle. It can run anywhere from 30 minutes to 2 hours shorter than the basic bread cycle, depending on the machine.
- **Delay-Bake or Timed-Bake Cycle.** Standard on just about every machine, this handy cycle allows you to measure ingredients into the bread pan now, then program the machine to complete the cycle up to 24 hours later. *Note that recipes calling for milk, butter, eggs, cheese, or other perishable ingredients should not be delayed more than 1 hour, for food safety reasons.*
- **Quick Bread or Cake Cycle.** For nonyeast breads, quick bread mixes, or simple cake recipes, this cycle simply mixes and bakes. The baking time can vary considerably among models.
- **Jam Cycle.** Simple fruit jams, chutneys, and fruit sauces can be made in the bread pan, which becomes a veritable saucepan for this cycle. Your jam concoction will be mixed and cooked for 1 to 1½ hours.

Baking Tips

What Size Recipe Should You Make?

Each of the recipes in this book is written with both 1½-pound and 2-pound yields. These options allow you to choose a recipe that fits the capacity of your bread pan. Because pan size can vary so much between models, you should use this guideline: for a 1½-pound loaf, the pan should have a liquid capacity of at least 10 cups. For the 2-pound loaf, a capacity of 12 cups or more is essential. To find out how much your pan can hold, simply measure water into your bread pan.

Ingredient Know-How

A wonderful loaf of bread is only as good as the ingredients that go into it. Follow these well-known rules: use only the freshest ingredients, and use the proper ingredients.

Flours and Grains

- **Bread Flour.** The type of flour recommended for bread machines, this white flour is a higher-protein flour than bleached or unbleached all-purpose flour. More protein in a flour ensures that a larger, higher-quality loaf will result. If you have only all-purpose flour on hand, you can use it, but try adding a "booster" such as 1 to 3 tablespoons of gluten flour or vital wheat gluten.
- **Whole-Grain Flours.** Milled from the entire kernel of the grain, whole wheat and rye flours contain more fiber, fat, vitamins, and minerals than bread or all-purpose flour. All whole wheat flour can be used in a bread, but the loaf will be somewhat smaller than bread made with bread flour and whole wheat flour combined. Rye flour has less gluten for bread structure, so it must be combined with bread flour or whole wheat flour in recipes.
- **Gluten Flour.** This high-protein, low-starch flour is often used for special diets. Added in small amounts to low-gluten flours (like rye flour) or low-protein all-purpose flour, gluten flour improves the texture of your bread.
- **Bran.** This is the outer layer of a kernel of grain, such as wheat, rye, corn, or wheat. Corn bran and wheat bran are highest in fiber. Bran cereals are an excellent way to add bran (and fiber) to bread.
- **Cornmeal.** Cornmeal is coarsely ground dried corn (white, yellow, or blue, depending on the type of corn used). Cornmeal can be added to bread recipes in small amounts; it adds a bit of sweetness to bread as well as a slightly crumbly texture.
- **Cracked Wheat.** It's just that—wheat kernels that have been cracked, or broken up. For the recipes in this book, the cracked wheat is cooked like a cereal, then added to the bread pan.
- **Oats.** This is a cereal grain with a nutty flavor that lends an interesting texture to breads. Quick-cooking oats or old-fashioned rolled oats are interchangeable in bread recipes.
- **Wheat Germ.** The true embryo of the wheat kernel, wheat germ adds a wonderful nutty taste and crunch to breads. It should not

replace flour in a recipe, nor should you need to reduce the amount of flour when adding it to a recipe.

Leavening Agents

(Be sure to observe the expiration dates on these products.)

- **Active Dry Yeast.** A highly stable yeast in dry form, this yeast is perfect for bread machines. Fed by sugar, warm liquid (around 80°F), and a pleasantly warm environment, yeast will multiply effectively, allowing bread to rise. One packet of active dry yeast contains 2¼ teaspoons yeast.
- **Bread Machine Yeast.** A strain of active dry yeast developed and packaged especially for bread machines, it comes in handy 4-ounce jars and is interchangeable with active dry yeast.
- **Fresh or Compressed Yeast.** Available in a refrigerated package, this highly perishable yeast is not recommended for use in bread machines.
- **Quick-Rise Yeast.** This is a fast-acting strain of dry yeast that requires only one rise, so it significantly shortens the entire bread-baking cycle. It is interchangeable with active dry yeast, but must be used in conjunction with the rapid-bake cycle in bread machines. If you choose to use quick-rise yeast, follow the directions on the package for the recommended temperature needed for the liquid in your recipe. I don't recommend using quick-rise yeast in sourdough breads, or in breads containing eggs, cheese, or two or more whole-grain flours, because these breads really need longer rising times to be successful in the bread machine.
- **Sourdough Starter.** A mixture of flour, water, sugar, and yeast, a starter is a mixture that is left to "sour," or ferment, for two to four days. During this time, it develops a sour flavor and a bubbly effervescence. Used as a leavener for yeast bread, a starter imparts a sour flavor and an open texture to bread. See Chapter 6 for sourdough starter and bread recipes for your bread machine.
- **Baking Powder.** Used in quick breads, not yeast breads, this is a type of chemical leavening that does not require a rising time. Quick breads and cakes made with baking powder can simply be mixed and baked.
- **Baking Soda.** Another type of chemical leavening used in quick breads, cakes, and muffins, baking soda activates when it comes in

contact with liquid ingredients. It cannot be substituted for baking powder, but is sometimes used together with it.

Bread Enhancers

- **Bread Fortifiers or Enhancers.** Formulated to produce breads with a better texture and a nice high rise, these ingredients are often recommended for whole-grain breads, which by their nature are lower in volume. The products also improve the nutrient content. Use as directed.
- **Dough Conditioners.** Made from inactive dry yeast, these products lend structural stability to the dough and also encourage greater yeast activity. Use as directed.
- **Flavor Enhancers.** Designed specifically for use with bread machines, some are designed for any bread dough, others are formulated for sweet dough. These enhance the flavors of grains and yeast in bread. Follow the package directions for use.
- **Vital Wheat Gluten.** This is a concentrated form of gluten—not a flour, but a dried gluten protein with very little starch left. It will improve the volume, shape, flavor, and texture of yeast breads, and also extend freshness. Follow the package directions for adding this baking aid to any bread recipe.

Baking Tips

A Simple Test for Yeast

Red Star Yeast recommends this simple test to determine the strength of your yeast: Test 1 package of active dry yeast or quick-rise yeast by measuring ½ cup of warm water (110–115°F) into a 1-cup measuring cup. Add 1 tablespoon granulated sugar and 1 package of the yeast (2¼ teaspoons) and stir until blended. After 10 minutes, if the yeast mixture has become activated and multiplied to the 1-cup mark, the yeast is very active. You can then use this mixture in your dough; just be certain to reduce the amount of liquid in your recipe by ½ cup.

Baking Tips

Judging the Temperature of Liquids

As you know, the temperature of liquid ingredients and purees is crucial to success because the right temperature allows the yeast to do its job. Even though many bread machines have a pre-warming function, most manufacturers call for room-temperature liquids to begin with. Assume that liquid at 80 to 90°F is the optimum. How do you determine that? You can invest in a thermometer, or just touch the liquid to the inside of your wrist (mothers of newborns are veterans at this!). It should feel comfortably warm. Liquid that is warmer than 100°F will feel too warm, and it will probably inhibit some of the yeast action. Cold milk heated in a microwave oven for 25 to 30 seconds and stirred should be close to room temperature. If you are using chilled mashed potatoes or a vegetable or fruit puree that's been refrigerated, mix them into the necessary liquid and warm the mixture in the microwave briefly.

Liquid Ingredients

- **Water.** Used in bread recipes, water produces a crisper crust. The softness or hardness of your water (in other words, the pH balance) can directly affect your bread dough. If you continually find yourself with unusually sticky bread dough (a sign of very soft water), or if you know you have extremely hard or soft water, switch to bottled or distilled water for use in bread machine recipes.
- **Milk.** Milk adds a certain richness to the flavor and texture of bread. It also adds to the keeping quality of bread and is responsible for a softer crust. Use any type of milk, from whole milk to nonfat milk, interchangeably. However, do not use unpasteurized milk unless it has been scalded first, since this milk contains enzymes that inhibit yeast action.

- **Nonfat Dry Milk.** This is skim milk minus the liquid. To substitute dry milk or powdered milk for liquid milk use this formula: 1/4 cup dry milk powder mixed with 1 cup water = 1 cup milk.
- **Buttermilk.** Buttermilk adds distinctive tangy taste and richness to bread. If you're out of buttermilk, here's an easy substitute: measure 1 tablespoon of vinegar or lemon juice into your measuring cup, then add regular milk to equal the amount of buttermilk needed. Let the mixture stand about 5 minutes, or until it curdles.
- **Fruit Juices.** By adding fruit juice to a recipe, you can increase the sweetness and fruit flavor of a loaf. Substitute fruit juice for half of the liquid in your recipe; experiment if you would like to use more.
- **Vegetable Juices.** Tomato juice and potato water (liquid drained off from cooked potatoes) produce very high loaves of bread with a slightly coarser texture. Breads made with these juices are typically of high quality, and they rise quickly. They are also very nutritious.

Salt

Talk about a flavor enhancer! Salt does many things besides rounding out the flavor of bread; it also helps to control the yeast action, so the bread rises just enough. It adds a golden color to the crust, too. I used common table salt in these recipes. "Light" salt is not recommended. For people on low-salt diets, try the Salt-Free White Bread recipe (page 28).

Sweeteners

- **Granulated Sugar.** Refined white sugar, most commonly used in bread machine recipes, enhances the action of the yeast. Too much sugar, however, slows down yeast and reduces bread volume.
- **Brown Sugar.** This is granulated sugar processed with molasses. Light brown sugar has less molasses flavor and a lighter color; dark brown sugar has more molasses flavor and a darker color. Light and dark brown sugars are interchangeable.
- **Powdered or Confectioners' Sugar.** This is pulverized refined white sugar. It is used when a very fine consistency is needed, such as in frostings and glazes.
- **Honey.** A liquid form of sugar produced by bees from flower nectar. Honey can be substituted for molasses in recipes, but should never be substituted for granulated or brown sugar in bread machine recipes, since honey is a liquid ingredient.
- **Molasses.** A thick brown syrup made from the juices of refined sugarcane. The flavor has been concentrated, or boiled down, to

produce a rich, heavy, sweet flavor. Light and dark varieties of molasses are available and are interchangeable.

- **Maple Syrup.** A natural syrup refined from the sap of maple trees, maple syrup can add a distinctive, caramel-maple flavor to breads. It can be used in place of honey or molasses, but it will produce a more delicate sweet flavor.

Fats and Oils

- **Butter or Margarine.** These solid fats add a lot of flavor and soften the texture of bread. Sweet breads contain a higher proportion of these fats. Use softened (but not melted) butter or margarine in recipes, and cut up these fats before adding them to the bread pan so they will be easily incorporated into the dough. Do not substitute low-fat spreads for bona fide butter or margarine.
- **Vegetable Oil.** Choose your favorite oil, whether it be corn, peanut, or canola, when vegetable oil is called for in bread machine recipes.
- **Olive Oil.** Any type of olive oil can be used when vegetable or olive oil is called for in recipes; note, however, that extra-virgin or flavored olive oils will add a stronger flavor and may not be appropriate for delicately flavored or sweet breads.
- **Flavored Oils.** Interesting oils such as garlic, walnut, and sesame can add unique flavor to breads. It's fun to experiment with these oils in recipes to find which you like best; substitute for vegetable oil. (Note: do not use chili oils; they are far too spicy for bread doughs.)

Eggs

I used extra-large eggs in all the recipes in this book. If large eggs are all you have on hand, check the dough very carefully during the kneading process; you may have to add more liquid. To use egg substitute, you may use ¼ cup of the liquid egg substitute for each egg needed. Use eggs at room temperature or rinse them under warm water for a minute to take the chill off refrigerated eggs.

Fruits and Vegetables

- **Dried Fruits.** Chop them before adding them to your bread machine dough. Since the kneading paddle can pulverize chopped dried fruit, add the fruit to the dough near the end of the kneading cycle, so the pieces will be lightly but efficiently distributed throughout the dough. Adding dried fruit too late in the cycle will result in a layer of dried fruit at the bottom of the loaf.

- **Fresh Fruit.** Do not substitute fresh fruit for dried because it contains water, which can cause a heavy loaf or gum layers. Follow the recipe exactly when fresh fruit is called for.
- **Pureed Fruits and Vegetables.** Used in many recipes in this book; you'll find that pureed fruits and vegetables in the jar (found in the baby food section of your market) are wonderful convenience products. Or you can try canned, or frozen, thawed vegetables, well drained and pureed in your food processor or blender.
- **Mashed Potatoes.** Mashed potatoes are a nice addition to many breads. You can use any type of potato, including sweet potato, when mashed potatoes are listed. Remember that if the mashed potatoes are freshly made, or have been refrigerated, you need to bring them up or down to the proper (80–90°F) temperature.

Nuts and Seeds

- **Chopped or Sliced Nuts.** Your favorite nuts can be used interchangeably in bread recipes. Try walnuts, hazelnuts, almonds, pine nuts, pecans, macadamia nuts, peanuts, or Brazil nuts.
- **Toasted Nuts.** Use your toaster oven to quickly toast a small amount. Or you can place nuts on a baking sheet with sides in a 350°F oven for 8 to 10 minutes until they turn a golden brown color.
- **Seeds.** Sesame, caraway, poppy, and sunflower seeds are as versatile as nuts. To toast seeds, just put them into a small nonstick skillet and toast them over medium heat, stirring constantly, until golden.

Herbs and Spices

- **Dried Herbs and Spices.** Use them straight from the jar. There is no need to crush dried herbs; the kneading action of the machine will distribute them throughout the dough. Be sure your dried herbs and spices are fresh; they should generally be stored no longer than three months.
- **Five-Spice Powder.** This spice powder, available in the Asian section of supermarkets or in specialty markets, is a wonderful substitute for cinnamon or nutmeg in any of the recipes in this book. It's a combination of anise, fennel, Szechuan pepper, ground cinnamon, and cloves, but may also contain a dash of ginger.

- **Fresh Herbs.** Use these wherever a dried herb is listed. Follow this equivalent: 1 tablespoon chopped fresh herbs = 1 teaspoon dried herbs. When using fresh herbs, use the leaves only, not the stems.
- **Garlic.** Fresh garlic tends to inhibit yeast action, so these recipes call for garlic salt to add garlic flavor.
- **Saffron.** An expensive spice, saffron is harvested from the autumn crocus. Marketed in "thread" form, it needs to be dissolved in the warm liquid that's called for in the recipe in order for the spice to be well distributed during kneading. It adds a golden color and a distinctive flavor to bread. You can substitute turmeric for the same yellow color and a bit of the same flavor.

Chocolate and Cocoa

- **Chocolate Chips.** Also called chocolate morsels, either milk chocolate or semisweet can be used. If chocolate chips are added at the beginning of the cycle, they will melt and color all of the dough. If added later (as when nuts and dried fruits are added), they will cause more of a marbled appearance in dough.
- **Semisweet Chocolate.** Sometimes called bittersweet chocolate, semisweet chocolate has more cocoa butter and sugar in it than sweet chocolate does. It is used in melted form in the recipes in this book. Be sure to allow melted chocolate to cool to room temperature before adding it to the bread machine. One square of chocolate is equivalent to 1 ounce of chocolate.
- **Unsweetened Chocolate.** This is simply chocolate without sugar or flavoring added, so the flavor is quite bitter. Buy unsweetened chocolate in 1-ounce squares, or you can purchase the melted product that comes in handy individual packets.
- **Unsweetened Cocoa Powder.** Cocoa powder is created by pressing most of the fat out of pure chocolate. Do not substitute a presweetened cocoa powder or an instant cocoa mix for unsweetened cocoa powder. To measure it, just scoop it out of its container.

How to Measure Ingredients Accurately

Having on hand a set of dry and liquid measuring cups and measuring spoons is a must for accurate measuring. With "dry" measuring cups, you measure right to the top and level off. Glass or "liquid" measuring cups have measuring lines you can use to precisely measure any wet or liquid ingredients.

Baking Tips

Helpful Measurements

1½ teaspoons = ½ tablespoon

3 teaspoons = 1 tablespoon

4 tablespoons = ¼ cup

5⅓ tablespoons = ⅓ cup

16 tablespoons = 1 cup = 8 ounces = ½ pint

2 cups = 16 ounces = 1 pint = ½ quart

4 cups = 32 ounces = 2 pints = 1 quart

Metric/U.S. Measurement Equivalents

⅛ teaspoon = 0.5 ml

¼ teaspoon = 1.25 ml

½ teaspoon = 2.5 ml

1 teaspoon = 5 ml

1¼ teaspoons = 6.25 ml

1½ teaspoons = 7.5 ml

2 teaspoons = 10 ml

1 tablespoon = 15 ml

¼ cup = 50 ml

⅓ cup = 75 ml

½ cup = 125 ml

⅔ cup = 150 ml

¾ cup = 175 ml

1 cup = 250 ml

2 cups = 1 pint

2 pints = 1 litre

1 ounce = 28 grams

1 pound = 0.45 kilograms

To measure flour, spoon the flour lightly into the appropriate dry measuring cup to just above the top of the cup; don't sift the flour or tap the cup on the counter to "settle" it. Use a table knife to smoothly level off the excess. Use this same technique when measuring dry ingredients into measuring spoons. Scooping a measuring cup into a canister of flour means you'll be measuring "heavy"; this method packs almost 1/4 cup more flour into the cup. You can also use dry measuring cups for purees or peanut butter.

For liquid ingredients, place the glass measuring cup on the counter or a level surface. Pour the liquid into it, and read the measurement you need at eye level. If you come across an odd measurement in a recipe, such as 3/4 cup + 1 tablespoon liquid, use the measuring marks on the cup, or measure 3/4 cup, then use a tablespoon measure to add the additional tablespoon of liquid.

Bread Machine Techniques for Success

The Dough Is the Thing!

Check the dough after the first 5 minutes of the kneading process by lifting the cover and inserting your finger into it, if necessary. It's a good-looking doughball you're after—one nice, rounded ball of dough shaped around the kneading paddle(s) that is only slightly sticky to the touch. It should not look dry or crumbly, nor should it be wet or mushy looking. A tablespoon or two of flour or liquid added to your dough during the kneading process (if necessary) can mean the difference between a nicely risen loaf with a domed top and a coarsely textured loaf that's concave in the center.

Add liquid, a tablespoon at a time, to dough that appears too dry—dry dough does not cling together or has lots of residual dough in the corners of the bread pan. If necessary, insert a rubber spatula in the sides and corners of the bread pan to scrape up all the unmixed bits of dough. Watch carefully, and add 1 to 2 tablespoons of liquid if you don't see a cohesive ball of dough forming.

Add flour, a tablespoon at a time, if the dough is sticking to the sides of the pan or feels very moist when you insert your finger into it. Scrape the pan sides and corners with your trusty rubber spatula to be certain that all the dry ingredients have mixed into the dough. Continue adding flour, just a tablespoon at a time, watching the kneading action until you have your dough ball.

Crust

You have three choices for baking breads in the machine: light, medium, or dark crust setting. Experimentation will tell you which setting works best for you. For the recipes in this book, I used the medium setting; however, I've recommended either the light or dark setting when it seemed more appropriate to a specific recipe.

Removing Bread From the Pan

No matter which yeast bread setting you choose, remove the bread from the machine (and the pan) as soon as the cycle is completed. Leaving the bread in the pan can result in a loaf with a wrinkled or collapsed top and a soggy bottom. If the bread sticks to the pan, do not use metal utensils to remove it. Allow the loaf to stand in the pan for five or ten minutes. With a potholder, jiggle the kneading paddle(s) under the pan and turn it a half turn in both directions. Then shake the pan vigorously to release the loaf. Remove the kneading paddle(s) with a pot holder, tongs, or the handle end of a wooden spoon. Next time, spray the kneading paddle and the pan sides with vegetable oil cooking spray; this usually makes removal easier.

For quick bread and cake recipes, allow the bread to stand in the pan for 15 to 20 minutes before trying to remove it. Otherwise, the kneading paddle(s) causes the hot, tender loaf to break in the center as you are trying to remove it.

Whatever type of bread you make, cool your just-baked loaf on a rack to allow for air circulation as it cools. To serve the bread warm, wait 20 minutes before slicing it; then use a serrated knife to cut neat, clean slices.

Preparing Bread Doughs

In Chapter 7, you'll find nine different dough recipes, each with several filling and shaping variations. For all of these recipes, you'll use the Dough cycle, then remove the dough from the machine to shape, fill, and bake the dough conventionally.

When you remove the dough from the bread pan, transfer it to a lightly floured surface or countertop and fold the dough over or knead it about ten or twelve times to remove excess gas. If you have problems shaping or rolling the dough, cover the dough with plastic wrap or a towel and let it "rest" for 15 minutes. Then try again.

After shaping, the dough will probably need to rise one more time. Cover the dough loosely with plastic wrap or a dampened cotton (not terry) kitchen towel—to keep air from drying it out, but leaving room for expansion—and place it in a warm or draft-free location. Set your timer for the minimum rising time stated in the recipe (usually 30 minutes) and check the dough by observing its size. Or, insert the tip of your index finger into a corner of the dough—if it bounces back right away, it probably needs 15 more minutes of rising time. If the dent remains, it's ready to bake.

Converting Your Own Recipes for the Bread Machine

Most of the familiar bread recipes you have made from scratch should work well in your bread machine. You may have to make a few adjustments, however. Here are some simple guidelines to follow:

- Start by comparing your own recipe to a similar recipe in this book. Most handmade recipes make two loaves of yeast bread. Cutting the recipe in half will probably leave you with ingredient proportions similar to either the 1½- or the 2-pound recipe.
- The amount of flour is key because that determines the proportions of all other ingredients in the final recipe. A 1½-pound recipe should have 3 to 3⅓ cups of flour; a 2-pound recipe will call for 3 ½ to 4 cups of flour.
- If your recipe calls for all-purpose flour, substitute bread flour.
- If your recipe contains more than one type of flour, reduce all of the flours equally, but be sure the total amount of flour in the recipe fits the capacity of your machine.
- If you are cutting your own recipe in half and you are left with some odd measurements, you can choose to go up or down on the measure to make it even. For example, if you don't want to try and measure ⅞ cup of flour, go up to 1 cup or down to ¾ cup, and reduce or increase the liquid a bit to compensate.
- Refer to the ingredients in and cycles used for the bread recipes in this book as representative guidelines for converting your own recipes.
- Most important, watch the dough ball formation during the first few minutes of kneading, so you can fine-tune your recipe to the machine.
- If you've followed all of these tips, but the bread doesn't seem to bake up very well, use the recipe with the Dough cycle. Remove the

dough and shape it and bake it in your conventional oven—you'll still save lots of time and energy by using your bread machine.

- Take notes along the way, and know that you may have to try a recipe two or three times in the machine to perfect it. Then you can enjoy Aunt Elaine's feather-light rolls, or Aunt Tillie's coffee bread more easily (and more often) than ever before!

Using Bread Mixes in Your Machine

In the baking section of your supermarket, you'll find several brands of bread machine mixes in a wide array of flavors. Expect the same quality that you would get if you used a cake mix instead of making the cake from scratch.

In addition to yeast bread mixes, I found that the quick bread mixes, originally developed for your conventional oven, are quite successful in bread machines with a quick bread or cake setting. The quality of these mixes is excellent, and because the quick bread cycle is so much shorter than the yeast bread cycles, it makes even more sense to save time with good mixes like these.

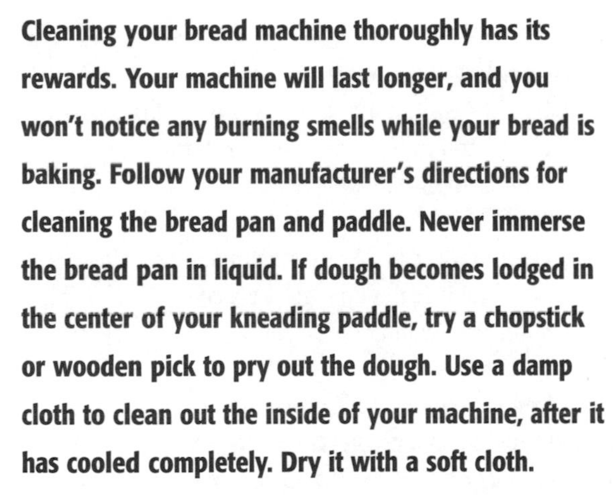

Baking Tips

Bread Machine Maintenance

Cleaning your bread machine thoroughly has its rewards. Your machine will last longer, and you won't notice any burning smells while your bread is baking. Follow your manufacturer's directions for cleaning the bread pan and paddle. Never immerse the bread pan in liquid. If dough becomes lodged in the center of your kneading paddle, try a chopstick or wooden pick to pry out the dough. Use a damp cloth to clean out the inside of your machine, after it has cooled completely. Dry it with a soft cloth.

Bread Machine Baking Troubleshooting

Try these solutions to common bread machine problems.

The machine is on, but the dough is not being mixed.

1. Your machine may be in a preheating cycle.
   Check the manual or read notations on the control panel.
2. The kneading paddle has not been inserted properly.
   Unplug machine, adjust the kneading paddle(s), or push it(them) down fully on the stem(s).

The loaf rose too high, or rose and collapsed while baking.

1. The recipe was too large for the bread pan, causing bread to rise to the top of machine, then fall.
   Try the 1½-pound recipe.
2. Not enough salt was used, or it was left out.
   Use the amount of salt recommended in recipe, or increase salt by ¼ teaspoon.
3. You are baking at a high altitude.
   See manufacturer's suggestions for high-altitude baking.
4. Too much yeast or the wrong type was used.
   Use yeast amount given in recipe; if necessary, reduce yeast by ⅛-¼ teaspoon.
5. You are baking in humid weather conditions.
   In high humidity, reduce liquid by 1-2 tablespoons, and/or reduce yeast by ⅛-¼ teaspoon.

The loaf is shorter than average; or the texture is heavy and dense.

1. Breads with whole-grain flours or cereals are shorter in volume.
   Use some bread flour in place of a portion of the whole-grain flour.
2. The dough was too dry, not enough liquid used.
   Add 1-2 tablespoons additional liquid.
3. The yeast was old.
   Discard yeast that is past the expiration date; use fresh yeast.
4. Sugar was omitted, or not enough was used.
   Add recommended amount of sugar.
5. Too much flour was used.
   Reduce flour amount by 1-2 tablespoons.
6. Too many additional ingredients were added, such as nuts or dried fruit.
   Use ¼ cup nuts or chopped ingredients per cup of flour in recipe.
7. The yeast came in contact with liquids before the machine cycle began.
   Keep yeast separate from liquid ingredients.
8. The liquid was too cold or too hot.

Measure temperature of liquid, or use all liquids at room temperature (80°F).

The loaf has a dip in the center.

1. Too much liquid was used.
   Reduce liquid by 1-2 tablespoons.
2. Not enough flour was used.
   Add 1-2 tablespoons more flour
3. Too much yeast was used.
   Reduce yeast by 1/8-1/4 teaspoon.
4. Fruits or vegetables added were not well drained.
   Squeeze fruits and vegetables dry, or drain well on paper towels before using.

Loaf has a rough, uneven, or gnarled appearance.

1. Too much flour was used, or the dough was too dry.
   Reduce the amount of flour, or add 1-2 tablespoons of liquid.
2. An all whole-grain recipe was used with lots of fruits and nuts added.
   Lighten a whole-grain recipe by substituting bread flour for some of the whole-grains, and use 1/4 cup chopped fruit or nuts per cup of flour.

There are large, uneven holes in the bread, or the bread has a coarse texture.

1. Too much yeast was used.
   Reduce yeast by 1/8-1/4 teaspoon.
2. Quick-rise yeast was used.
   Use regular active dry or bread machine yeast on a regular cycle.
3. Not enough salt was used.
   Use recommended amount of salt.

Bread has gummy layers in it, or the bottom crust is soggy.

1. Too much liquid and not enough flour was used.
   Reduce liquid by 2 tablespoons.
2. The loaf was left too long in the pan after baking.
   Remove bread from pan promptly at the end of the cycle.

The machine makes grinding noises during kneading.

1. Too much flour or whole grains were used.
   Reduce flour by 2 tablespoons, or substitute some bread flour for a portion of the whole grains used.
2. Not enough liquid was used to make a smooth dough ball.
   Add 1-2 tablespoons liquid and observe the dough ball.
3. Kneading paddle(s) was not properly inserted in the pan.
   Push kneading paddle(s) firmly down into the bread pan.

CHAPTER 2

Bread Classics

CLASSIC WHITE BREAD

BUTTERMILK WHITE BREAD

RICH EGG BREAD

OVERNIGHT WHITE BREAD

WHITE BREAD PLUS

FAT-FREE WHITE BREAD

SALT-FREE WHITE BREAD

CRUSTY FRENCH BREAD

BEST RAISIN BREAD

CINNAMON RAISIN LOAF

CHALLAH WITH HONEY & RAISINS

FRENCH ONION BREAD

CHEDDAR ONION BREAD

DILL COTTAGE CHEESE LOAF

THREE-HERB BREAD

SALLY LUNN BREAD

ENGLISH MUFFIN BREAD

POTATO BREAD

HONEY OATMEAL WHEAT BREAD

ANADAMA (CORNMEAL) BREAD

Classic White Bread

For white bread aficionados, this fine-textured loaf will make you proud.

1½-POUND	INGREDIENTS	2-POUND
¾ cup + 2 tablespoons	**Milk**	1 cup
¼ cup	**Water**	⅓ cup
1½ tablespoons	**Butter or margarine, softened**	2 tablespoons
1½ tablespoons	**Sugar**	3 tablespoons
1½ teaspoons	**Salt**	2 teaspoons
3¼ cups	**Bread flour, unsifted**	4 cups
2 teaspoons	**Active dry yeast or bread machine yeast**	2½ teaspoons

CYCLE BASIC
CRUST SETTING AS DESIRED

1 If your machine does not have a preheat cycle, combine milk and water and heat in microwave on HIGH power for 30 seconds (or heat in a saucepan for 1 minute to 80°F). Add to the bread pan with remaining ingredients according to the manufacturer's directions for your machine. Set the CYCLE, LOAF SIZE, and CRUST SETTING. Press START.

2 After about 5 minutes of kneading, check the consistency of your dough. If dough is not in a smooth round ball, open lid and with machine ON, add liquid a tablespoon at a time if too dry, or add flour a tablespoon at a time if too wet.

3 Remove the bread promptly from the pan when the machine beeps or on completing the cycle. Cool on rack before slicing.

Buttermilk White Bread

Buttermilk adds a velvety texture and rich flavor to this bread.

1 1/2-POUND	INGREDIENTS	2-POUND
1 cup + 2 tablespoons	**Buttermilk**	1 1/3 cups
1 1/2 tablespoons	**Butter or margarine, softened**	2 tablespoons
2 tablespoons	**Sugar**	3 tablespoons
1 1/4 teaspoons	**Salt**	1 1/2 teaspoons
3 1/4 cups	**Bread flour, unsifted**	4 cups
1 1/2 teaspoons	**Active dry yeast or bread machine yeast**	2 teaspoons

CYCLE BASIC
CRUST SETTING AS DESIRED

1 If your machine does not have a preheat cycle, heat buttermilk in microwave on HIGH power for 30 seconds (or heat in a saucepan for 1 minute to 80°F). Add to the bread pan with remaining ingredients according to the manufacturer's directions for your machine. Set the CYCLE, LOAF SIZE, and CRUST SETTING. Press START.

2 After about 5 minutes of kneading, check the consistency of your dough. If dough is not in a smooth round ball, open lid and with machine ON, add liquid a tablespoon at a time if too dry, or add flour a tablespoon at a time if too wet.

3 Remove the bread promptly from the pan when the machine beeps or on completing the cycle. Cool on rack before slicing.

Baking Tips

No buttermilk on hand? Just measure 1 tablespoon of vinegar into your measuring cup, then add regular milk to the measure of buttermilk you need. Let the mixture stand for 5 minutes to curdle; then use in your recipe.

Rich Egg Bread

For best results, use extra-large eggs for this lovely, wholesome loaf. You can use egg substitute in place of the egg, if you prefer (use 1/4 cup substitute for each egg used).

1 1/2-POUND	INGREDIENTS	2-POUND
1 cup	**Milk***	1 cup
1	**Egg(s)**	2
1 1/2 tablespoons	**Butter or margarine, softened**	2 tablespoons
2 tablespoons	**Sugar**	3 tablespoons
1 1/2 teaspoons	**Salt**	2 teaspoons
3 1/4 cups	**Bread flour, unsifted**	4 cups
2 teaspoons	**Active dry yeast or bread machine yeast**	2 1/2 teaspoons

*Use the same amount for either size loaf.

CYCLE BASIC
CRUST SETTING MEDIUM RECOMMENDED

1. If your machine does not have a preheat cycle, heat milk in microwave on HIGH power for 30 seconds (or heat in a saucepan for 1 minute to 80°F). Add to the bread pan with remaining ingredients according to the manufacturer's directions. Set the CYCLE, LOAF SIZE, and CRUST SETTING. Press START.

2. After about 5 minutes of kneading, check the consistency of your dough. If dough is not in a smooth round ball, open lid and with machine ON, add liquid a tablespoon at a time if too dry, or add flour a tablespoon at a time if too wet.

3. Remove the bread promptly from the pan when the machine beeps or on completing the cycle. Cool on rack before slicing.

Overnight White Bread

Try this recipe the next time you would like to wake up to a fresh hot loaf.

1 1/2-POUND	INGREDIENTS	2-POUND
1 cup + 2 tablespoons	**Water**	1 1/3 cups
1 1/2 tablespoons	**Nonfat dry milk**	2 tablespoons
1 1/2 tablespoons	**Sugar**	2 tablespoons
1 1/2 tablespoons	**Vegetable oil**	2 tablespoons
1 1/2 teaspoons	**Salt**	2 teaspoons
3 cups	**Bread flour, unsifted**	4 cups
1 1/2 teaspoons	**Active dry yeast or bread machine yeast**	2 teaspoons

CYCLE BASIC (DELAY-BAKE CAN BE USED)
CRUST SETTING AS DESIRED

1 Measure the ingredients into the bread pan according to the manufacturer's directions for your machine. Set the CYCLE, LOAF SIZE, and CRUST SETTING. Set the timer for completion as directed in the machine manual. Press START.

2 Remove the bread promptly from the pan when the machine beeps or on completing the cycle. Cool on rack before slicing.

Baking Tips

It's a bit of a gamble to pre-measure bread ingredients and set the machine to begin several hours later, because if you do not observe the condition of the dough after the first 5 minutes of kneading, you can't correct the consistency, if needed. However, this bread has proved to be nearly foolproof.

White Bread Plus

Look for dough conditioners and fortifiers in health food stores, food specialty shops, or baking catalogs.

1 1/2-POUND	INGREDIENTS	2-POUND
1 cup	**Milk***	1 cup
1	**Egg(s)**	2
1 1/2 tablespoons	**Butter or margarine, softened**	2 tablespoons
1 1/2 tablespoons	**Sugar**	2 tablespoons
1 tablespoon	**Vital gluten**	4 teaspoons
1 tablespoon	**Dough conditioner**	4 teaspoons
1 1/2 teaspoons	**Salt**	2 teaspoons
1 1/2 teaspoons	**Natural bread fortifier (optional)**	2 teaspoons
3 1/3 cups	**Bread flour, unsifted**	4 cups
2 1/2 teaspoons	**Active dry yeast or bread machine yeast**	3 teaspoons

*Use the same amount for either size loaf.

VARIATION

For Whole Wheat Bread Plus, use half whole wheat flour and half bread flour for either size loaf.

CYCLE BASIC
CRUST SETTING LIGHT RECOMMENDED

1 If your machine does not have a preheat cycle, heat milk in microwave on HIGH power for 30 seconds (or heat in a saucepan for 1 minute to 80°F). Add to the bread pan with remaining ingredients according to the manufacturer's directions for your machine. Set the CYCLE, LOAF SIZE, and CRUST SETTING. Press START.

2 After about 5 minutes of kneading, check the consistency of your dough. If dough is not in a smooth round ball, open lid and with machine ON, add liquid a tablespoon at a time if too dry, or add flour a tablespoon at a time if too wet.

3 Remove the bread promptly from the pan when the machine beeps or on completing the cycle. Cool on rack before slicing.

Fat-Free White Bread

This guilt-free bread rises very well, and the yogurt enhances the texture.

1 1/2-POUND	INGREDIENTS	2-POUND
1 cup	**Unflavored nonfat yogurt**	1 1/4 cups
1/3 cup	**Water**	1/2 cup
3 tablespoons	**Sugar**	1/4 cup
1 tablespoon	**Nonfat dry milk**	1 1/2 tablespoons
1 teaspoon	**Salt**	1 1/2 teaspoons
3 1/3 cups	**Bread flour, unsifted**	4 cups
2 teaspoons	**Active dry yeast or bread machine yeast**	2 1/4 teaspoons

CYCLE BASIC
CRUST SETTING AS DESIRED

1 If your machine does not have a preheat cycle, combine nonfat yogurt and water and heat in microwave on HIGH power for 30 seconds (or heat in a saucepan for 1 minute to 80°F). Add to the bread pan with remaining ingredients according to the manufacturer's directions for your machine. Set the CYCLE, LOAF SIZE, and CRUST SETTING. Press START.

2 After about 5 minutes of kneading, check the consistency of your dough. If dough is not in a smooth round ball, open lid and with machine ON, add liquid a tablespoon at a time if too dry, or add flour a tablespoon at a time if too wet.

3 Remove the bread promptly from the pan when the machine beeps or on completing the cycle. Cool on rack before slicing.

Salt-Free White Bread

This bread will have a light crust color owing to the lack of salt, so try a dark crust setting to compensate.

1 1/2-POUND	INGREDIENTS	2-POUND
1 cup + 2 tablespoons	**Warm water (80°F)**	1 1/4 cups
3 tablespoons	**Oil**	4 tablespoons
3 1/3 cups	**Bread flour, unsifted**	4 cups
2 teaspoons	**Active dry yeast or bread machine yeast**	2 1/4 teaspoons

CYCLE BASIC (DELAY-BAKE CAN BE USED)
CRUST SETTING DARK RECOMMENDED

1 Measure ingredients into the bread pan according to the manufacturer's directions for your machine. Set the CYCLE, LOAF SIZE, and CRUST SETTING. Press START.

2 After about 5 minutes of kneading, check the consistency of your dough. If dough is not in a smooth round ball, open lid and with machine ON, add liquid a tablespoon at a time if too dry, or add flour a tablespoon at a time if too wet.

3 Remove the bread promptly from the pan when the machine beeps or on completing the cycle. Cool on rack before slicing.

Baking Tips

If eating salt-free bread with salt-free butter pleases your doctor but not your taste-buds, try sprinkling your buttered bread with some Cinnamon Sugar (page 206), or try making one of the easy jams in Chapter 10.

Crusty French Bread

This is a very good bread machine version of classic French bread. For conventionally baked French rolls, baguettes, and breadsticks, see the French Bread and Roll Dough recipe (page 150).

1½-POUND	INGREDIENTS	2-POUND
1 cup + 2 tablespoons	**Warm water (80°F)**	1⅓ cups
1 tablespoon	**Vegetable oil**	2 tablespoons
1½ tablespoons	**Sugar**	2 tablespoons
1 teaspoon	**Salt**	1½ teaspoons
3¼ cups	**Bread flour, unsifted**	4 cups
1¼ teaspoons	**Active dry yeast or bread machine yeast**	1½ teaspoons

CYCLE BASIC OR FRENCH
(DELAY-BAKE CAN BE USED)
CRUST SETTING LIGHT TO MEDIUM

1 Measure ingredients into the bread pan according to the manufacturer's directions for your machine. Set the CYCLE, LOAF SIZE, and CRUST SETTING. Press START.

2 After about 5 minutes of kneading, check the consistency of your dough. If dough is not in a smooth round ball, open lid and with machine ON, add liquid a tablespoon at a time if too dry, or add flour a tablespoon at a time if too wet.

3 Remove the bread promptly from the pan when the machine beeps or on completing the cycle. Cool on rack before slicing.

Best Raisin Bread

For toast, peanut butter sandwiches, or to just spread with butter, you can't beat the old-fashioned goodness of this raisin bread.

1 1/2-POUND	INGREDIENTS	2-POUND
1 cup	**Milk**	1 cup + 2 tablespoons
2 tablespoons	**Water***	2 tablespoons
1 1/2 tablespoons	**Butter or margarine, softened**	2 tablespoons
2 1/2 tablespoons	**Sugar**	3 tablespoons
1 1/4 teaspoons	**Salt**	1 3/4 teaspoons
3 1/3 cups	**Bread flour, unsifted**	4 cups
2 teaspoons	**Active dry yeast or bread machine yeast**	2 1/4 teaspoons
1/2 cup	**Dark or golden raisins or currants**	2/3 cup

*Use the same amount for either size loaf.

CYCLE BASIC OR RAISIN/NUT
CRUST SETTING AS DESIRED

1 If your machine does not have a preheat cycle, combine milk and water and heat in microwave on HIGH power for 30 seconds (or heat in a saucepan for 1 minute to 80°F). Add to the bread pan with remaining ingredients (except raisins or currants) according to the manufacturer's directions for your machine. Measure raisins or currants to add at the beep or according to manufacturer's directions. Set the CYCLE, LOAF SIZE, and CRUST SETTING. Press START.

2 After about 5 minutes of kneading, check the consistency of your dough. If dough is not in a smooth round ball, open lid and with machine ON, add liquid a tablespoon at a time if too dry, or add flour a tablespoon at a time if too wet.

3 Remove the bread promptly from the pan when the machine beeps or on completing the cycle. Cool on rack before slicing.

Cinnamon Raisin Loaf

Finish off this bread with an easy butter and cinnamon-sugar topping right after the baking cycle ends.

1 1/2-POUND	INGREDIENTS	2-POUND
1 cup	**Milk**	1 cup + 2 tablespoons
2 tablespoons	**Water***	2 tablespoons
1 1/2 tablespoons	**Butter or margarine, softened**	2 tablespoons
2 tablespoons	**Brown sugar**	3 tablespoons
1 1/2 teaspoons	**Salt**	2 teaspoons
1/2 teaspoon	**Ground cinnamon**	3/4 teaspoon
3 1/4 cups	**Bread flour, unsifted**	4 cups
1 1/2 teaspoons	**Active dry yeast or bread machine yeast**	2 1/4 teaspoons
1/2 cup	**Dark or golden raisins**	2/3 cup

*Use the same amount for either size loaf.

TOPPING

Brush loaf while hot with 1 tablespoon melted butter; sprinkle with 2 teaspoons Cinnamon Sugar (page 206).

CYCLE BASIC OR RAISIN/NUT
CRUST SETTING AS DESIRED

1 If your machine does not have a preheat cycle, combine milk and water and heat in microwave on HIGH power for 30 seconds (or heat in a saucepan for 1 minute to 80°F). Add to the bread pan with remaining ingredients (except raisins) according to the manufacturer's directions for your machine. Measure raisins to add at the beep or according to manufacturer's directions. Set the CYCLE, LOAF SIZE, and CRUST SETTING. Press START.

2 After about 5 minutes of kneading, check the consistency of your dough. If dough is not in a smooth round ball, open lid and with machine ON, add liquid a tablespoon at a time if too dry, or add flour a tablespoon at a time if too wet.

3 Remove the bread promptly from the pan when the machine beeps or on completing the cycle. If desired, add topping to crust (recipe above) while bread is hot. Cool on rack before slicing.

Challah with Honey & Raisins

This rich egg bread gets authentic flavor and golden color from saffron. It is a rather expensive spice, so you can omit the saffron, if you prefer.

1 1/2-POUND	INGREDIENTS	2-POUND
1/4 teaspoon	**Crushed saffron threads***	1/4 teaspoon
3/4 cup	**Milk**	3/4 cup + 2 tablespoons
1	**Egg(s)**	2
2 tablespoons	**Honey**	3 tablespoons
1 1/2 tablespoons	**Butter or margarine, softened**	2 tablespoons
1 1/2 teaspoons	**Salt**	2 teaspoons
3 1/3 cups	**Bread flour, unsifted**	4 cups
1 1/2 teaspoons	**Active dry yeast or bread machine yeast**	2 1/4 teaspoons
1/2 cup	**Golden raisins**	2/3 cup

* Use the same amount for either size loaf.

CYCLE BASIC OR RAISIN/NUT
CRUST SETTING AS DESIRED

1 Stir the saffron into the milk. If your machine does not have a preheat cycle, heat milk mixture in microwave on HIGH power for 30 seconds (or heat in a saucepan for 1 minute to 80°F). Add to the bread pan with the remaining ingredients (except the raisins) according to the manufacturer's directions for your machine. Measure raisins to add at the beep or according to manufacturer's directions. Set the CYCLE, LOAF SIZE, and CRUST SETTING. Press START.

2 After about 5 minutes of kneading, check the consistency of your dough. If dough is not in a smooth round ball, open lid and with machine ON, add liquid a tablespoon at a time if too dry, or add flour a tablespoon at a time if too wet.

3 Remove the bread promptly from the pan when the machine beeps or on completing the cycle. Cool on rack before slicing.

French Onion Bread

Now here's a great reason to keep dry onion soup mix on hand! This is best served warm.

1 1/2-POUND	INGREDIENTS	2-POUND
1 cup + 2 tablespoons	**Warm water (80°F)**	1 1/4 cups
1 1/2 tablespoons	**Olive oil**	2 tablespoons
2 1/2 tablespoons	**Dry onion soup mix**	3 1/2 tablespoons
1 1/2 tablespoons	**Sugar**	2 tablespoons
1/2 teaspoon	**Salt**	1 teaspoon
3 1/4 cups	**Bread flour, unsifted**	4 cups
1 1/2 teaspoons	**Active dry yeast or bread machine yeast**	2 teaspoons

CYCLE BASIC
CRUST SETTING AS DESIRED

1. Measure ingredients into the bread pan according to the manufacturer's directions for your machine. Set the CYCLE, LOAF SIZE, and CRUST SETTING. Press START.

2. After about 5 minutes of kneading, check the consistency of your dough. If dough is not in a smooth round ball, open lid and with machine ON, add liquid a tablespoon at a time if too dry, or add flour a tablespoon at a time if too wet.

3. Remove the bread promptly from the pan when the machine beeps or on completing the cycle. Cool on rack before slicing.

Baking Tips

It's elementary, but true: having the right equipment in the kitchen makes all the difference. To make nice, clean slices from your freshly baked loaf, use a good quality serrated knife. Allow the bread to cool at least 20 minutes before slicing.

Cheddar Onion Bread

Talk about comfort food! This fragrant bread, redolent of cheese and onion, is the perfect partner for a pot of soup or a healthy salad.

1 1/2-POUND	INGREDIENTS	2-POUND
1 cup + 2 tablespoons	**Milk**	1 1/3 cups
1 1/2 tablespoons	**Oil**	2 tablespoons
1/4 cup	**Grated onion**	1/3 cup
1/2 cup	**Shredded sharp cheddar cheese**	2/3 cup
1 1/2 tablespoons	**Sugar**	2 tablespoons
1 1/2 teaspoons	**Salt**	2 teaspoons
1/4 teaspoon	**Garlic salt***	1/4 teaspoon
3 1/3 cups	**Bread flour, unsifted**	4 cups
2 1/4 teaspoons	**Active dry yeast or bread machine yeast**	2 1/2 teaspoons

*Use the same amount for either size loaf.

CYCLE SWEET
CRUST SETTING AS DESIRED

1. If your machine does not have a preheat cycle, heat milk in microwave on HIGH power for 30 seconds (or heat in a saucepan for 1 minute to 80°F). Add to the bread pan with remaining ingredients according to the manufacturer's directions for your machine. Set the CYCLE, LOAF SIZE, and CRUST SETTING. Press START.

2. After about 5 minutes of kneading, check the consistency of your dough. If dough is not in a smooth round ball, open lid and with machine ON, add liquid a tablespoon at a time if too dry, or add flour a tablespoon at a time if too wet.

3. Remove the bread promptly from the pan when the machine beeps or on completing the cycle. Cool on rack before slicing.

Dill Cottage Cheese Loaf

This bread is delicious warm! Brush the crust with melted butter after baking, if you like.

1 1/2-POUND	INGREDIENTS	2-POUND
3/4 cup	**Creamed cottage cheese**	1 cup
1/3 cup	**Warm water (80°F)**	1/2 cup
2 teaspoons	**Butter or margarine, softened**	1 tablespoon
1 tablespoon	**Sugar**	2 tablespoons
1 1/2 teaspoons	**Dill seed**	2 teaspoons
1 teaspoon	**Salt**	1 1/4 teaspoons
1/4 teaspoon	**Lemon pepper seasoning**	1/2 teaspoon
1/8 teaspoon	**Baking soda**	1/4 teaspoon
3 1/3 cups	**Bread flour, unsifted**	4 cups
2 1/4 teaspoons	**Active dry yeast or bread machine yeast**	3 teaspoons

CYCLE SWEET
CRUST SETTING AS DESIRED

1. If your machine does not have a preheat cycle, combine cottage cheese and water and heat in microwave on HIGH power for 30 seconds (or heat in a saucepan for 1 minute to 80°F). Add to the bread pan with remaining ingredients according to the manufacturer's directions for your machine. Set the CYCLE, LOAF SIZE, and CRUST SETTING. Press START.

2. After about 5 minutes of kneading, check the consistency of your dough. If dough is not in a smooth round ball, open lid and with machine ON, add liquid a tablespoon at a time if too dry, or add flour a tablespoon at a time if too wet.

3. Remove the bread promptly from the pan when the machine beeps or on completing the cycle. Cool on rack before slicing.

Three-Herb Bread

Try this aromatic herb bread warm the first day, then make grilled cheese sandwiches with it the next day.

1½-POUND	INGREDIENTS	2-POUND
1 cup	**Buttermilk**	1¼ cups
2 tablespoons	**Water***	2 tablespoons
1½ tablespoons	**Butter or margarine, softened**	2 tablespoons
1½ tablespoons	**Sugar**	2 tablespoons
4 teaspoons	**Minced fresh chives**	2 tablespoons
1¼ teaspoons	**Salt**	1½ teaspoons
¾ teaspoon	**Dried basil**	1 teaspoon
¾ teaspoon	**Dried thyme, rosemary, or oregano**	1 teaspoon
3¼ cups	**Bread flour, unsifted**	4 cups
1½ teaspoons	**Active dry yeast or bread machine yeast**	2 teaspoons

*Use the same amount for either size loaf.

CYCLE BASIC
CRUST SETTING MEDIUM RECOMMENDED

1 If your machine does not have a preheat cycle, combine buttermilk and water and heat in microwave on HIGH power for 30 seconds (or heat in a saucepan for 1 minute to 80°F). Add to the bread pan with remaining ingredients according to the manufacturer's directions for your machine. Set the CYCLE, LOAF SIZE, and CRUST SETTING. Press START.

2 After about 5 minutes of kneading, check the consistency of your dough. If dough is not in a smooth round ball, open lid and with machine ON, add liquid a tablespoon at a time if too dry, or add flour a tablespoon at a time if too wet.

3 Remove the bread promptly from the pan when the machine beeps or on completing the cycle. Cool on rack before slicing.

Sally Lunn Bread

Sally Lunn lived in eighteenth-century Bath, England, and sold her own piping hot tea cakes. Try this bread toasted with a cup of hot tea, in the English tradition.

1 1/2-POUND	INGREDIENTS	2-POUND
3/4 cup	**Milk**	3/4 cup + 2 tablespoons
1	**Egg(s)**	2
1 1/2 tablespoons	**Butter or margarine, softened**	2 tablespoons
3 tablespoons	**Sugar**	1/4 cup
1 teaspoon	**Salt**	1 1/2 teaspoons
3 1/3 cups	**Bread flour, unsifted**	4 cups
2 1/4 teaspoons	**Active dry yeast or bread machine yeast**	2 3/4 teaspoons

CYCLE SWEET
CRUST SETTING AS DESIRED

1. If your machine does not have a preheat cycle, heat milk in microwave on HIGH power for 30 seconds (or heat in a saucepan for 1 minute to 80°F). Add to the bread pan with remaining ingredients according to the manufacturer's directions for your machine. Set the CYCLE, LOAF SIZE, and CRUST SETTING. Press START.

2. After about 5 minutes of kneading, check the consistency of your dough. If dough is not in a smooth round ball, open lid and with machine ON, add liquid a tablespoon at a time if too dry, or add flour a tablespoon at a time if too wet.

3. Remove the bread promptly from the pan when the machine beeps or on completing the cycle. Cool on rack before slicing.

English Muffin Bread

This recipe gives a loaf of medium volume, with an English muffin taste and texture.

1 1/2-POUND	INGREDIENTS	2-POUND
1 cup + 2 tablespoons	**Milk**	1 1/4 cups
1 tablespoon	**Water***	1 tablespoon
2 teaspoons	**Sugar**	1 tablespoon
1 1/4 teaspoons	**Salt**	1 3/4 teaspoons
1/4 teaspoon	**Baking soda***	1/4 teaspoon
3 1/3 cups	**Bread flour, unsifted**	4 cups
2 teaspoons	**Active dry yeast or bread machine yeast**	2 1/2 teaspoons

* Use the same amount for either size loaf.

CYCLE BASIC
CRUST SETTING MEDIUM RECOMMENDED

1. If your machine does not have a preheat cycle, heat milk in microwave on HIGH power for 30 seconds (or heat in a saucepan for 1 minute to 80°F). Add to the bread pan with remaining ingredients according to the manufacturer's directions for your machine. Set the CYCLE, LOAF SIZE, and CRUST SETTING. Press START.

2. After about 5 minutes of kneading, check the consistency of your dough. If dough is not in a smooth round ball, open lid and with machine ON, add liquid a tablespoon at a time if too dry, or add flour a tablespoon at a time if too wet.

3. Remove the bread promptly from the pan when the machine beeps or on completing the cycle. Cool on rack before slicing.

Potato Bread

Here's a great reason to make extra mashed potatoes for dinner tonight! The potato cooking liquid makes this bread rise tall.

1 1/2-POUND	INGREDIENTS	2-POUND
1/2 cup + 2 tablespoons	**Potato water or warm water (80°F)**	2/3 cup
1/2 cup	**Prepared mashed potatoes, room temperature**	2/3 cup
1 1/2 tablespoons	**Butter or margarine, softened**	2 tablespoons
2 tablespoons	**Sugar**	3 tablespoons
1 1/2 teaspoons	**Salt**	2 teaspoons
3 1/3 cups	**Bread flour, unsifted**	4 cups
2 teaspoons	**Active dry yeast or bread machine yeast**	2 1/2 teaspoons

VARIATION

For Potato Raisin Bread, add 1/2 cup raisins to the 1 1/2-pound recipe, or 2/3 cup raisins to the 2-pound recipe, according to the manufacturer's directions.

CYCLE BASIC
CRUST SETTING AS DESIRED

1 Measure ingredients into the bread pan according to the manufacturer's directions for your machine. Set the CYCLE, LOAF SIZE, and CRUST SETTING. Press START.

2 After about 5 minutes of kneading, check the consistency of your dough. If dough is not in a smooth round ball, open lid and with machine ON, add liquid a tablespoon at a time if too dry, or add flour a tablespoon at a time if too wet.

3 Remove the bread promptly from the pan when the machine beeps or on completing the cycle. Cool on rack before slicing.

Honey Oatmeal Wheat Bread

Honey adds moistness, rather than an overpowering sweetness, to this bread.

1½-POUND	INGREDIENTS	2-POUND
1 cup + 2 tablespoons	Milk	1⅓ cups
2 tablespoons	Honey	3 tablespoons
1½ tablespoons	Butter or margarine, softened	2 tablespoons
⅔ cup	Oatmeal, dry	1 cup
1¼ teaspoons	Salt	1½ teaspoons
1¼ cups	Bread flour, unsifted	1¾ cups
1 cup	Whole wheat flour	1½ cups
2 teaspoons	Active dry yeast or bread machine yeast	2¼ teaspoons

CYCLE WHOLE WHEAT
CRUST SETTING AS DESIRED

1 If your machine does not have a preheat cycle, heat milk in microwave on HIGH power for 30 seconds (or heat in a saucepan for 1 minute to 80°F). Add to the bread pan with remaining ingredients according to the manufacturer's directions for your machine. Set the CYCLE, LOAF SIZE, and CRUST SETTING. Press START.

2 After about 5 minutes of kneading, check the consistency of your dough. If dough is not in a smooth round ball, open lid and with machine ON, add liquid a tablespoon at a time if too dry, or add flour a tablespoon at a time if too wet.

3 Remove the bread promptly from the pan when the machine beeps or on completing the cycle. Cool on rack before slicing.

Baking Tips

Whole grain flours have more of the fatty wheat kernel in them; hence they can become rancid fairly quickly. Store these flours in your refrigerator for up to 6 months, or indefinitely in your freezer.

Anadama (Cornmeal) Bread

An all-American bread that originated in New England, this yeast bread flavored with corn and molasses has many variations. Try a slice of this warm with Honey-Orange Butter (page 208).

1 1/2-POUND	INGREDIENTS	2-POUND
1 cup	**Warm water (80°F)**	1 cup + 2 tablespoons
2 tablespoons	**Molasses**	3 tablespoons
1 1/2 tablespoons	**Vegetable oil**	2 tablespoons
1/2 cup	**Yellow cornmeal***	1/2 cup
1 1/2 teaspoons	**Salt**	2 1/2 teaspoons
2 1/2 cups	**Bread flour, unsifted**	4 cups
2 teaspoons	**Active dry yeast or bread machine yeast**	2 1/2 teaspoons

*Use the same amount for either size loaf.

CYCLE BASIC (DELAY-BAKE CAN BE USED)
CRUST SETTING AS DESIRED

1 Measure ingredients into the bread pan according to the manufacturer's directions for your machine. Set the CYCLE, LOAF SIZE, and CRUST SETTING. Press START.

2 After about 5 minutes of kneading, check the consistency of your dough. If dough is not in a smooth round ball, open lid and with machine ON, add liquid a tablespoon at a time if too dry, or add flour a tablespoon at a time if too wet.

3 Remove the bread promptly from the pan when the machine beeps or on completing the cycle. Cool on rack before slicing.

CHAPTER

3

Whole-Grain, Wheat, and Rye Breads

BASIC WHOLE WHEAT BREAD

WHOLE WHEAT BUTTERMILK BREAD

100% WHOLE WHEAT BREAD

FRENCH WHEAT BREAD

WHOLE WHEAT WALNUT RAISIN BREAD

DUTCH BROWN BREAD

ROSEMARY WHEAT BREAD

TOASTED NUT WHEAT BREAD

WHOLE WHEAT POTATO SPICE BREAD

SEDONA SUNFLOWER SEED BREAD

PEANUT BUTTER OAT BREAD

WHOLE WHEAT TRAIL BREAD

CRACKED WHEAT BREAD

IRISH OAT 'N' WHEAT BREAD

GRANOLA HONEY-NUT LOAF

FOUR-GRAIN LOAF

WHOLE-GRAIN SESAME LOAF

CLASSIC CARAWAY RYE BREAD

RYE WALNUT BREAD

GERMAN PUMPERNICKEL RYE BREAD

BEER RYE BREAD

SWEDISH RYE BREAD

CZECH PEASANT BREAD

CHEDDAR BACON RYE BREAD

RUSSIAN BLACK BREAD

CORNMEAL RYE BREAD

Basic Whole Wheat Bread

A whole-grain bread that's perfect for lunchtime sandwiches, or toasted and drizzled with honey.

1 1/2-POUND	INGREDIENTS	2-POUND
1 cup	**Warm water (80°F)**	1 1/2 cups
1 1/2 tablespoons	**Butter or margarine, softened**	2 tablespoons
3 tablespoons	**Brown sugar, packed**	1/4 cup
1 1/2 tablespoons	**Nonfat dry milk**	2 tablespoons
1 teaspoon	**Salt**	1 1/4 teaspoons
2 cups	**Bread flour, unsifted**	2 3/4 cups
1 cup	**Whole wheat flour**	1 1/4 cups
2 1/4 teaspoons	**Active dry yeast or bread machine yeast**	1 tablespoon

CYCLE WHOLE WHEAT
CRUST SETTING AS DESIRED

1 Measure ingredients into the bread pan according to the manufacturer's directions for your machine. Set the CYCLE, LOAF SIZE, and CRUST SETTING. Press START.

2 After about 5 minutes of kneading, check the consistency of your dough. If dough is not in a smooth round ball, open lid and with machine ON, add liquid a tablespoon at a time if too dry, or add flour a tablespoon at a time if too wet.

3 Remove the bread promptly from the pan when the machine beeps or on completing the cycle. Cool on rack before slicing.

Whole Wheat Buttermilk Bread

If you prefer a heartier grain, switch the proportions of bread flour and whole wheat flour used here; however, your loaf will be somewhat shorter.

1 1/2-POUND	INGREDIENTS	2-POUND
1/2 cup	**Buttermilk**	2/3 cup
1/2 cup	**Water***	1/2 cup
2 tablespoons	**Molasses**	2 1/2 tablespoons
1 1/2 tablespoons	**Butter or margarine, softened**	2 tablespoons
1 1/4 teaspoons	**Salt**	1 1/2 teaspoons
2 cups	**Bread flour, unsifted**	2 1/2 cups
1 1/4 cups	**Whole wheat flour, unsifted**	1 1/2 cups
2 1/4 teaspoons	**Active dry yeast or bread machine yeast**	2 1/2 teaspoons

*Use the same amount for either size loaf.

CYCLE WHOLE WHEAT
CRUST SETTING AS DESIRED

1 If your machine does not have a preheat cycle, heat buttermilk and water in microwave on HIGH power for 30 seconds (or heat in a saucepan for 1 minute to 80°F). Add to the bread pan with remaining ingredients according to the manufacturer's directions for your machine. Set the CYCLE, LOAF SIZE, and CRUST SETTING. Press START.

2 After about 5 minutes of kneading, check the consistency of your dough. If dough is not in a smooth round ball, open lid and with machine ON, add liquid a tablespoon at a time if too dry, or add flour a tablespoon at a time if too wet.

3 Remove the bread promptly from the pan when the machine beeps or on completing the cycle. Cool on rack before slicing.

100% Whole Wheat Bread

This loaf is moist and hearty with a delicious wheat flavor.

1 1/2-POUND	INGREDIENTS	2-POUND
1 1/4 cups	**Milk**	1 1/3 cups
1 1/2 tablespoons	**Butter or margarine, softened**	2 tablespoons
3 tablespoons	**Brown sugar, packed**	1/4 cup
1 1/2 teaspoons	**Salt**	2 teaspoons
1 teaspoon	**Vanilla extract**	1 1/2 teaspoons
3 cups	**Whole wheat flour, unsifted**	4 cups
2 1/2 teaspoons	**Active dry yeast or bread machine yeast**	3 teaspoons

CYCLE WHOLE WHEAT
CRUST SETTING AS DESIRED

1. If your machine does not have a preheat cycle, heat milk in microwave on HIGH power for 30 seconds (or heat in a saucepan for 1 minute to 80°F). Add to the bread pan with remaining ingredients according to the manufacturer's directions for your machine. Set the CYCLE, LOAF SIZE, and CRUST SETTING. Press START.

2. After about 5 minutes of kneading, check the consistency of your dough. If dough is not in a smooth round ball, open lid and with machine ON, add liquid a tablespoon at a time if too dry, or add flour a tablespoon at a time if too wet.

3. Remove the bread promptly from the pan when the machine beeps or on completing the cycle. Cool on rack before slicing.

French Wheat Bread

This is a light whole wheat bread with French bread character.

1 1/2-POUND	INGREDIENTS	2-POUND
1 cup + 2 tablespoons	**Warm water (80°F)**	1 1/3 cups
1 tablespoon	**Vegetable oil**	2 tablespoons
1 1/2 tablespoons	**Sugar**	2 tablespoons
1 teaspoon	**Salt**	1 1/2 teaspoons
2 cups	**Bread flour, unsifted**	2 1/2 cups
1 1/4 cups	**Whole wheat flour, unsifted**	1 1/2 cups
1 1/4 teaspoons	**Active dry yeast or bread machine yeast**	1 1/2 teaspoons

CYCLE WHOLE WHEAT
(DELAY-BAKE CAN BE USED)
CRUST SETTING AS DESIRED

1. Add warm water to the bread pan with remaining ingredients according to the manufacturer's directions for your machine. Set the CYCLE, LOAF SIZE, and CRUST SETTING. Press START.

2. After about 5 minutes of kneading, check the consistency of your dough. If dough is not in a smooth round ball, open lid and with machine ON, add liquid a tablespoon at a time if too dry, or add flour a tablespoon at a time if too wet.

3. Remove the bread promptly from the pan when the machine beeps or on completing the cycle. Cool on rack before slicing.

To prevent sogginess, be sure to turn your bread out of the baking pan as soon as the cycle ends. Cool your loaf on a rack so air can circulate.

Whole Wheat Walnut Raisin Bread

This is a superb choice for peanut butter sandwiches or morning toast.

1 1/2-POUND	INGREDIENTS	2-POUND
1 cup + 2 tablespoons	**Milk**	1 1/3 cups
1 1/2 tablespoons	**Butter or margarine, softened**	2 tablespoons
1 1/2 tablespoons	**Sugar**	2 tablespoons
1 1/2 teaspoons	**Salt**	2 teaspoons
1 teaspoon	**Vanilla extract**	1 1/2 teaspoons
1 1/2 cups	**Whole wheat flour, unsifted**	2 cups
1 1/2 cups	**Bread flour, unsifted**	1 3/4 cups
2 teaspoons	**Active dry yeast or bread machine yeast**	2 1/2 teaspoons
1/2 cup	**Chopped walnuts or pecans**	2/3 cup
1/2 cup	**Raisins**	2/3 cup

CYCLE WHOLE WHEAT OR RAISIN NUT
CRUST SETTING AS DESIRED

1 If your machine does not have a preheat cycle, heat milk in microwave on HIGH power for 30 seconds (or heat in a saucepan for 1 minute to 80°F). Add to the bread pan with remaining ingredients (except nuts and raisins) according to the manufacturer's directions for your machine. Measure nuts and raisins to add at the beep or according to manufacturer's directions. Set the CYCLE, LOAF SIZE, and CRUST SETTING. Press START.

2 After about 5 minutes of kneading, check the consistency of your dough. If dough is not in a smooth round ball, open lid and with machine ON, add liquid a tablespoon at a time if too dry, or add flour a tablespoon at a time if too wet.

3 Remove the bread promptly from the pan when the machine beeps or on completing the cycle. Cool on rack before slicing.

Dutch Brown Bread

Molasses lends this lightly sweetened dark bread
a European flavor.

1½-POUND	INGREDIENTS	2-POUND
1 cup	**Warm water (80°F)**	1 cup + 2 tablespoons
1	**Egg(s)**	2
3 tablespoons	**Dark molasses**	¼ cup
1½ tablespoons	**Butter or margarine, softened**	2 tablespoons
1 teaspoon	**Ground cinnamon**	1¼ teaspoons
1 teaspoon	**Salt**	1½ teaspoons
1¾ cups	**Whole wheat flour, unsifted**	2¼ cups
1 cup	**Bread flour, unsifted**	1½ cups
2¼ teaspoons	**Active dry yeast or bread machine yeast**	3 teaspoons

CYCLE WHOLE WHEAT
CRUST SETTING AS DESIRED

1. Add warm water to the bread pan with remaining ingredients according to the manufacturer's directions for your machine. Set the CYCLE, LOAF SIZE, and CRUST SETTING. Press START.

2. After about 5 minutes of kneading, check the consistency of your dough. If dough is not in a smooth round ball, open lid and with machine ON, add liquid a tablespoon at a time if too dry, or add flour a tablespoon at a time if too wet.

3. Remove the bread promptly from the pan when the machine beeps or on completing the cycle. Cool on rack before slicing.

Rosemary Wheat Bread

The distinctive aroma of rosemary marries well with the whole grain flavor. You don't have to crush the dried rosemary; let the bread machine do it for you.

1 1/2-POUND	INGREDIENTS	2-POUND
1 1/4 cups	**Milk**	1 1/3 cups
2 tablespoons	**Olive or vegetable oil**	2 1/2 tablespoons
2 tablespoons	**Sugar**	3 tablespoons
1 1/2 teaspoons	**Crushed dried rosemary**	2 teaspoons
1 1/2 teaspoons	**Salt**	2 teaspoons
2 cups	**Whole wheat flour**	2 1/4 cups
1 cup	**Bread flour, unsifted**	1 1/2 cups
2 1/2 teaspoons	**Active dry yeast or bread machine yeast**	3 teaspoons

CYCLE WHOLE WHEAT
CRUST SETTING AS DESIRED

1 If your machine does not have a preheat cycle, heat milk in microwave on HIGH power for 30 seconds (or heat in a saucepan for 1 minute to 80°F). Add to the bread pan with remaining ingredients according to the manufacturer's directions for your machine. Set the CYCLE, LOAF SIZE, and CRUST SETTING. Press START.

2 After about 5 minutes of kneading, check the consistency of your dough. If dough is not in a smooth round ball, open lid and with machine ON, add liquid a tablespoon at a time if too dry, or add flour a tablespoon at a time if too wet.

3 Remove the bread promptly from the pan when the machine beeps or on completing the cycle. Cool on rack before slicing.

Toasted Nut Wheat Bread

This bread is super for grilled cheese
and tomato sandwiches.

1 1/2-POUND	INGREDIENTS	2-POUND
1 cup + 2 tablespoons	**Warm water (80°F)**	1 1/4 cups
1 1/2 tablespoons	**Walnut or vegetable oil**	2 tablespoons
2 tablespoons	**Honey**	2 1/2 tablespoons
1 1/2 teaspoons	**Salt**	2 teaspoons
1 1/2 cups	**Whole wheat flour, unsifted**	2 cups
1 1/2 cups	**Bread flour, unsifted**	2 cups
2 teaspoons	**Active dry yeast or bread machine yeast**	2 1/2 teaspoons
1/2 cup	**Toasted walnuts, almonds, or pecans**	3/4 cup

CYCLE WHOLE WHEAT OR RAISIN/NUT
(DELAY-BAKE CAN BE USED)
CRUST SETTING LIGHT TO MEDIUM

1. Measure all ingredients, except nuts, into the bread pan according to the manufacturer's directions for your machine. Measure nuts to add at the beep or when manufacturer directs. Set the CYCLE, LOAF SIZE, and CRUST SETTING. Press START.

2. After about 5 minutes of kneading, check the consistency of your dough. If dough is not in a smooth round ball, open lid and with machine ON, add liquid a tablespoon at a time if too dry, or add flour a tablespoon at a time if too wet.

3. Remove the bread promptly from the pan when the machine beeps or on completing the cycle. Cool on rack before slicing.

Baking Tips

Toasting nuts is easy—just spread them on a tray in your toaster oven or toast them on a baking sheet in a 350°F oven for 5 to 10 minutes (stir them once or twice) until golden brown.

Whole Wheat Potato Spice Bread

Potatoes and the water they're cooked in give this bread a wonderful texture and good keeping quality.

1 1/2-POUND	INGREDIENTS	2-POUND
1/2 cup + 2 tablespoons	**Potato water or plain water**	2/3 cup
1/2 cup	**Prepared mashed potatoes, at room temperature**	2/3 cup
1 1/2 tablespoons	**Butter or margarine, softened**	2 tablespoons
2 tablespoons	**Sugar**	3 tablespoons
1 teaspoon	**Salt**	1 1/2 teaspoons
1/2 teaspoon	**Ground cinnamon**	3/4 teaspoon
1/4 teaspoon	**Ground nutmeg**	1/2 teaspoon
1 3/4 cups	**Bread flour, unsifted**	2 cups
1 1/2 cups	**Whole wheat flour, unsifted**	2 cups
2 teaspoons	**Active dry yeast or bread machine yeast**	2 1/4 teaspoons
1/2 cup	**Dark or golden raisins**	3/4 cup

CYCLE WHOLE WHEAT OR RAISIN/NUT
CRUST SETTING AS DESIRED

1 If your machine does not have a preheat cycle, heat potato water mixed with potatoes in microwave on HIGH power for 30 seconds (or heat in a saucepan for 1 minute to 80°F). Add to the bread pan with remaining ingredients (except raisins) according to the manufacturer's directions for your machine. Measure raisins to add at the beep or when manufacturer directs. Set the CYCLE, LOAF SIZE, and CRUST SETTING. Press START.

2 After about 5 minutes of kneading, check the consistency of your dough. If dough is not in a smooth round ball, open lid and with machine ON, add liquid a tablespoon at a time if too dry, or add flour a tablespoon at a time if too wet.

3 Remove the bread promptly from the pan when the machine beeps or on completing the cycle. Cool on rack before slicing.

Sedona Sunflower Seed Bread

This full-flavored loaf with a hint of orange flavor is a nice change from plain whole wheat bread. It is reminiscent of the loaves that Arizona pioneers might have set out among the red rocks to rise.

1 1/2-POUND	INGREDIENTS	2-POUND
1 1/4 cups	**Buttermilk**	1 1/3 cups
1 1/2 tablespoons	**Vegetable oil**	2 tablespoons
2 tablespoons	**Honey**	2 1/2 tablespoons
1/4 cup	**Sunflower seeds**	1/3 cup
1/4 cup	**Toasted wheat germ***	1/4 cup
2 teaspoons	**Grated orange peel**	1 tablespoon
1 1/4 teaspoons	**Salt**	1 1/2 teaspoons
1 1/2 cups	**Bread flour, unsifted**	2 cups
1 1/2 cups	**Whole wheat flour, unsifted**	2 cups
2 1/4 teaspoons	**Active dry yeast or bread machine yeast**	3 teaspoons

*Use the same amount for either size loaf.

CYCLE WHOLE WHEAT
CRUST SETTING AS DESIRED

1. If your machine does not have a preheat cycle, heat buttermilk in microwave on HIGH power for 30 seconds (or heat in a saucepan for 1 minute to 80°F). Add to the bread pan with remaining ingredients according to the manufacturer's directions for your machine. Set the CYCLE, LOAF SIZE, and CRUST SETTING. Press START.

2. After about 5 minutes of kneading, check the consistency of your dough. If dough is not in a smooth round ball, open lid and with machine ON, add liquid a tablespoon at a time if too dry, or add flour a tablespoon at a time if too wet.

3. Remove the bread promptly from the pan when the machine beeps or on completing the cycle. Cool on rack before slicing.

Peanut Butter Oat Bread

Peanut butter lovers, unite!

1 1/2-POUND	INGREDIENTS	2-POUND
1 1/4 cups	**Warm water (80°F)**	1 1/3 cups
1/2 cup	**Peanut butter***	1/2 cup
1/3 cup	**Oatmeal, dry**	1/2 cup
1/4 cup	**Brown sugar, packed**	1/3 cup
1 teaspoon	**Salt**	1 1/4 teaspoons
2 1/4 cups	**Bread flour, unsifted**	2 1/3 cups
1 cup	**Whole wheat flour, unsifted**	1 1/2 cups
1 1/2 teaspoons	**Active dry yeast or bread machine yeast**	2 1/4 teaspoons

*Use the same amount for either size loaf.

CYCLE WHOLE WHEAT (DELAY-BAKE CAN BE USED)
CRUST SETTING LIGHT RECOMMENDED

1 Add warm water to the bread pan with remaining ingredients according to the manufacturer's directions for your machine. Set the CYCLE, LOAF SIZE, and CRUST SETTING. Press START.

2 After about 5 minutes of kneading, check the consistency of your dough. If dough is not in a smooth round ball, open lid and with machine ON, add liquid a tablespoon at a time if too dry, or add flour a tablespoon at a time if too wet.

3 Remove the bread promptly from the pan when the machine beeps or on completing the cycle. Cool on rack before slicing.

Baking Tips

Make it a habit to check for the kneading paddle when you remove your loaf from the pan. If it stays in the loaf unnoticed and you slice against it, you may wind up scratching off some of the Teflon coating.

Whole Wheat Trail Bread

You can use any type of trail mix, purchased or homemade, for this pleasantly sweet loaf.

1 1/2-POUND	INGREDIENTS	2-POUND
1 cup	**Milk**	1 1/4 cups
3 tablespoons	**Butter or margarine, softened and cut up**	1/4 cup
1/4 cup	**Brown sugar, packed**	1/4 cup + 1 tablespoon
1 teaspoon	**Vanilla extract**	1 1/2 teaspoons
1 1/4 teaspoons	**Salt**	1 1/2 teaspoons
1 1/2 cups	**Bread flour, unsifted**	1 3/4 cups
1 1/2 cups	**Whole wheat flour, unsifted**	2 cups
2 1/4 teaspoons	**Active dry yeast or bread machine yeast**	2 1/2 teaspoons
2/3 cup	**Trail mix**	1 cup

CYCLE WHOLE WHEAT OR RAISIN/NUT
CRUST SETTING AS DESIRED

1 If your machine does not have a preheat cycle, heat milk in microwave on HIGH power for 30 seconds (or heat in a saucepan for 1 minute to 80°F). Add to the bread pan with remaining ingredients (except trail mix) according to the manufacturer's directions for your machine. Measure trail mix to add at the beep or when manufacturer directs. Set the CYCLE, LOAF SIZE, and CRUST SETTING. Press START.

2 After about 5 minutes of kneading, check the consistency of your dough. If dough is not in a smooth round ball, open lid and with machine ON, add liquid a tablespoon at a time if too dry, or add flour a tablespoon at a time if too wet.

3 Remove the bread promptly from the pan when the machine beeps or on completing the cycle. Cool on rack before slicing.

Cracked Wheat Bread

You can purchase just the amount of cracked wheat needed here from the bins at health food stores.

1 1/2-POUND	INGREDIENTS	2-POUND
3/4 cup	**Warm water (80°F)**	3/4 cup + 2 tablespoons
1/2 cup	**Cracked wheat, cooked and cooled (recipe below)**	3/4 cup
1 1/2 tablespoons	**Vegetable oil**	2 tablespoons
1 1/2 tablespoons	**Molasses or honey**	2 tablespoons
1 1/2 teaspoons	**Salt**	2 teaspoons
1 3/4 cups	**Bread flour, unsifted***	1 3/4 cups
1 1/2 cups	**Whole wheat flour, unsifted**	2 cups
2 1/2 teaspoons	**Active dry yeast or bread machine yeast**	3 teaspoons

*Use the same amount for either size loaf.

CRACKED WHEAT

To cook cracked wheat: for 1 1/2-pound loaf, cook 1/2 cup cracked wheat in 1 cup simmering water; for 2-pound loaf, cook 3/4 cup cracked wheat in 1 1/2 cups simmering water. Cook for 12 to 15 minutes, or until thick, stirring frequently. Cool to 80°F or room temperature.

CYCLE WHOLE WHEAT OR BASIC
CRUST SETTING AS DESIRED

1 Add warm water to the bread pan with remaining ingredients according to the manufacturer's directions for your machine. Set the CYCLE, LOAF SIZE, and CRUST SETTING. Press START.

2 After about 5 minutes of kneading, check the consistency of your dough. If dough is not in a smooth round ball, open lid and with machine ON, add liquid a tablespoon at a time if too dry, or add flour a tablespoon at a time if too wet.

3 Remove the bread promptly from the pan when the machine beeps or on completing the cycle. Cool on rack before slicing.

Irish Oat 'n' Wheat Bread

This bread is far and away a favorite with my family.

1 1/2-POUND	INGREDIENTS	2-POUND
1 cup	**Warm water (80°F)**	1 1/4 cups
1 1/2 tablespoons	**Vegetable oil**	2 tablespoons
1 1/2 tablespoons	**Cider vinegar**	2 tablespoons
1 1/2 tablespoons	**Nonfat dry milk**	2 tablespoons
2 tablespoons	**Molasses**	3 tablespoons
2 tablespoons	**Honey**	3 tablespoons
1 1/2 teaspoons	**Salt**	2 teaspoons
1 3/4 cups	**Bread flour, unsifted**	2 1/3 cups
1 cup	**Whole wheat flour, unsifted***	1 cup
1/2 cup	**Oatmeal, dry**	2/3 cup
2 1/4 teaspoons	**Active dry yeast or bread machine yeast**	3 teaspoons

*Use the same amount for either size loaf.

CYCLE WHOLE WHEAT OR BASIC
(DELAY-BAKE CAN BE USED)
CRUST SETTING AS DESIRED

1. Add warm water to the bread pan with remaining ingredients according to the manufacturer's directions for your machine. Set the CYCLE, LOAF SIZE, and CRUST SETTING. Press START.

2. After about 5 minutes of kneading, check the consistency of your dough. If dough is not in a smooth round ball, open lid and with machine ON, add liquid a tablespoon at a time if too dry, or add flour a tablespoon at a time if too wet.

3. Remove the bread promptly from the pan when the machine beeps or on completing the cycle. Cool on rack before slicing.

Granola Honey-Nut Loaf

It doesn't get more wholesome than this!

1 1/2-POUND	INGREDIENTS	2-POUND
1 1/4 cups	**Buttermilk**	1 1/2 cups
1 1/2 tablespoons	**Butter or margarine, softened**	2 tablespoons
1 1/2 tablespoons	**Honey**	2 tablespoons
1 1/2 teaspoons	**Salt**	2 teaspoons
1 1/2 cups	**Bread flour, unsifted**	2 cups
1 cup	**Whole wheat flour, unsifted**	1 1/2 cups
1/3 cup	**Oatmeal, dry**	1/2 cup
1/3 cup	**Granola cereal**	1/2 cup
2 1/4 teaspoons	**Active dry yeast or bread machine yeast**	2 1/2 teaspoons
1/2 cup	**Chopped walnuts**	2/3 cup

CYCLE WHOLE WHEAT OR RAISIN/NUT
CRUST SETTING AS DESIRED

1 If your machine does not have a preheat cycle, heat buttermilk in microwave on HIGH power for 30 seconds (or heat in a saucepan for 1 minute to 80°F). Add to the bread pan with remaining ingredients (except walnuts) according to the manufacturer's directions for your machine. Measure walnuts to add at the beep or when manufacturer directs. Set the CYCLE, LOAF SIZE, and CRUST SETTING. Press START.

2 After about 5 minutes of kneading, check the consistency of your dough. If dough is not in a smooth round ball, open lid and with machine ON, add liquid a tablespoon at a time if too dry, or add flour a tablespoon at a time if too wet.

3 Remove the bread promptly from the pan when the machine beeps or on completing the cycle. Cool on rack before slicing.

Four-Grain Loaf

If your machine produces a vertical loaf, stick with the 1½-pound version of this recipe. The 2-pound loaf is best suited to machines with horizontal pans with a capacity of at least 12 cups.

1½-POUND	INGREDIENTS	2-POUND
1¼ cups	**Warm water (80°F)**	1⅓ cups
1½ tablespoons	**Butter or margarine, softened**	2 tablespoons
2½ tablespoons	**Maple syrup**	3 tablespoons
¼ cup	**All-Bran cereal**	⅓ cup
¼ cup	**Toasted wheat germ**	⅓ cup
¼ cup	**Sunflower seeds**	⅓ cup
1¼ teaspoons	**Salt**	1½ teaspoons
2 cups	**Bread flour, unsifted**	2¼ cups
1¼ cups	**Whole wheat flour, unsifted**	1⅓ cups
2¼ teaspoons	**Active dry yeast or bread machine yeast**	3 teaspoons

CYCLE WHOLE WHEAT
CRUST SETTING AS DESIRED

1 Measure ingredients into the bread pan according to the manufacturer's directions for your machine. Set the CYCLE, LOAF SIZE, and CRUST SETTING. Press START.

2 After about 5 minutes of kneading, check the consistency of your dough. If dough is not in a smooth round ball, open lid and with machine ON, add liquid a tablespoon at a time if too dry, or add flour a tablespoon at a time if too wet.

3 Remove the bread promptly from the pan when the machine beeps or on completing the cycle. Cool on rack before slicing.

Whole-Grain Sesame Loaf

Nonfat dry milk gives this bread a dark crust.

1 1/2-POUND	INGREDIENTS	2-POUND
1 cup	**Warm water (80°F)**	1 1/4 cups
1 1/2 tablespoons	**Butter or margarine, softened**	2 tablespoons
3 tablespoons	**Honey**	1/4 cup
3 tablespoons	**Sesame seed**	1/4 cup
1 1/2 tablespoons	**Nonfat dry milk**	2 tablespoons
1 1/4 teaspoons	**Salt**	1 1/2 teaspoons
1 1/3 cups	**Bread flour, unsifted**	2 cups
1 cup	**Whole wheat flour, unsifted**	1 1/4 cups
1/2 cup	**Rye flour, unsifted**	3/4 cup
2 1/4 teaspoons	**Active dry yeast or bread machine yeast**	3 teaspoons

CYCLE WHOLE WHEAT
CRUST SETTING AS DESIRED

1 Measure ingredients into the bread pan according to the manufacturer's directions for your machine. Set the CYCLE, LOAF SIZE, and CRUST SETTING. Press START.

2 After about 5 minutes of kneading, check the consistency of your dough. If dough is not in a smooth round ball, open lid and with machine ON, add liquid a tablespoon at a time if too dry, or add flour a tablespoon at a time if too wet.

3 Remove the bread promptly from the pan when the machine beeps or on completing the cycle. Cool on rack before slicing.

Classic Caraway Rye Bread

A lovely basic rye bread. Note that the loaf will be about half the height of your best white bread, since rye flour doesn't have the amount of gluten that gives bread high volume.

1 1/2-POUND	INGREDIENTS	2-POUND
3/4 cup	**Milk**	3/4 cup + 2 tablespoons
1/4 cup	**Water**	1/3 cup
1 1/2 tablespoons	**Butter or margarine, softened**	2 tablespoons
2 tablespoons	**Honey**	3 tablespoons
1 1/2 teaspoons	**Salt**	2 teaspoons
1 1/2 teaspoons	**Caraway seed**	2 teaspoons
1 3/4 cups	**Bread flour, unsifted**	2 1/4 cups
1 1/2 cups	**Rye flour, unsifted**	1 3/4 cups
2 1/4 teaspoons	**Active dry yeast or bread machine yeast**	2 3/4 teaspoons

CYCLE WHOLE WHEAT
CRUST SETTING AS DESIRED

1. If your machine does not have a preheat cycle, heat milk and water in microwave on HIGH power for 30 seconds (or heat in a saucepan for 1 minute to 80°F). Add to the bread pan with remaining ingredients according to the manufacturer's directions for your machine. Set the CYCLE, LOAF SIZE, and CRUST SETTING. Press START.

2. After about 5 minutes of kneading, check the consistency of your dough. If dough is not in a smooth round ball, open lid and with machine ON, add liquid a tablespoon at a time if too dry, or add flour a tablespoon at a time if too wet.

3. Remove the bread promptly from the pan when the machine beeps or on completing the cycle. Cool on rack before slicing.

Rye Walnut Bread

Try pieces of this bread dipped in olive oil.

1 1/2-POUND	INGREDIENTS	2-POUND
1 cup + 2 tablespoons	**Warm water (80°F)**	1 1/3 cups
1 1/2 tablespoons	**Butter or margarine, softened**	2 tablespoons
3 tablespoons	**Brown sugar, packed**	1/4 cup
1 teaspoon	**Ground cardamom (optional)**	1 1/4 teaspoons
1 teaspoon	**Salt**	1 1/2 teaspoons
2 1/3 cups	**Bread flour, unsifted**	2 1/2 cups
1 cup	**Rye flour, unsifted**	1 1/2 cups
2 1/4 teaspoons	**Active dry yeast or bread machine yeast**	3 teaspoons
1/2 cup	**Chopped walnuts, pecans, or almonds**	3/4 cup

CYCLE WHOLE WHEAT OR RAISIN/NUT
CRUST SETTING AS DESIRED

1 Measure ingredients (except nuts) into the bread pan according to the manufacturer's directions for your machine. Measure nuts to add at the beep or when manufacturer directs. Set the CYCLE, LOAF SIZE, and CRUST SETTING. Press START.

2 After about 5 minutes of kneading, check the consistency of your dough. If dough is not in a smooth round ball, open lid and with machine ON, add liquid a tablespoon at a time if too dry, or add flour a tablespoon at a time if too wet.

3 Remove the bread promptly from the pan when the machine beeps or on completing the cycle. Cool on rack before slicing.

Baking Tips

Olive oil is the new "in" replacement for butter on bread. Check your supermarket shelf; you'll be amazed at the intriguing variety of flavored oils available. Try one for your next dinner party.

German Pumpernickel Rye Bread

My maternal grandmother (we called her Nana) would have loved this version of her favorite bread. It is a natural for a Reuben, ham, or egg salad sandwich.

1 1/2-POUND	INGREDIENTS	2-POUND
1 cup + 2 tablespoons	**Warm water (80°F)**	1 1/3 cups
1 1/2 tablespoons	**Olive or vegetable oil**	2 tablespoons
1 1/2 tablespoons	**Molasses**	2 tablespoons
1 tablespoon	**Unsweetened cocoa powder**	4 teaspoons
1 1/2 teaspoons	**Salt**	2 teaspoons
1/2 teaspoon	**Anise seed***	1/2 teaspoon
1/4 teaspoon	**Fennel seed**	1/2 teaspoon
1/4 teaspoon	**Ground coriander**	1/2 teaspoon
1 cup	**Bread flour, unsifted**	1 1/2 cups
1 cup	**Rye flour, unsifted**	2/3 cup
1 cup	**Whole wheat flour, unsifted**	1 1/3 cups
2 1/4 teaspoons	**Active dry yeast or bread machine yeast**	3 teaspoons

*Use the same amount for either size loaf.

CYCLE WHOLE WHEAT (DELAY-BAKE CAN BE USED)
CRUST SETTING AS DESIRED

1 Measure ingredients into the bread pan according to the manufacturer's directions for your machine. Set the CYCLE, LOAF SIZE, and CRUST SETTING. Press START.

2 After about 5 minutes of kneading, check the consistency of your dough. If dough is not in a smooth round ball, open lid and with machine ON, add liquid a tablespoon at a time if too dry, or add flour a tablespoon at a time if too wet.

3 Remove the bread promptly from the pan when the machine beeps or on completing the cycle. Cool on rack before slicing.

Beer Rye Bread

Beer lends a slightly sour flavor to this hearty rye.
The bread is spicy and mildly sweet. You can
use either regular or nonalcoholic beer in this recipe.

1 1/2-POUND	INGREDIENTS	2-POUND
1/3 cup	**Warm water (80°F)**	1/2 cup + 2 tablespoons
1/2 cup	**Beer, room temperature**	1/2 cup + 2 tablespoons
1 1/2 tablespoons	**Butter or margarine, softened**	2 tablespoons
2 tablespoons	**Molasses**	3 tablespoons
1 1/2 teaspoons	**Salt***	1 1/2 teaspoons
1/4 teaspoon	**Ground cloves**	1/2 teaspoon
1/4 teaspoon	**Ground ginger***	1/4 teaspoon
2 cups	**Bread flour, unsifted**	2 1/4 cups
1 1/4 cups	**Rye flour, unsifted**	1 3/4 cups
2 1/4 teaspoons	**Active dry yeast or bread machine yeast**	3 teaspoons

*Use the same amount for either size loaf.

CYCLE WHOLE WHEAT
CRUST SETTING AS DESIRED

1 Measure ingredients into the bread pan according to the manufacturer's directions for your machine. Set the CYCLE, LOAF SIZE, and CRUST SETTING. Press START.

2 After about 5 minutes of kneading, check the consistency of your dough. If dough is not in a smooth round ball, open lid and with machine ON, add liquid a tablespoon at a time if too dry, or add flour a tablespoon at a time if too wet.

3 Remove the bread promptly from the pan when the machine beeps or on completing the cycle. Cool on rack before slicing.

Swedish Rye Bread

Watch this dough carefully during the first 5 minutes of kneading. The large amount of rye flour makes it a bit trickier to achieve the smooth ball of dough that's ideal.

1 1/2-POUND	INGREDIENTS	2-POUND
3/4 cup + 2 tablespoons	**Warm water (80°F)**	1 cup + 2 tablespoons
1 1/2 tablespoons	**Butter or margarine, softened**	2 tablespoons
2 tablespoons	**Molasses**	3 tablespoons
1 1/2 teaspoons	**Salt**	2 teaspoons
1 1/2 teaspoons	**Grated orange or lemon peel**	2 1/2 teaspoons
1/2 teaspoon	**Anise seed**	3/4 teaspoon
2 cups	**Bread flour, unsifted**	2 1/4 cups
1 1/4 cups	**Rye flour, unsifted**	1 3/4 cups
2 teaspoons	**Active dry yeast or bread machine yeast**	2 1/2 teaspoons

CYCLE WHOLE WHEAT
CRUST SETTING AS DESIRED

1 Measure ingredients into the bread pan according to the manufacturer's directions for your machine. Set the CYCLE, LOAF SIZE, and CRUST SETTING. Press START.

2 After about 5 minutes of kneading, check the consistency of your dough. If dough is not in a smooth round ball, open lid and with machine ON, add liquid a tablespoon at a time if too dry, or add flour a tablespoon at a time if too wet.

3 Remove the bread promptly from the pan when the machine beeps or on completing the cycle. Cool on rack before slicing.

Czech Peasant Bread

This makes a smaller loaf, but it has a lot of flavor.
Great with cheese, fruit, and a glass of wine.

1 1/2-POUND	INGREDIENTS	2-POUND
3/4 cup + 2 tablespoons	**Warm water (80°F)**	1 cup + 2 tablespoons
1 1/2 tablespoons	**Butter or margarine, softened**	2 tablespoons
2 tablespoons	**Cider vinegar**	3 tablespoons
2 tablespoons	**Molasses**	3 tablespoons
1/2 oz. (1/2 square)	**Unsweetened chocolate, melted and cooled**	1 oz. (1 square)
1 1/2 teaspoons	**Caraway seed**	2 teaspoons
1 teaspoon	**Instant coffee crystals**	1 1/4 teaspoons
1 teaspoon	**Salt**	1 1/2 teaspoons
3/4 teaspoon	**Onion powder**	1 teaspoon
2 1/3 cups	**Bread flour, unsifted**	2 2/3 cups
1 cup	**Rye flour, unsifted**	1 1/3 cups
2 1/4 teaspoons	**Active dry yeast or bread machine yeast**	3 teaspoons

CYCLE WHOLE WHEAT
CRUST SETTING AS DESIRED

1 Measure ingredients into the bread pan according to the manufacturer's directions for your machine. Set the CYCLE, LOAF SIZE, and CRUST SETTING. Press START.

2 After about 5 minutes of kneading, check the consistency of your dough. If dough is not in a smooth round ball, open lid and with machine ON, add liquid a tablespoon at a time if too dry, or add flour a tablespoon at a time if too wet.

3 Remove the bread promptly from the pan when the machine beeps or on completing the cycle. Cool on rack before slicing.

Cheddar Bacon Rye Bread

You can purchase crumbled cooked bacon in the salad dressing section of your supermarket.

1 1/2-POUND	INGREDIENTS	2-POUND
1 cup + 2 tablespoons	**Milk**	1 1/3 cups
1/2 cup	**Shredded sharp cheddar cheese**	2/3 cup
1/4 cup	**Crumbled cooked bacon**	3/4 cup
1 1/2 tablespoons	**Vegetable oil**	2 tablespoons
1 1/2 tablespoons	**Sugar**	2 tablespoons
1 1/2 teaspoons	**Salt***	1 1/2 teaspoons
1 3/4 cups	**Bread flour, unsifted**	2 1/4 cups
1 1/2 cups	**Rye flour, unsifted**	1 3/4 cups
2 1/4 teaspoons	**Actlve dry yeast or bread machine yeast**	2 3/4 teaspoons

*Use the same amount for either size loaf.

CYCLE WHOLE WHEAT
CRUST SETTING AS DESIRED

1 If your machine does not have a preheat cycle, heat milk in microwave on HIGH power for 30 seconds (or heat in a saucepan for 1 minute to 80°F). Add to the bread pan with remaining ingredients according to the manufacturer's directions for your machine. Set the CYCLE, LOAF SIZE, and CRUST SETTING. Press START.

2 After about 5 minutes of kneading, check the consistency of your dough. If dough is not in a smooth round ball, open lid and with machine ON, add liquid a tablespoon at a time if too dry, or add flour a tablespoon at a time if too wet.

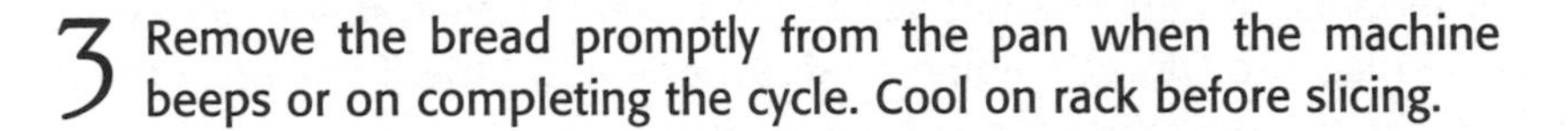

3 Remove the bread promptly from the pan when the machine beeps or on completing the cycle. Cool on rack before slicing.

Russian Black Bread

Cut this delicious dark bread into triangles and spread with chive cream cheese and a sliver of smoked salmon topped with capers. Or skip the salmon and substitute a slice of tomato and a sprinkling of dill.

1½-POUND	INGREDIENTS	2-POUND
1 cup + 2 tablespoons	**Warm water* (80°F)**	1 cup + 2 tablespoons
3 tablespoons	**Molasses**	¼ cup
1½ tablespoons	**Vegetable oil**	2 tablespoons
2 teaspoons	**Sugar**	1 tablespoon
2 teaspoons	**Unsweetened cocoa powder**	1 tablespoon
1½ teaspoons	**Salt**	2 teaspoons
1 teaspoon	**Instant coffee powder**	2 teaspoons
½ teaspoon	**Fennel seed**	¾ teaspoon
2¼ cups	**Bread flour, unsifted**	2½ cups
1 cup	**Rye flour, unsifted**	1½ cups
½ cup	**Bran cereal, crushed**	¾ cup
2¼ teaspoons	**Active dry yeast or bread machine yeast**	1 tablespoon

*Use the same amount for either size loaf.

CYCLE WHOLE WHEAT
(DELAY-BAKE CAN BE USED)
CRUST SETTING AS DESIRED

1 Measure ingredients into the bread pan according to the manufacturer's directions for your machine. Set the CYCLE, LOAF SIZE, and CRUST SETTING. Press START.

2 After about 5 minutes of kneading, check the consistency of your dough. If dough is not in a smooth round ball, open lid and with machine ON, add liquid a tablespoon at a time if too dry, or add flour a tablespoon at a time if too wet.

3 Remove the bread promptly from the pan when the machine beeps or on completing the cycle. Cool on rack before slicing.

Cornmeal Rye Bread

This bread will remind you of your favorite deli.
A short but very satisfying loaf of rye.

1 1/2-POUND	INGREDIENTS	2-POUND
3/4 cup	**Milk**	3/4 cup + 2 tablespoons
1/4 cup	**Water**	1/2 cup
1 1/2 tablespoons	**Butter or margarine, softened**	2 tablespoons
2 tablespoons	**Molasses**	3 tablespoons
1 1/2 teaspoons	**Salt**	2 teaspoons
1 3/4 cups	**Bread flour, unsifted**	2 1/4 cups
1 cup	**Rye flour, unsifted**	1 1/2 cups
1/4 cup	**Yellow cornmeal**	1/3 cup
2 teaspoons	**Active dry yeast or bread machine yeast**	2 1/2 teaspoons

CYCLE WHOLE WHEAT
CRUST SETTING AS DESIRED

1 If your machine does not have a preheat cycle, heat milk and water in microwave on HIGH power for 30 seconds (or heat in a saucepan for 1 minute to 80°F). Add to the bread pan with remaining ingredients according to the manufacturer's directions for your machine. Set the CYCLE, LOAF SIZE, and CRUST SETTING. Press START.

2 After about 5 minutes of kneading, check the consistency of your dough. If dough is not in a smooth round ball, open lid and with machine ON, add liquid a tablespoon at a time if too dry, or add flour a tablespoon at a time if too wet.

3 Remove the bread promptly from the pan when the machine beeps or on completing the cycle. Cool on rack before slicing.

CHAPTER

4

Sweet Breads for the Sweet

APPLESAUCE RAISIN BREAD

APPLE-CINNAMON BREAD

APPLE BUTTER BREAD

BRIOCHE LOAF (FRENCH SWEET BREAD)

LEMON YOGURT POPPYSEED BREAD

HONEY FIVE-SPICE BREAD

ORANGE MARMALADE BREAD

SWEET CARROT-APRICOT BREAD

PINEAPPLE CREAM CHEESE LOAF

HAWAIIAN COCONUT BREAD

TOASTED COCONUT-PINEAPPLE-MACADAMIA LOAF

APRICOT AND PRUNE BREAD

SWEET PRUNE LOAF

SPICED PUMPKIN LOAF

ZUCCHINI SPICE BREAD

PEAR-CARDAMOM BREAD

TOASTED ALMOND BREAD

ROCKY ROAD BREAD

NUTTY CHOCOLATE CHIP BREAD

LAURA'S PEANUT BUTTER-CHOCOLATE BREAD

CHOCOLATE CHERRY LOAF

DOUBLE CHOCOLATE-ALMOND BREAD

CHOCOLATE AND CINNAMON RAISIN BREAD

Applesauce Raisin Bread

For a triple apple experience, spread toasted slices of this delicious bread with apple butter or applesauce.

1 1/2-POUND	INGREDIENTS	2-POUND
2/3 cup	**Applesauce**	3/4 cup
1/3 cup	**Apple juice**	1/2 cup
3 tablespoons	**Butter or margarine, softened and cut up**	1/4 cup
3 tablespoons	**Sugar**	1/4 cup
1 1/4 teaspoons	**Salt***	1 1/4 teaspoons
1 teaspoon	**Ground cinnamon**	1 1/2 teaspoons
1/4 teaspoon	**Ground nutmeg***	1/4 teaspoon
3 1/4 cups	**Bread flour, unsifted**	3 3/4 cups
2 1/4 teaspoons	**Active dry yeast or bread machine yeast**	2 1/2 teaspoons
2/3 cup	**Raisins**	3/4 cup

*Use the same amount for either size loaf.

CYCLE SWEET OR RAISIN/NUT
CRUST SETTING AS DESIRED

1. If your machine does not have a preheat cycle, combine applesauce and apple juice and heat in microwave on HIGH power for 30 seconds (or heat in a saucepan for 1 minute to 80°F). Add to the bread pan with remaining ingredients according to the manufacturer's directions for your machine. Set the CYCLE, LOAF SIZE, and CRUST setting. Press START.

2. After about 5 minutes of kneading, check the consistency of your dough. If dough is not in a smooth round ball, open lid and with machine ON, add liquid a tablespoon at a time if too dry, or add flour a tablespoon at a time if too wet.

3. Remove the bread promptly from the pan when the machine beeps or on completing the cycle. Cool on rack before slicing.

Apple-Cinnamon Bread

Do not substitute fresh or canned apples for dried ones.

1 1/2-POUND	INGREDIENTS	2-POUND
1/2 cup	**Milk**	2/3 cup
1/4 cup	**Apple juice**	1/3 cup
3 tablespoons	**Butter or margarine, softened and cut up**	1/4 cup
1/4 cup	**Brown sugar, packed**	1/3 cup
1 teaspoon	**Ground cinnamon**	1 1/4 teaspoons
1 1/4 teaspoons	**Salt**	1 1/2 teaspoons
2 1/2 cups	**Bread flour, unsifted**	3 cups
2 1/4 teaspoons	**Active dry yeast or bread machine yeast**	2 1/2 teaspoons
2/3 cup	**Chopped dried apples or pears**	1 cup

TOPPING

Brush crust with 1 tablespoon melted butter and sprinkle with 2 teaspoons Cinnamon Sugar (page 206).

CYCLE SWEET OR RAISIN/NUT
CRUST SETTING AS DESIRED

1 If your machine does not have a preheat cycle, combine milk and apple juice and heat in microwave on HIGH power for 30 seconds (or heat in a saucepan for 1 minute to 80°F). Add to the bread pan with remaining ingredients (except the chopped dried apples or pears) according to the manufacturer's directions for your machine. Measure the chopped dried apples or pears to add at the beep or when manufacturer directs. Set the CYCLE, LOAF SIZE, and CRUST setting. Press START.

2 After about 5 minutes of kneading, check the consistency of your dough. If dough is not in a smooth round ball, open lid and with machine ON, add liquid a tablespoon at a time if too dry, or add flour a tablespoon at a time if too wet.

3 Remove the bread promptly from the pan when the machine beeps or on completing the cycle. If desired, add Topping to crust of bread. Cool on rack before slicing.

Apple Butter Bread

If you can find it, peach butter, sometimes available next to the apple butter in your supermarket jam and jelly section, is also great in this bread.

1 1/2-POUND	INGREDIENTS	2-POUND
3/4 cup	**Warm water (80°F)**	3/4 cup + 2 tablespoons
1/3 cup	**Apple or peach butter**	1/2 cup
3 tablespoons	**Butter or margarine, softened and cut up**	1/4 cup
1 teaspoon	**Vanilla extract**	1 1/2 teaspoons
3 tablespoons	**Sugar**	1/4 cup
1 1/4 teaspoons	**Salt**	1 1/2 teaspoons
1/4 teaspoon	**Ground nutmeg**	1/2 teaspoon
3 1/4 cups	**Bread flour, unsifted**	3 3/4 cups
2 1/2 teaspoons	**Active dry yeast or bread machine yeast**	3 teaspoons

CYCLE SWEET
CRUST SETTING LIGHT RECOMMENDED

1 Measure ingredients into the bread pan according to the manufacturer's directions for your machine. Set the CYCLE, LOAF SIZE, and CRUST setting. Press START.

2 After about 5 minutes of kneading, check the consistency of your dough. If dough is not in a smooth round ball, open lid and with machine ON, add liquid a tablespoon at a time if too dry, or add flour a tablespoon at a time if too wet.

3 Remove the bread promptly from the pan when the machine beeps or on completing the cycle. Cool on rack before slicing.

Brioche Loaf (French Sweet Bread)

This delightfully sweet loaf is tailor-made for breakfast or a tea break. It rises high, so do not use the 2-pound recipe unless your bread machine has a horizontal bread pan with a capacity of at least 12 cups.

1 1/2-POUND	INGREDIENTS	2-POUND
1/2 cup	**Water***	1/2 cup
1/2 cup	**Milk***	1/2 cup
1	**Egg(s)**	2
1/4 cup	**Butter or margarine, softened and cut up**	1/3 cup
1/4 cup	**Sugar**	1/3 cup
1 teaspoon	**Grated lemon peel**	1 1/2 teaspoons
3/4 teaspoon	**Salt**	1 teaspoon
3 1/3 cups	**Bread flour, unsifted**	4 cups
2 1/2 teaspoons	**Active dry yeast or bread machine yeast**	3 teaspoons

*Use the same amount for either size loaf.

CYCLE SWEET
CRUST SETTING AS DESIRED

1 If your machine does not have a preheat cycle, combine water and milk and heat in microwave on HIGH power for 30 seconds (or heat in a saucepan for 1 minute to 80°F). Add to the bread pan with remaining ingredients according to the manufacturer's directions for your machine. Set the CYCLE, LOAF SIZE, and CRUST SETTING. Press START.

2 After about 5 minutes of kneading, check the consistency of your dough. If dough is not in a smooth round ball, open lid and with machine ON, add liquid a tablespoon at a time if too dry, or add flour a tablespoon at a time if too wet.

3 Remove the bread promptly from the pan when the machine beeps or on completing the cycle. Cool on rack before slicing.

Lemon Yogurt Poppyseed Bread

Adding yogurt is such an easy way to achieve great lemon flavor. For lemon-lovers only!

1 1/2-POUND	INGREDIENTS	2-POUND
1 cup	**Lemon yogurt**	1 1/2 cups
1/4 cup	**Water**	2 tablespoons
2 tablespoons	**Butter or margarine, softened**	3 tablespoons
3 tablespoons	**Sugar**	1/4 cup
1 tablespoon	**Poppyseed**	4 teaspoons
1 teaspoon	**Salt**	1 1/2 teaspoons
3 1/3 cups	**Bread flour, unsifted**	4 cups
2 teaspoons	**Active dry yeast or bread machine yeast**	2 1/2 teaspoons

CYCLE SWEET
CRUST SETTING AS DESIRED

1 If your machine does not have a preheat cycle, combine lemon yogurt and water and heat in microwave on HIGH power for 30 seconds (or heat in a saucepan for 1 minute to 80°F). Add to the bread pan with remaining ingredients according to the manufacturer's directions for your machine. Set the CYCLE, LOAF SIZE, and CRUST SETTING. Press START.

2 After about 5 minutes of kneading, check the consistency of your dough. If dough is not in a smooth round ball, open lid and with machine ON, add liquid a tablespoon at a time if too dry, or add flour a tablespoon at a time if too wet.

3 Remove the bread promptly from the pan when the machine beeps or on completing the cycle. Cool on rack before slicing.

Honey Five-Spice Bread

Five-spice powder is a mixture of spices that varies, but often contains cinnamon, anise, fennel, Szechuan pepper, and cloves. It is sometimes labeled "Chinese five-spice powder." You'll find it in spice sections or the Asian food section of larger supermarkets or specialty food markets. You can substitute ground cinnamon in a pinch.

1 1/2-POUND	INGREDIENTS	2-POUND
3/4 cup + 2 tablespoons	**Milk**	1 cup + 2 tablespoons
1 tablespoon	**Vegetable oil**	1 1/2 tablespoons
1/4 cup	**Honey**	1/3 cup
1 teaspoon	**Salt**	1 1/4 teaspoons
3/4 teaspoon	**Five-spice powder or ground cinnamon**	1 1/4 teaspoons
2 1/3 cups	**Bread flour, unsifted**	2 1/2 cups
1 cup	**Whole wheat flour, unsifted**	1 1/3 cups
2 1/4 teaspoons	**Active dry yeast or bread machine yeast**	2 1/2 teaspoons

CYCLE SWEET OR WHOLE WHEAT
CRUST SETTING AS DESIRED

1 If your machine does not have a preheat cycle, heat milk in microwave on HIGH power for 30 seconds (or heat in a saucepan for 1 minute to 80°F). Add to the bread pan with remaining ingredients according to the manufacturer's directions for your machine. Set the CYCLE, LOAF SIZE, and CRUST SETTING. Press START.

2 After about 5 minutes of kneading, check the consistency of your dough. If dough is not in a smooth round ball, open lid and with machine ON, add liquid a tablespoon at a time if too dry, or add flour a tablespoon at a time if too wet.

3 Remove the bread promptly from the pan when the machine beeps or on completing the cycle. Cool on rack before slicing.

Orange Marmalade Bread

Apricot preserve is also wonderful in this loaf.

1 1/2-POUND	INGREDIENTS	2-POUND
1/2 cup	**Warm water (80°F)**	2/3 cup
1/2 cup	**Orange marmalade or apricot preserve***	1/2 cup
1/4 cup	**Butter or margarine, softened and cut up**	1/3 cup
1	**Egg(s)**	2
1 teaspoon	**Salt**	1 1/4 teaspoons
1 teaspoon	**Grated lemon peel**	1 1/2 teaspoons
3 1/3 cups	**Bread flour, unsifted**	4 cups
2 1/4 teaspoons	**Active dry yeast or bread machine yeast**	3 teaspoons

*Use the same amount for either size loaf.

CYCLE SWEET
CRUST SETTING AS DESIRED

1 If your machine does not have a preheat cycle, combine water and marmalade or preserves and heat in microwave on HIGH power for 30 seconds (or heat in a saucepan for 1 minute to 80°F). Add to the bread pan with remaining ingredients according to the manufacturer's directions for your machine. Set the CYCLE, LOAF SIZE, and CRUST SETTING. Press START.

2 After about 5 minutes of kneading, check the consistency of your dough. If dough is not in a smooth round ball, open lid and with machine ON, add liquid a tablespoon at a time if too dry, or add flour a tablespoon at a time if too wet.

3 Remove the bread promptly from the pan when the machine beeps or on completing the cycle. Cool on rack before slicing.

Sweet Carrot-Apricot Bread

No dried apricots in your cupboard?
Try substituting chopped dates, dried figs, prunes,
or dried peaches for the apricots.

1 1/2-POUND	INGREDIENTS	2-POUND
3/4 cup	**Warm water (80°F)**	3/4 cup + 2 tablespoons
3/4 cup	**Finely grated carrots**	1 cup
1/4 cup	**Butter or margarine, softened and cut up**	1/3 cup
3 tablespoons	**Honey**	1/4 cup
1 teaspoon	**Salt**	1 1/2 teaspoons
1 teaspoon	**Grated orange peel**	2 teaspoons
1/2 teaspoon	**Ground nutmeg**	3/4 teaspoon
3 1/4 cups	**Bread flour, unsifted**	4 cups
2 1/4 teaspoons	**Active dry yeast or bread machine yeast**	2 1/2 teaspoons
2/3 cup	**Chopped dried apricots**	1 cup

CYCLE SWEET OR RAISIN/NUT
CRUST SETTING AS DESIRED

1 Measure ingredients (except dried apricots) into the bread pan according to the manufacturer's directions for your machine. Measure dried apricots to add at the beep or when manufacturer directs. Set the CYCLE, LOAF SIZE, and CRUST SETTING. Press START.

2 After about 5 minutes of kneading, check the consistency of your dough. If dough is not in a smooth round ball, open lid and with machine ON, add liquid a tablespoon at a time if too dry, or add flour a tablespoon at a time if too wet.

3 Remove the bread promptly from the pan when the machine beeps or on completing the cycle. Cool on rack before slicing.

Pineapple Cream Cheese Loaf

This recipe produces a large loaf with a tender, almost cakelike texture and a mild cheese flavor. It's so good you'll want to eat it without butter.

1 1/2-POUND	INGREDIENTS	2-POUND
1/3 cup	**Water***	1/3 cup
1/2 cup	**Soft cream cheese,* room temperature, cut up**	1/2 cup
1/2 cup	**Crushed canned pineapple and juice**	2/3 cup
3 tablespoons	**Sugar**	4 tablespoons
1 1/2 teaspoons	**Grated orange or lemon peel**	2 teaspoons
1 1/4 teaspoons	**Salt**	1 1/2 teaspoons
3 1/3 cups	**Bread flour, unsifted**	3 2/3 cups
2 1/4 teaspoons	**Active dry yeast or bread machine yeast**	2 1/2 teaspoons

*Use the same amount for either size loaf.

CYCLE SWEET
CRUST SETTING AS DESIRED

1 If your machine does not have a preheat cycle, combine water with soft cream cheese and heat in microwave on HIGH power for 30 seconds (or heat in a saucepan for 1 minute to 80°F). Add to the bread pan with remaining ingredients according to the manufacturer's directions for your machine. Set the CYCLE, LOAF SIZE, and CRUST SETTING. Press START.

2 After about 5 minutes of kneading, check the consistency of your dough. If dough is not in a smooth round ball, open lid and with machine ON, add liquid a tablespoon at a time if too dry, or add flour a tablespoon at a time if too wet.

3 Remove the bread promptly from the pan when the machine beeps or on completing the cycle. Cool on rack before slicing.

Hawaiian Coconut Bread

Serve this loaf with a summer fresh fruit salad and a glass of iced tea.

1 1/2-POUND	INGREDIENTS	2-POUND
3/4 cup	**Warm water (80°F)**	3/4 cup + 1 tablespoon
1/2 cup	**Crushed canned pineapple and juice***	1/2 cup
3 tablespoons	**Butter or margarine, softened and cut up**	1/4 cup
1/4 cup	**Sugar**	1/3 cup
1 1/4 teaspoons	**Salt**	1 1/2 teaspoons
1/2 teaspoon	**Coconut extract (optional)**	1 teaspoon
3 1/3 cups	**Bread flour, unsifted**	3 2/3 cups
3/4 cup	**Shredded coconut***	3/4 cup
2 1/4 teaspoons	**Active dry yeast or bread machine yeast**	2 1/2 teaspoons
1/2 cup	**Golden raisins**	2/3 cup

*Use the same amount for either size loaf.

CYCLE SWEET OR RAISIN/NUT
CRUST SETTING AS DESIRED

1 Measure ingredients (except raisins) into the bread pan according to the manufacturer's directions for your machine. Measure raisins to add at the beep or when manufacturer directs. Set the CYCLE, LOAF SIZE, and CRUST SETTING. Press START.

2 After about 5 minutes of kneading, check the consistency of your dough. If dough is not in a smooth round ball, open lid and with machine ON, add liquid a tablespoon at a time if too dry, or add flour a tablespoon at a time if too wet.

3 Remove the bread promptly from the pan when the machine beeps or on completing the cycle. Cool on rack before slicing.

Toasted Coconut-Pineapple-Macadamia Loaf

If macadamia nuts are too rich for your budget, substitute almonds. The toasted coconut lends a bit of crunch and tropical flavor.

1 1/2-POUND	INGREDIENTS	2-POUND
2/3 cup	**Milk**	3/4 cup
1/2 cup	**Crushed canned pineapple and juice**	2/3 cup
1/4 cup	**Butter or margarine, softened and cut up**	1/3 cup
1/4 cup	**Sugar**	1/3 cup
1 1/4 teaspoons	**Salt**	1 1/2 teaspoons
2/3 cup	**Shredded coconut, toasted**	1 cup
3 1/3 cups	**Bread flour, unsifted**	4 cups
2 teaspoons	**Active dry yeast or bread machine yeast**	2 1/4 teaspoons
2/3 cup	**Chopped macadamia nuts or almonds**	3/4 cup

CYCLE SWEET OR RAISIN/NUT
CRUST SETTING AS DESIRED

1 If your machine does not have a preheat cycle, heat milk in microwave on HIGH power for 30 seconds (or heat in a saucepan for 1 minute to 80°F). Add to the bread pan with remaining ingredients (except the macadamia nuts or almonds) according to the manufacturer's directions for your machine. Measure macadamia nuts or almonds to add at the beep or when manufacturer directs. Set the CYCLE, LOAF SIZE, and CRUST SETTING. Press START.

2 After about 5 minutes of kneading, check the consistency of your dough. If dough is not in a smooth round ball, open lid and with machine ON, add liquid a tablespoon at a time if too dry, or add flour a tablespoon at a time if too wet.

3 Remove the bread promptly from the pan when the machine beeps or on completing the cycle. Cool on rack before slicing.

Apricot and Prune Bread

This is a rich, somewhat heavy bread, but it is ever so sweet and worth every calorie.

1 1/2-POUND	INGREDIENTS	2-POUND
3/4 cup	**Milk**	1 cup
1/4 cup	**Butter or margarine, softened and cut up**	1/3 cup
1	**Egg(s)**	2
1/4 cup	**Sugar**	1/3 cup
1 1/4 teaspoons	**Salt**	1 1/2 teaspoons
1 teaspoon	**Ground cinnamon**	1 1/2 teaspoons
3 cups	**Bread flour, unsifted**	3 3/4 cups
2 teaspoons	**Active dry yeast or bread machine yeast**	2 1/4 teaspoons
1/2 cup	**Chopped pitted prunes**	2/3 cup
1/2 cup	**Chopped dried apricots**	2/3 cup

CYCLE SWEET OR RAISIN/NUT
CRUST SETTING LIGHT RECOMMENDED

1 If your machine does not have a preheat cycle, heat milk in microwave on HIGH power for 30 seconds (or heat in a saucepan for 1 minute to 80°F). Add to the bread pan with remaining ingredients (except pitted prunes and dried apricots) according to the manufacturer's directions for your machine. Measure pitted prunes or dried apricots to add at the beep or when manufacturer directs. Set the CYCLE, LOAF SIZE, and CRUST SETTING. Press START.

2 After about 5 minutes of kneading, check the consistency of your dough. If dough is not in a smooth round ball, open lid and with machine ON, add liquid a tablespoon at a time if too dry, or add flour a tablespoon at a time if too wet.

3 Remove the bread promptly from the pan when the machine beeps or on completing the cycle. Cool on rack before slicing.

Sweet Prune Loaf

With the whole wheat flour, this bread will have a somewhat lower volume, but it is rich and sweet.

1 1/2-POUND	INGREDIENTS	2-POUND
1/2 cup	**Milk**	2/3 cup
1/4 cup	**Prune juice**	1/3 cup
2 tablespoons	**Butter or margarine, softened**	3 tablespoons
3 tablespoons	**Brown sugar, packed**	1/4 cup
1 teaspoon	**Salt**	1 1/4 teaspoons
1 1/2 cups	**Bread flour, unsifted**	2 cups
1 cup	**Whole wheat flour, unsifted***	1 cup
2 teaspoons	**Active dry yeast or bread machine yeast**	2 1/4 teaspoons
1/2 cup	**Chopped pitted prunes**	2/3 cup

*Use the same amount for either size loaf.

CYCLE SWEET, WHOLE WHEAT OR RAISIN/NUT
CRUST SETTING AS DESIRED

1 If your machine does not have a preheat cycle, combine milk and prune juice and heat in microwave on HIGH power for 30 seconds (or heat in a saucepan for 1 minute to 80°F). Add to the bread pan with remaining ingredients (except the pitted prunes) according to the manufacturer's directions for your machine. Measure pitted prunes to add at the beep or when manufacturer directs. Set the CYCLE, LOAF SIZE, and CRUST SETTING. Press START.

2 After about 5 minutes of kneading, check the consistency of your dough. If dough is not in a smooth round ball, open lid and with machine ON, add liquid a tablespoon at a time if too dry, or add flour a tablespoon at a time if too wet.

3 Remove the bread promptly from the pan when the machine beeps or on completing the cycle. Cool on rack before slicing.

Spiced Pumpkin Loaf

Try the Honey-Orange Butter (page 208) or Cinnamon Honey Butter (page 208) on slices of this mildly sweet bread. Use canned pumpkin or baby food pumpkin puree in the jar.

1 1/2-POUND	INGREDIENTS	2-POUND
1/2 cup + 2 tablespoons	**Milk***	1/2 cup + 2 tablespoons
3/4 cup	**Canned pumpkin puree**	1 cup
1 1/2 tablespoons	**Vegetable oil**	2 tablespoons
1/4 cup	**Sugar**	1/3 cup
1 teaspoon	**Salt**	1 1/4 teaspoons
1 teaspoon	**Ground cinnamon**	1 1/4 teaspoons
1/4 teaspoon	**Ground nutmeg**	1/2 teaspoon
3 1/3 cups	**Bread flour, unsifted**	3 2/3 cups
1 1/2 teaspoons	**Active dry yeast or bread machine yeast**	2 teaspoons

*Use the same amount for either size loaf.

CYCLE SWEET
CRUST SETTING AS DESIRED

1 If your machine does not have a preheat cycle, heat milk in microwave on HIGH power for 30 seconds (or heat in a saucepan for 1 minute to 80°F). Add to the bread pan with remaining ingredients according to the manufacturer's directions for your machine. Set the CYCLE, LOAF SIZE, and CRUST SETTING. Press START.

2 After about 5 minutes of kneading, check the consistency of your dough. If dough is not in a smooth round ball, open lid and with machine ON, add liquid a tablespoon at a time if too dry, or add flour a tablespoon at a time if too wet.

3 Remove the bread promptly from the pan when the machine beeps or on completing the cycle. Cool on rack before slicing.

Zucchini Spice Bread

This is a yeast-bread version of the familiar quick bread. Whole wheat flour makes it extra-wholesome.

1 1/2-POUND	INGREDIENTS	2-POUND
2/3 cup	**Warm water (80°F)**	1 cup
1/2 cup	**Finely shredded raw zucchini**	2/3 cup
1 tablespoon	**Vegetable oil**	1 1/2 tablespoons
3 tablespoons	**Sugar**	1/4 cup
1 teaspoon	**Salt**	1 1/4 teaspoons
1/2 teaspoon	**Ground cinnamon**	1 teaspoon
1/8 teaspoon	**Ground nutmeg**	1/4 teaspoon
1/8 teaspoon	**Ground cloves**	1/4 teaspoon
1 1/2 cups	**Bread flour, unsifted**	2 cups
3/4 cup	**Whole wheat flour, unsifted**	1 cup
1 1/2 teaspoons	**Active dry yeast or bread machine yeast**	2 teaspoons
1/2 cup	**Raisins**	2/3 cup

CYCLE WHOLE WHEAT OR RAISIN/NUT
CRUST SETTING LIGHT RECOMMENDED

1 Measure the ingredients (except raisins) into the bread pan according to the manufacturer's directions for your machine. Measure raisins to add at the beep or when manufacturer directs. Set the CYCLE, LOAF SIZE, and CRUST SETTING. Press START.

2 After about 5 minutes of kneading, check the consistency of your dough. If dough is not in a smooth round ball, open lid and with machine ON, add liquid a tablespoon at a time if too dry, or add flour a tablespoon at a time if too wet.

3 Remove the bread promptly from the pan when the machine beeps or on completing the cycle. Cool on rack before slicing.

Pear-Cardamom Bread

Inspired by a Scandinavian bread, this loaf bakes up best when made with baby-food pureed pears. Try it for chicken salad sandwiches!

1½-POUND	INGREDIENTS	2-POUND
¾ cup	**Milk**	¾ cup + 2 tablespoons
⅔ cup or one 6-ounce jar	**Pureed pears***	⅔ cup or one 6-ounce jar
2 tablespoons	**Butter or margarine, softened**	2½ tablespoons
¼ cup	**Brown sugar, packed**	⅓ cup
1 teaspoon	**Grated lemon peel**	1½ teaspoons
1 teaspoon	**Salt**	1¼ teaspoons
1 teaspoon	**Ground cardamom**	1¼ teaspoons
3⅓ cups	**Bread flour, unsifted**	4 cups
2¼ teaspoons	**Active dry yeast or bread machine yeast**	3 teaspoons

*Use the same amount for either size loaf.

CYCLE SWEET
CRUST SETTING LIGHT TO MEDIUM RECOMMENDED

1 If your machine does not have a preheat cycle, heat milk in microwave on HIGH power for 30 seconds (or heat in a saucepan for 1 minute to 80°F). Add to the bread pan with remaining ingredients according to the manufacturer's directions for your machine. Set the CYCLE, LOAF SIZE, and CRUST SETTING. Press START.

2 After about 5 minutes of kneading, check the consistency of your dough. If dough is not in a smooth round ball, open lid and with machine ON, add liquid a tablespoon at a time if too dry, or add flour a tablespoon at a time if too wet.

3 Remove the bread promptly from the pan when the machine beeps or on completing the cycle. Cool on rack before slicing.

Toasted Almond Bread

See tips for toasting nuts (page 11). If you're nuts about almonds, you'll love this bread.

1 1/2-POUND	INGREDIENTS	2-POUND
1 cup	**Milk**	1 cup + 2 tablespoons
1	**Egg***	1
2 tablespoons	**Butter or margarine, softened**	3 tablespoons
1/4 cup	**Sugar**	1/3 cup
1 teaspoon	**Salt**	1 1/4 teaspoons
1/2 teaspoon	**Almond extract**	3/4 teaspoon
3 1/3 cups	**Bread flour, unsifted**	4 cups
2 teaspoons	**Active dry yeast or bread machine yeast**	2 1/2 teaspoons
2/3 cup	**Chopped toasted almonds or pine nuts***	2/3 cup

*Use the same amount for either size loaf.

CYCLE SWEET OR RAISIN/NUT
CRUST SETTING AS DESIRED

1 If your machine does not have a preheat cycle, heat milk in microwave on HIGH power for 30 seconds (or heat in a saucepan for 1 minute to 80°F). Add to the bread pan with remaining ingredients (except toasted almonds or pine nuts) according to the manufacturer's directions for your machine. Measure toasted almonds or pine nuts to add at the beep or when manufacturer directs. Set the CYCLE, LOAF SIZE, and CRUST SETTING. Press START.

2 After about 5 minutes of kneading, check the consistency of your dough. If dough is not in a smooth round ball, open lid and with machine ON, add liquid a tablespoon at a time if too dry, or add flour a tablespoon at a time if too wet.

3 Remove the bread promptly from the pan when the machine beeps or on completing the cycle. Cool on rack before slicing.

Rocky Road Bread

Yes, it's marshmallow creme, chocolate, and nuts—in bread!

1 1/2-POUND	INGREDIENTS	2-POUND
1 cup + 2 tablespoons	**Warm water (80°F)**	1 1/4 cups
1/3 cup	**Marshmallow creme**	1/2 cup
1 tablespoon	**Vegetable oil**	1 1/2 tablespoons
3 tablespoons	**Sugar**	1/4 cup
3 tablespoons	**Unsweetened cocoa powder**	1/4 cup
1 teaspoon	**Salt**	1 1/2 teaspoons
2 teaspoons	**Vanilla extract**	2 1/2 teaspoons
3 cups	**Bread flour, unsifted**	3 2/3 cups
2 teaspoons	**Active dry yeast or bread machine yeast**	2 1/2 teaspoons
1/2 cup	**Chopped nuts (any type)**	2/3 cup
1/2 cup	**Chocolate chips**	2/3 cup

CYCLE SWEET OR RAISIN/NUT
(DELAY-BAKE CAN BE USED)
CRUST SETTING AS DESIRED

1 Measure ingredients (except chopped nuts and chocolate chips) into the bread pan according to the manufacturer's directions for your machine. Measure chopped nuts and chocolate chips to add at the beep or when manufacturer directs. Set the CYCLE, LOAF SIZE, and CRUST SETTING. Press START.

2 After about 5 minutes of kneading, check the consistency of your dough. If dough is not in a smooth round ball, open lid and with machine ON, add liquid a tablespoon at a time if too dry, or add flour a tablespoon at a time if too wet.

3 Remove the bread promptly from the pan when the machine beeps or on completing the cycle. Cool on rack before slicing.

Nutty Chocolate Chip Bread

For extra fun, substitute M&M candies or Reese's Pieces for the chocolate chips.

1 1/2-POUND	INGREDIENTS	2-POUND
1 cup	**Milk**	1 1/4 cups
3 tablespoons	**Butter or margarine, softened and cut up**	1/4 cup
1/4 cup	**Brown sugar, packed**	1/3 cup
1 1/4 teaspoons	**Salt**	1 1/2 teaspoons
1 1/2 teaspoons	**Vanilla extract**	2 teaspoons
3 1/3 cups	**Bread flour, unsifted**	3 3/4 cups
2 teaspoons	**Active dry yeast or bread machine yeast**	2 1/2 teaspoons
2/3 cup	**Chocolate chips**	3/4 cup
1/2 cup	**Chopped nuts (any type)**	2/3 cup

CYCLE SWEET OR RAISIN/NUT
CRUST SETTING AS DESIRED

1 If your machine does not have a preheat cycle, heat milk in microwave on HIGH power for 30 seconds (or heat in a saucepan for 1 minute to 80°F). Add to the bread pan with remaining ingredients (except chocolate chips and chopped nuts) according to the manufacturer's directions for your machine. Measure chocolate chips and chopped nuts to add at the beep or when manufacturer directs. Set the CYCLE, LOAF SIZE, and CRUST SETTING. Press START.

2 After about 5 minutes of kneading, check the consistency of your dough. If dough is not in a smooth round ball, open lid and with machine ON, add liquid a tablespoon at a time if too dry, or add flour a tablespoon at a time if too wet.

3 Remove the bread promptly from the pan when the machine beeps or on completing the cycle. Cool on rack before slicing.

Laura's Peanut Butter-Chocolate Bread

I developed this bread for my godchild, Laura Hudson, who lives for peanut butter and chocolate! If your child's school lunches have lost their charm, try this bread for peanut butter and banana sandwiches. You'll get the parent-of-the-year award!

1½-POUND	INGREDIENTS	2-POUND
1 cup	**Warm water (80°F)**	1 cup + 2 tablespoons
½ cup	**Crunchy peanut butter***	½ cup
¼ cup	**Brown sugar, packed**	⅓ cup
1 teaspoon	**Salt**	1¼ teaspoons
1½ teaspoons	**Vanilla extract**	2 teaspoons
3⅓ cups	**Bread flour, unsifted**	4 cups
1½ teaspoons	**Active dry yeast or bread machine yeast**	2 teaspoons
⅔ cup	**Chocolate chips**	1 cup

*Use the same amount for either size loaf.

CYCLE SWEET OR RAISIN/NUT
(DELAY-BAKE CAN BE USED)
CRUST SETTING AS DESIRED

1 Measure ingredients (except chocolate chips) into the bread pan according to the manufacturer's directions for your machine. Measure chocolate chips to add at the beep or when manufacturer directs. Set the CYCLE, LOAF SIZE, and CRUST SETTING. Press START.

2 After about 5 minutes of kneading, check the consistency of your dough. If dough is not in a smooth round ball, open lid and with machine ON, add liquid a tablespoon at a time if too dry, or add flour a tablespoon at a time if too wet.

3 Remove the bread promptly from the pan when the machine beeps or on completing the cycle. Cool on rack before slicing.

Chocolate Cherry Loaf

This bread features the great flavor of dried cherries.
Maraschino cherries, well drained, are a good substitute.

1 1/2-POUND	INGREDIENTS	2-POUND
1/2 cup	**Milk**	3/4 cup
1/2 cup	**Water***	1/2 cup
1 1/2 tablespoons	**Butter or margarine, softened**	2 tablespoons
1/4 cup	**Sugar**	1/3 cup
3 tablespoons	**Unsweetened cocoa powder***	3 tablespoons
1 teaspoon	**Salt**	1 1/4 teaspoons
1 teaspoon	**Almond extract**	1 1/2 teaspoons
3 cups	**Bread flour, unsifted**	3 2/3 cups
2 teaspoons	**Active dry yeast or bread machine yeast**	2 1/4 teaspoons
2/3 cup	**Dried cherries or halved maraschino cherries, drained**	1 cup
1/2 cup	**Chocolate chips**	2/3 cup

*Use the same amount for either size loaf.

CYCLE SWEET OR RAISIN/NUT
CRUST SETTING LIGHT RECOMMENDED

1 If your machine does not have a preheat cycle, heat milk and water in microwave on HIGH power for 30 seconds (or heat in a saucepan for 1 minute to 80°F). Add to the bread pan with remaining ingredients (except cherries and chocolate chips) according to the manufacturer's directions for your machine. Measure cherries and chocolate chips to add at the beep or when manufacturer directs. Set the CYCLE, LOAF SIZE, and CRUST SETTING. Press START.

2 After about 5 minutes of kneading, check the consistency of your dough. If dough is not in a smooth round ball, open lid and with machine ON, add liquid a tablespoon at a time if too dry, or add flour a tablespoon at a time if too wet.

3 Remove the bread promptly from the pan when the machine beeps or on completing the cycle. Cool on rack before slicing.

Double Chocolate-Almond Bread

A marvelous bread for brunch or afternoon coffee or tea.

1 1/2-POUND	INGREDIENTS	2-POUND
1 cup + 2 tablespoons	**Milk**	1 1/4 cups
1 1/2 tablespoons	**Butter or margarine, softened**	2 tablespoons
1/4 cup	**Sugar**	1/3 cup
3 tablespoons	**Unsweetened cocoa powder***	3 tablespoons
1 teaspoon	**Salt**	1 1/4 teaspoons
1 teaspoon	**Almond extract**	1 1/2 teaspoons
3 cups	**Bread flour, unsifted**	3 2/3 cups
2 teaspoons	**Active dry yeast or bread machine yeast**	2 1/4 teaspoons
1/2 cup	**Slivered almonds**	2/3 cup
1/2 cup	**Chocolate chips**	2/3 cup

*Use the same amount for either size loaf.

CYCLE SWEET OR RAISIN/NUT
CRUST SETTING AS DESIRED

1. If your machine does not have a preheat cycle, heat milk in microwave on HIGH power for 30 seconds (or heat in a saucepan for 1 minute to 80°F). Add to the bread pan with remaining ingredients (except slivered almonds and chocolate chips) according to the manufacturer's directions for your machine. Measure slivered almonds and chocolate chips to add at the beep or when manufacturer directs. Set the CYCLE, LOAF SIZE, and CRUST SETTING. Press START.

2. After about 5 minutes of kneading, check the consistency of your dough. If dough is not in a smooth round ball, open lid and with machine ON, add liquid a tablespoon at a time if too dry, or add flour a tablespoon at a time if too wet.

3. Remove the bread promptly from the pan when the machine beeps or on completing the cycle. Cool on rack before slicing.

Chocolate and Cinnamon Raisin Bread

Cinnamon-covered raisins are now available in the dried fruit section of larger markets. If you can't find the coated raisins, use plain ones and add ground cinnamon, using the same amount of cinnamon as chocolate extract.

1 1/2-POUND	INGREDIENTS	2-POUND
1 cup	**Milk**	1 cup + 2 tablespoons
1 1/2 tablespoons	**Butter or margarine, softened**	2 tablespoons
3 tablespoons	**Brown sugar, packed**	1/4 cup
3 tablespoons	**Unsweetened cocoa powder***	3 tablespoons
1 teaspoon	**Salt**	1 1/4 teaspoons
1 teaspoon	**Chocolate or vanilla extract**	1 1/2 teaspoons
3 cups	**Bread flour, unsifted**	3 2/3 cups
2 1/4 teaspoons	**Active dry yeast or bread machine yeast**	2 1/2 teaspoons
3/4 cup	**Cinnamon-coated raisins or plain raisins**	1 cup
1/2 cup	**Chocolate chips**	2/3 cup

*Use the same amount for either size loaf.

CYCLE SWEET OR RAISIN/NUT
CRUST SETTING LIGHT RECOMMENDED

1 If your machine does not have a preheat cycle, heat milk in microwave on HIGH power for 30 seconds (or heat in a saucepan for 1 minute to 80°F). Add to the bread pan with remaining ingredients (except raisins and chocolate chips) according to the manufacturer's directions for your machine. Measure raisins and chocolate chips to add at the beep or when manufacturer directs. Set the CYCLE, LOAF SIZE, and CRUST SETTING. Press START.

2 After about 5 minutes of kneading, check the consistency of your dough. If dough is not in a smooth round ball, open lid and with machine ON, add liquid a tablespoon at a time if too dry, or add flour a tablespoon at a time if too wet.

3 Remove the bread promptly from the pan when the machine beeps or on completing the cycle. Cool on rack before slicing.

Baking Tips

Chocolate Substitution Guide

It's a good idea to use the type of chocolate that's called for in a recipe, but try these substitutes in a pinch:

- **1 square (1 ounce) unsweetened chocolate, melted = 3 tablespoons unsweetened cocoa powder + 1 tablespoon cooking oil or solid shortening**
- **1 square (1 ounce) semisweet chocolate, melted = 1 square (1 ounce) unsweetened chocolate + 1 tablespoon sugar**

CHAPTER

5

Vegetable, Cheese, and Herb Breads

BRIOCHE AU FROMAGE (CHEESE BRIOCHE)

DOUBLE CHEESE BREAD

CREAM CHEESE 'N' CHIVE BREAD

MAYTAG BLUE CHEESE BREAD

ITALIAN CHEESE AND GARLIC BREAD

GREEK OLIVE BREAD WITH FETA

CHEDDAR, BACON, AND ONION BREAD

JALAPEÑO CHEESE BREAD

PARMESAN HERB BREAD

BASIL PESTO BREAD

RED PEPPER PESTO BREAD

GAZPACHO BREAD

ITALIAN TOMATO BREAD

SUN-DRIED TOMATO OLIVE BREAD

YEAST CORN BREAD WITH CHIPOTLE CHILE

SPINACH POTATO BREAD WITH BASIL

SWEET POTATO WHEAT BREAD

SQUASH AND WALNUT BREAD

SWISS BEER BREAD

ROSEMARY CARROT BREAD

BACK-AT-THE-RANCH BREAD

TARRAGON MUSTARD BREAD

GREEN ONION-POPPYSEED LOAF

Brioche au Fromage (Cheese Brioche)

Here is a cheesy adaptation of the richest of all yeast breads. Because it is a moist bread, high in fat, it's a good keeper.

1 1/2-POUND	INGREDIENTS	2-POUND
1/3 cup	**Milk**	1/2 cup
1/3 cup	**Water**	1/2 cup
1	**Egg***	1
1/2 cup	**Shredded Gruyère or Swiss cheese**	2/3 cup
1/4 cup	**Butter or margarine, softened and cut up**	1/3 cup
1 tablespoon	**Sugar**	1 1/2 tablespoons
1 1/4 teaspoons	**Salt**	1 1/2 teaspoons
2 3/4 cups	**Bread flour, unsifted**	3 1/2 cups
1 1/2 teaspoons	**Active dry yeast or bread machine yeast**	2 teaspoons

*Use the same amount for either size loaf.

CYCLE SWEET
CRUST SETTING AS DESIRED

1 If your machine does not have a pre-heat cycle, combine milk and water and heat in microwave on HIGH power for 30 seconds (or heat in a saucepan for 1 minute to 80°F). Add to the bread pan with remaining ingredients according to the manufacturer's directions for your machine. Set the CYCLE, LOAF SIZE, and CRUST SETTING. Press START.

2 After about 5 minutes of kneading, check the consistency of your dough. If dough is not in a smooth round ball, open lid and with machine ON, add liquid a tablespoon at a time if too dry, or add flour a tablespoon at a time if too wet.

3 Remove the bread promptly from the pan when the machine beeps or on completing the cycle. Cool on rack before slicing.

Double Cheese Bread

If you like jalapeño jack cheese, you can substitute it for regular Monterey jack in this recipe—it will add a nice kick to this flavor-filled bread.

1 1/2-POUND	INGREDIENTS	2-POUND
1 cup + 2 tablespoons	**Milk**	1 1/3 cups
1 1/2 tablespoons	**Vegetable oil**	2 tablespoons
1 1/2 tablespoons	**Sugar***	1 1/2 tablespoons
1 1/2 tablespoons	**Fresh chopped parsley**	2 tablespoons
1 teaspoon	**Salt**	1 1/2 teaspoons
1/2 teaspoon	**Garlic salt***	1/2 teaspoon
3 1/3 cups	**Bread flour, unsifted**	4 cups
1/4 cup	**Shredded sharp cheddar cheese**	1/3 cup
1/4 cup	**Shredded Monterey jack, mozzarella, or Swiss cheese**	1/3 cup
2 1/4 teaspoons	**Active dry yeast or bread machine yeast**	2 1/2 teaspoons

*Use the same amount for either size loaf.

CYCLE SWEET
CRUST SETTING AS DESIRED

1 If your machine does not have a preheat cycle, heat milk in microwave on HIGH power for 30 seconds (or heat in a saucepan for 1 minute to 80°F). Add to the bread pan with remaining ingredients according to the manufacturer's directions for your machine. Set the CYCLE, LOAF SIZE, and CRUST SETTING. Press START.

2 After about 5 minutes of kneading, check the consistency of your dough. If dough is not in a smooth round ball, open lid and with machine ON, add liquid a tablespoon at a time if too dry, or add flour a tablespoon at a time if too wet.

3 Remove the bread promptly from the pan when the machine beeps or on completing the cycle. Cool on rack before slicing.

Cream Cheese 'n' Chive Bread

This recipe produces a lovely high loaf with a wonderful texture and a mild cheese and onion flavor.

1½-POUND**	INGREDIENTS	2-POUND**
¾ cup	**Warm water (80°F)**	¾ cup + 2 tablespoons
½ cup	**Soft cream cheese*, cut up, room temperature**	½ cup
1½ tablespoons	**Sugar**	2 tablespoons
1½ tablespoons	**Chives, chopped**	2 tablespoons
1¼ teaspoons	**Salt**	1½ teaspoons
3 cups	**Bread flour, unsifted**	3½ cups
2 teaspoons	**Active dry yeast or bread machine yeast**	2¼ teaspoons

*Use the same amount for either size loaf.

**Use the 1½-pound recipe if your bread machine has a vertical bread pan. The 2-pound recipe can be used with bread machines with horizontal bread pans that have at least a 12-cup capacity.

CYCLE SWEET
CRUST SETTING AS DESIRED

1 Measure ingredients into the bread pan according to the manufacturer's directions for your machine. Set the CYCLE, LOAF SIZE, and CRUST SETTING. Press START.

2 After about 5 minutes of kneading, check the consistency of your dough. If dough is not in a smooth round ball, open lid and with machine ON, add liquid a tablespoon at a time if too dry, or add flour a tablespoon at a time if too wet.

3 Remove the bread promptly from the pan when the machine beeps or on completing the cycle. Cool on rack before slicing.

Maytag Blue Cheese Bread

Maytag, Iowa, is known for producing a superb blue cheese that carries that town's name. The blue cheese flavor is best when the bread is warm. If you enjoy sourdough breads, you might also want to try Blue Cheese Sourdough Bread (page 134).

1 1/2-POUND	INGREDIENTS	2-POUND
1 cup	**Buttermilk**	1 1/4 cups
1/3 cup	**Crumbled blue cheese**	1/2 cup
2 teaspoons	**Oil**	1 tablespoon
2 tablespoons	**Fresh chopped parsley**	3 tablespoons
1 tablespoon	**Sugar**	1 1/2 tablespoons
1 1/4 teaspoons	**Salt**	1 1/2 teaspoons
3 cups	**Bread flour, unsifted**	3 2/3 cups
1 1/2 teaspoons	**Active dry yeast or bread machine yeast**	2 teaspoons

CYCLE SWEET
CRUST SETTING AS DESIRED

1. If your machine does not have a preheat cycle, heat buttermilk in microwave on HIGH power for 30 seconds (or heat in a saucepan for 1 minute to 80°F). Add to the bread pan with remaining ingredients according to the manufacturer's directions for your machine. Set the CYCLE, LOAF SIZE, and CRUST SETTING. Press START.

2. After about 5 minutes of kneading, check the consistency of your dough. If dough is not in a smooth round ball, open lid and with machine ON, add liquid a tablespoon at a time if too dry, or add flour a tablespoon at a time if too wet.

3. Remove the bread promptly from the pan when the machine beeps or on completing the cycle. Cool on rack before slicing.

Italian Cheese and Garlic Bread

If you like, brush this loaf with olive oil and dust with grated Parmesan cheese as soon as you have removed it from the bread pan. Serve warm.

1 1/2-POUND	INGREDIENTS	2-POUND
3/4 cup	**Milk**	1 1/4 cups
1 tablespoon	**Olive or vegetable oil**	1 1/2 tablespoons
1/4 cup	**Shredded provolone or mozzarella cheese***	1/4 cup
3 tablespoons	**Grated Parmesan cheese**	1/4 cup
1 tablespoon	**Sugar**	1 1/2 tablespoons
1 teaspoon	**Garlic salt***	1 teaspoon
1/2 teaspoon	**Salt**	1 teaspoon
2 2/3 cups	**Bread flour, unsifted**	3 1/3 cups
1 1/2 teaspoons	**Active dry yeast or bread machine yeast**	2 teaspoons

*Use the same amount for either size loaf.

CYCLE SWEET
CRUST SETTING AS DESIRED

1 If your machine does not have a preheat cycle, heat milk in microwave on HIGH power for 30 seconds (or heat in a saucepan for 1 minute to 80°F). Add to the bread pan with remaining ingredients according to the manufacturer's directions for your machine. Set the CYCLE, LOAF SIZE, and CRUST SETTING. Press START.

2 After about 5 minutes of kneading, check the consistency of your dough. If dough is not in a smooth round ball, open lid and with machine ON, add liquid a tablespoon at a time if too dry, or add flour a tablespoon at a time if too wet.

3 Remove the bread promptly from the pan when the machine beeps or on completing the cycle. Cool on rack before slicing.

Greek Olive Bread with Feta

This bread will make you want to dance! Buy the feta cheese in blocks or already crumbled. It also comes flavored with herbs, which you can substitute for the plain feta cheese.

1 1/2-POUND	INGREDIENTS	2-POUND
1 cup	**Buttermilk**	1 1/4 cups
1/3 cup	**Crumbled feta cheese**	1/2 cup
2 teaspoons	**Olive or vegetable oil**	1 tablespoon
1 tablespoon	**Sugar**	1 1/2 tablespoons
1 1/4 teaspoons	**Salt**	1 1/2 teaspoons
3 cups	**Bread flour, unsifted**	3 2/3 cups
2 teaspoons	**Active dry yeast or bread machine yeast**	2 1/2 teaspoons
1/2 cup	**Halved pitted Greek or ripe olives**	2/3 cup

VARIATION

Add 1 tablespoon drained capers.

CYCLE BASIC OR RASIN/NUT
CRUST SETTING AS DESIRED

1 If your machine does not have a preheat cycle, heat buttermilk in microwave on HIGH power for 30 seconds (or heat in a saucepan for 1 minute to 80°F). Add to the bread pan with remaining ingredients (except olives) according to the manufacturer's directions for your machine. Measure olives to add at the beep or when manufacturer directs. Set the CYCLE, LOAF SIZE, and CRUST SETTING. Press START.

2 After about 5 minutes of kneading, check the consistency of your dough. If dough is not in a smooth round ball, open lid and with machine ON, add liquid a tablespoon at a time if too dry, or add flour a tablespoon at a time if too wet.

3 Remove the bread promptly from the pan when the machine beeps or on completing the cycle. Cool on rack before slicing.

Cheddar, Bacon, and Onion Bread

The sharper your cheddar, the stronger the flavor.

1 1/2-POUND	INGREDIENTS	2-POUND
3/4 cup + 2 tablespoons	**Milk**	1 cup
1/3 cup	**Shredded cheddar cheese**	1/2 cup
1/3 cup	**Chopped onion**	1/2 cup
1/4 cup	**Crumbled cooked bacon**	1/3 cup
2 teaspoons	**Vegetable oil**	1 tablespoon
1 tablespoon	**Sugar**	1 1/2 tablespoons
1/2 teaspoon	**Salt***	1/2 teaspoon
2 1/2 cups	**Bread flour, unsifted**	3 cups
1 1/2 teaspoons	**Active dry yeast or bread machine yeast**	2 teaspoons

*Use the same amount for either size loaf.

CYCLE SWEET
CRUST SETTING AS DESIRED

1 If your machine does not have a preheat cycle, heat milk in microwave on HIGH power for 30 seconds (or heat in a saucepan for 1 minute to 80°F). Add to the bread pan with remaining ingredients according to the manufacturer's directions for your machine. Set the CYCLE, LOAF SIZE, and CRUST SETTING. Press START.

2 After about 5 minutes of kneading, check the consistency of your dough. If dough is not in a smooth round ball, open lid and with machine ON, add liquid a tablespoon at a time if too dry, or add flour a tablespoon at a time if too wet.

3 Remove the bread promptly from the pan when the machine beeps or on completing the cycle. Cool on rack before slicing.

Jalapeño Cheese Bread

This bread is the perfect partner for a bowl of chili.

1 1/2-POUND	INGREDIENTS	2-POUND
3/4 cup + 2 tablespoons	**Milk**	1 cup
2 teaspoons	**Vegetable oil**	1 tablespoon
1/2 cup	**Shredded Swiss, cheddar, or Monterey jack cheese**	2/3 cup
1 1/2 tablespoons	**Finely chopped jalapeño or mild green chile**	2 tablespoons
1 tablespoon	**Diced pimiento**	1 1/2 tablespoons
1 tablespoon	**Sugar**	1 1/2 tablespoons
1 teaspoon	**Salt**	1 1/4 teaspoons
2 1/2 cups	**Bread flour, unsifted**	3 cups
1 1/2 teaspoons	**Active dry yeast or bread machine yeast**	2 teaspoons

CYCLE SWEET
CRUST SETTING AS DESIRED

1. If your machine does not have a preheat cycle, heat milk in microwave on HIGH power for 30 seconds (or heat in a saucepan for 1 minute to 80°F). Add to the bread pan with remaining ingredients according to the manufacturer's directions for your machine. Set the CYCLE, LOAF SIZE, and CRUST SETTING. Press START.

2. After about 5 minutes of kneading, check the consistency of your dough. If dough is not in a smooth round ball, open lid and with machine ON, add liquid a tablespoon at a time if too dry, or add flour a tablespoon at a time if too wet.

3. Remove the bread promptly from the pan when the machine beeps or on completing the cycle. Cool on rack before slicing.

Parmesan Herb Bread

Try slices of this bread topped with the Roasted Garlic Spread (page 214).

1½-POUND	INGREDIENTS	2-POUND
1 cup + 2 tablespoons	**Milk**	1¼ cups
1½ tablespoons	**Olive or vegetable oil**	2 tablespoons
½ cup	**Grated Parmesan or Romano cheese***	½ cup
1½ tablespoons	**Sugar**	2 tablespoons
1 teaspoon	**Salt**	1¼ teaspoons
1 teaspoon	**Dried thyme, basil, or dill**	1½ teaspoons
3⅓ cups	**Bread flour, unsifted**	4 cups
2¼ teaspoons	**Active dry yeast or bread machine yeast**	2½ teaspoons

*Use the same amount for either size loaf.

CYCLE SWEET
CRUST SETTING AS DESIRED

1 If your machine does not have a preheat cycle, heat milk in microwave on HIGH power for 30 seconds (or heat in a saucepan for 1 minute to 80°F). Add to the bread pan with remaining ingredients according to the manufacturer's directions for your machine. Set the CYCLE, LOAF SIZE, and CRUST SETTING. Press START.

2 After about 5 minutes of kneading, check the consistency of your dough. If dough is not in a smooth round ball, open lid and with machine ON, add liquid a tablespoon at a time if too dry, or add flour a tablespoon at a time if too wet.

3 Remove the bread promptly from the pan when the machine beeps or on completing the cycle. Cool on rack before slicing.

Basil Pesto Bread

Cover and refrigerate leftover pesto to toss with pasta or stir into a salad dressing.

1 1/2-POUND	INGREDIENTS	2-POUND
1 cup	**Warm water (80°F)**	1 cup + 2 tablespoons
1/3 cup	**Basil Pesto (recipe below)**	1/2 cup
1 1/2 tablespoons	**Sugar**	2 tablespoons
1 teaspoon	**Salt**	1 1/2 teaspoons
3 1/3 cups	**Bread flour, unsifted**	4 cups
2 teaspoons	**Active dry yeast or bread machine yeast**	2 1/4 teaspoons

BASIL PESTO

In blender container or food processor bowl, place 1/2 cup chopped fresh basil leaves, 1/3 cup olive oil or vegetable oil, 1/4 cup grated Parmesan cheese, 1 tablespoon lemon juice, and 1 minced garlic clove. Cover and process until smooth. Makes 2/3 cup. Refrigerate any leftovers. Or use purchased refrigerated pesto brought to room temperature.

CYCLE BASIC
CRUST SETTING AS DESIRED

1. Measure ingredients into the bread pan according to the manufacturer's directions for your machine. Set the CYCLE, LOAF SIZE, and CRUST SETTING. Press START.

2. After about 5 minutes of kneading, check the consistency of your dough. If dough is not in a smooth round ball, open lid and with machine ON, add liquid a tablespoon at a time if too dry, or add flour a tablespoon at a time if too wet.

3. Remove the bread promptly from the pan when the machine beeps or on completing the cycle. Cool on rack before slicing.

Red Pepper Pesto Bread

Use your leftover pesto to spread on slices of the warm bread.

1 1/2-POUND	INGREDIENTS	2-POUND
3/4 cup + 2 tablespoons	**Warm water (80°F)**	1 cup + 2 tablespoons
1/3 cup	**Red Pepper Pesto (recipe below)**	1/2 cup
1 1/2 tablespoons	**Sugar**	2 tablespoons
1 teaspoon	**Salt**	1 1/2 teaspoons
3 1/4 cups	**Bread flour, unsifted**	3 3/4 cups
2 1/4 teaspoons	**Active dry yeast or bread machine yeast**	2 1/2 teaspoons

RED PEPPER PESTO

In blender container or food processor bowl, place 1 chopped red bell pepper, 1/2 cup chopped fresh basil leaves, 1/2 cup olive oil or vegetable oil, 1/3 cup grated Parmesan cheese, and 1 minced garlic clove. Cover and process until smooth. Refrigerate any leftovers. Makes 1 1/3 cups.

CYCLE BASIC
CRUST SETTING AS DESIRED

1 Measure ingredients into the bread pan according to the manufacturer's directions for your machine. Set the CYCLE, LOAF SIZE, and CRUST SETTING. Press START.

2 After about 5 minutes of kneading, check the consistency of your dough. If dough is not in a smooth round ball, open lid and with machine ON, add liquid a tablespoon at a time if too dry, or add flour a tablespoon at a time if too wet.

3 Remove the bread promptly from the pan when the machine beeps or on completing the cycle. Cool on rack before slicing.

Gazpacho Bread

This delightful bread is well worth the bit of extra effort to chop a few ingredients. Its pale orange color makes these slices a great addition to a bread basket.

1 1/2-POUND	INGREDIENTS	2-POUND
1/2 cup	**V-8 juice**	2/3 cup
1/3 cup	**Water**	1/2 cup
1 tablespoon	**Olive or vegetable oil**	1 1/2 tablespoons
1/3 cup	**Chopped red or green bell pepper***	1/3 cup
2 tablespoons	**Chopped green onion (scallion)**	3 tablespoons
1 tablespoon	**Chopped cilantro**	1 1/2 tablespoons
1 tablespoon	**Sugar**	1 1/2 tablespoons
1/2 teaspoon	**Salt***	1/2 teaspoon
1/4 teaspoon	**Garlic salt***	1/4 teaspoon
2 3/4 cups	**Bread flour, unsifted**	3 1/2 cups
1 1/4 teaspoons	**Active dry yeast or bread machine yeast**	1 1/2 teaspoons

*Use the same amount for either size loaf.

CYCLE BASIC
CRUST SETTING AS DESIRED

1 If your machine does not have a preheat cycle, combine V-8 juice and water and heat mixture in microwave on HIGH power for 30 seconds (or heat in a saucepan for 1 minute to 80°F). Add to the bread pan with remaining ingredients according to the manufacturer's directions for your machine. Set the CYCLE, LOAF SIZE, and CRUST SETTING. Press START.

2 After about 5 minutes of kneading, check the consistency of your dough. If dough is not in a smooth round ball, open lid and with machine ON, add liquid a tablespoon at a time if too dry, or add flour a tablespoon at a time if too wet.

3 Remove the bread promptly from the pan when the machine beeps or on completing the cycle. Cool on rack before slicing.

Italian Tomato Bread

Buy seasoned canned diced tomatoes for a quick, easy addition to this loaf.

1 1/2-POUND	INGREDIENTS	2-POUND
2/3 cup	**Canned diced tomatoes with Italian seasonings in juice**	3/4 cup
1/2 cup	**Water***	1/2 cup
1 1/2 tablespoons	**Olive or vegetable oil**	2 tablespoons
2 tablespoons	**Sugar**	2 1/2 tablespoons
1/2 teaspoon	**Salt**	3/4 teaspoon
3 1/3 cups	**Bread flour, unsifted**	3 1/2 cups
2 1/4 teaspoons	**Active dry yeast or bread machine yeast***	2 1/4 teaspoons

*Use the same amount for either size loaf.

CYCLE BASIC
CRUST SETTING AS DESIRED

1 If your machine does not have a preheat cycle, combine diced tomatoes with juice and water and heat in microwave on HIGH power for 30 seconds (or heat in a saucepan for 1 minute to 80°F). Add to the bread pan with remaining ingredients according to the manufacturer's directions for your machine. Set the CYCLE, LOAF SIZE, and CRUST SETTING. Press START.

2 After about 5 minutes of kneading, check the consistency of your dough. If dough is not in a smooth round ball, open lid and with machine ON, add liquid a tablespoon at a time if too dry, or add flour a tablespoon at a time if too wet.

3 Remove the bread promptly from the pan when the machine beeps or on completing the cycle. Cool on rack before slicing.

Sun-Dried Tomato Olive Bread

Drain the sun-dried tomatoes well on paper towels to eliminate excess oil.

1 1/2-POUND	INGREDIENTS	2-POUND
3/4 cup	**Milk**	1 cup
1/2 cup	**Sliced olives, any type**	2/3 cup
1/3 cup	**Oil-packed, sun-dried tomatoes, drained and chopped**	1/2 cup
1 tablespoon	**Olive or vegetable oil**	1 1/2 tablespoons
1 1/2 tablespoons	**Sugar**	2 tablespoons
1/2 teaspoon	**Salt**	3/4 teaspoon
2 2/3 cups	**Bread flour, unsifted**	3 cups
1 1/2 teaspoons	**Active dry yeast or bread machine yeast**	2 teaspoons

CYCLE BASIC
CRUST SETTING AS DESIRED

1. If your machine does not have a preheat cycle, heat milk in microwave on HIGH power for 30 seconds (or heat in a saucepan for 1 minute to 80°F). Add to the bread pan with remaining ingredients according to the manufacturer's directions for your machine. Set the CYCLE, LOAF SIZE, and CRUST SETTING. Press START.

2. After about 5 minutes of kneading, check the consistency of your dough. If dough is not in a smooth round ball, open lid and with machine ON, add liquid a tablespoon at a time if too dry, or add flour a tablespoon at a time if too wet.

3. Remove the bread promptly from the pan when the machine beeps or on completing the cycle. Cool on rack before slicing.

Yeast Corn Bread with Chipotle Chile

Choose your own level of hotness for this cheesy corn bread.

1 1/2-POUND	INGREDIENTS	2-POUND
1 cup	**Milk**	1 1/4 cups
1 1/2 tablespoons	**Butter or margarine, softened**	2 tablespoons
1/3 cup	**Shredded cheddar cheese**	1/2 cup
1/4 cup	**Sliced green onions (scallions)**	1/2 cup
4–5 teaspoons	**Minced canned chipotle chiles in adobo sauce**	1 1/2–2 tablespoons
2 tablespoons	**Sugar**	3 tablespoons
1 1/4 teaspoons	**Salt**	1 1/2 teaspoons
2 1/3 cups	**Bread flour, unsifted**	3 1/4 cups
2/3 cup	**Yellow cornmeal**	1 cup
2 teaspoons	**Active dry yeast or bread machine yeast**	2 1/4 teaspoons

CYCLE SWEET
CRUST SETTING AS DESIRED

1 If your machine does not have a preheat cycle, heat milk in microwave on HIGH power for 30 seconds (or heat in a saucepan for 1 minute to 80°F). Add to the bread pan with remaining ingredients according to the manufacturer's directions for your machine. Set the CYCLE, LOAF SIZE, and CRUST SETTING. Press START.

2 After about 5 minutes of kneading, check the consistency of your dough. If dough is not in a smooth round ball, open lid and with machine ON, add liquid a tablespoon at a time if too dry, or add flour a tablespoon at a time if too wet.

3 Remove the bread promptly from the pan when the machine beeps or on completing the cycle. Cool on rack before slicing.

Baking Tips

Chipotle chiles come canned in adobo sauce, a spicy vinegar-herb mixture. Look for them in the Hispanic food section of large supermarkets. Chipotle (pronounced chip-OAT-lay) chiles are actually smoked jalapeños. They have a sweet, smoky, somewhat hot flavor.

Spinach Potato Bread with Basil

A light-textured bread with a pale green color. Use frozen chopped spinach, cooked according to package directions, then squeeze out all the liquid before measuring. If you have any of this bread left after a couple of days, make salad croutons (pages 244 and 245).

1 1/2-POUND	INGREDIENTS	2-POUND
3/4 cup	**Warm water (80°F)**	1 cup
1/3 cup	**Chopped cooked spinach, squeezed dry**	1/2 cup
1 1/2 tablespoons	**Olive or vegetable oil**	2 tablespoons
1 1/2 tablespoons	**Sugar**	2 tablespoons
1 teaspoon	**Salt**	1 1/4 teaspoons
1/2 teaspoon	**Dried basil**	1 teaspoon
3 cups	**Bread flour, unsifted**	3 1/2 cups
1/4 cup	**Instant mashed potato flakes**	1/3 cup
1 1/2 teaspoons	**Active dry yeast or bread machine yeast**	2 1/4 teaspoons

CYCLE BASIC
CRUST SETTING AS DESIRED

1 Measure ingredients into the bread pan according to the manufacturer's directions for your machine. Set the CYCLE, LOAF SIZE, and CRUST SETTING. Press START.

2 After about 5 minutes of kneading, check the consistency of your dough. If dough is not in a smooth round ball, open lid and with machine ON, add liquid a tablespoon at a time if too dry, or add flour a tablespoon at a time if too wet.

3 Remove the bread promptly from the pan when the machine beeps or on completing the cycle. Cool on rack before slicing.

Sweet Potato Wheat Bread

This bread has a dense texture, somewhat like a corn bread.

1½-POUND	INGREDIENTS	2-POUND
⅔ cup	**Milk**	¾ cup + 2 tablespoons
½ cup	**Cooked mashed sweet potatoes, room temperature**	⅔ cup
1½ tablespoons	**Butter or margarine, softened**	2 tablespoons
1½ tablespoons	**Honey**	2 tablespoons
1 teaspoon	**Salt**	1½ teaspoons
1 teaspoon	**Grated orange peel**	1½ teaspoons
1¾ cups	**Bread flour, unsifted**	2 cups
1½ cups	**Whole wheat flour, unsifted**	2 cups
2 teaspoons	**Active dry yeast or bread machine yeast**	2¼ teaspoons

CYCLE WHOLE WHEAT
CRUST SETTING AS DESIRED

1 If your machine does not have a preheat cycle, combine milk and potatoes and heat in microwave on HIGH power for 30 seconds (or heat in a saucepan for 1 minute to 80°F). Add to the bread pan with remaining ingredients according to the manufacturer's directions for your machine. Set the CYCLE, LOAF SIZE, and CRUST SETTING. Press START.

2 After about 5 minutes of kneading, check the consistency of your dough. If dough is not in a smooth round ball, open lid and with machine ON, add liquid a tablespoon at a time if too dry, or add flour a tablespoon at a time if too wet.

3 Remove the bread promptly from the pan when the machine beeps or on completing the cycle. Cool on rack before slicing.

Squash and Walnut Bread

Pureed baby-food is a convenient way to add squash or sweet potatoes to bread doughs.

1 1/2-POUND	INGREDIENTS	2-POUND
1/2 cup	**Water***	1/2 cup
2/3 cup**	**Mashed cooked squash or sweet potatoes, room temperature**	3/4 cup**
1 1/2 tablespoons	**Vegetable oil**	2 tablespoons
1 1/2 tablespoons	**Brown sugar, packed**	2 tablespoons
1 1/4 teaspoons	**Salt**	1 1/2 teaspoons
1/2 teaspoon	**Dried thyme**	3/4 teaspoon
3 1/4 cups	**Bread flour, unsifted**	3 3/4 cups
2 1/4 teaspoons	**Active dry yeast or bread machine yeast**	2 1/2 teaspoons
1/2 cup	**Chopped walnuts**	2/3 cup

*Use the same amount for either size loaf.

**Or 1 - 6 oz. jar baby food for 1 1/2-pound loaf; 1 - 6 oz. jar plus 1 heaping teaspoon for 2-pound loaf.

CYCLE BASIC OR RAISIN/NUT
CRUST SETTING AS DESIRED

1. If your machine does not have a preheat cycle, combine water and potatoes and heat in microwave on HIGH power for 30 seconds (or heat in a saucepan for 1 minute to 80°F). Add to the bread pan with remaining ingredients (except walnuts) according to the manufacturer's directions for your machine. Measure walnuts to add at the beep or when manufacturer directs. Set the CYCLE, LOAF SIZE, and CRUST SETTING. Press START.

2. After about 5 minutes of kneading, check the consistency of your dough. If dough is not in a smooth round ball, open lid and with machine ON, add liquid a tablespoon at a time if too dry, or add flour a tablespoon at a time if too wet.

3. Remove the bread promptly from the pan when the machine beeps or on completing the cycle. Cool on rack before slicing.

Swiss Beer Bread

Serve this cheese bread with a hearty soup or stew.
The beer lends a great flavor and texture.

1 1/2-POUND	INGREDIENTS	2-POUND
1 cup	**Beer, room temperature**	1 1/4 cups
1/2 cup	**Shredded Swiss cheese**	2/3 cup
1 1/2 tablespoons	**Vegetable oil**	2 tablespoons
1 1/2 tablespoons	**Sugar**	2 tablespoons
1 1/4 teaspoons	**Salt**	1 1/2 teaspoons
3 1/3 cups	**Bread flour, unsifted**	3 3/4 cups
2 1/4 teaspoons	**Active dry yeast or bread machine yeast***	2 1/4 teaspoons

*Use the same amount for either size loaf.

CYCLE SWEET OR BASIC
CRUST SETTING AS DESIRED

1 If your machine does not have a preheat cycle, heat beer in microwave on HIGH power for 30 seconds (or heat in a saucepan for 1 minute to 80°F). Add to the bread pan with remaining ingredients according to the manufacturer's directions for your machine. Set the CYCLE, LOAF SIZE, and CRUST SETTING. Press START.

2 After about 5 minutes of kneading, check the consistency of your dough. If dough is not in a smooth round ball, open lid and with machine ON, add liquid a tablespoon at a time if too dry, or add flour a tablespoon at a time if too wet.

3 Remove the bread promptly from the pan when the machine beeps or on completing the cycle. Cool on rack before slicing.

Rosemary Carrot Bread

Substitute mashed cooked sweet potatoes or squash for the carrots, if you like.

1 1/2-POUND	INGREDIENTS	2-POUND
3/4 cup	**Mashed cooked carrots, room temperature**	1 cup
1/2 cup	**Milk**	1/2 cup + 2 tablespoons
1 1/2 tablespoons	**Olive or vegetable oil**	2 tablespoons
1 1/2 tablespoons	**Sugar**	2 tablespoons
1 teaspoon	**Dried rosemary**	1 1/2 teaspoons
1 teaspoon	**Salt**	1 1/4 teaspoons
3 1/3 cups	**Bread flour, unsifted**	3 2/3 cups
1 1/2 teaspoons	**Active dry yeast or bread machine yeast**	2 teaspoons

CYCLE BASIC
CRUST SETTING AS DESIRED

1 If your machine does not have a preheat cycle, combine carrots and milk and heat in microwave on HIGH power for 30 seconds (or heat in a saucepan for 1 minute to 80°F). Add to the bread pan with remaining ingredients according to the manufacturer's directions for your machine. Set the CYCLE, LOAF SIZE, and CRUST SETTING. Press START.

2 After about 5 minutes of kneading, check the consistency of your dough. If dough is not in a smooth round ball, open lid and with machine ON, add liquid a tablespoon at a time if too dry, or add flour a tablespoon at a time if too wet.

3 Remove the bread promptly from the pan when the machine beeps or on completing the cycle. Cool on rack before slicing.

Back-at-the-Ranch Bread

Ranch dressing gives this bread a garlic and herb flavor.
The crust gets pretty dark unless the light setting is used.

1 1/2-POUND	INGREDIENTS	2-POUND
1 cup + 2 tablespoons	**Milk**	1 1/3 cups
1 1/2 tablespoons	**Vegetable oil**	2 tablespoons
2 1/2 tablespoons	**Dry ranch dressing mix**	3 tablespoons
2 tablespoons	**Sugar**	2 1/2 tablespoons
3 cups	**Bread flour, unsifted**	3 3/4 cups
2 1/4 teaspoons	**Active dry yeast or bread machine yeast**	2 1/2 teaspoons

CYCLE BASIC
CRUST SETTING LIGHT RECOMMENDED

1 If your machine does not have a preheat cycle, heat milk in microwave on HIGH power for 30 seconds (or heat in a saucepan for 1 minute to 80°F). Add to the bread pan with remaining ingredients according to the manufacturer's directions for your machine. Set the CYCLE, LOAF SIZE, and CRUST SETTING. Press START.

2 After about 5 minutes of kneading, check the consistency of your dough. If dough is not in a smooth round ball, open lid and with machine ON, add liquid a tablespoon at a time if too dry, or add flour a tablespoon at a time if too wet.

3 Remove the bread promptly from the pan when the machine beeps or on completing the cycle. Cool on rack before slicing.

Be sure to cool your loaf thoroughly before you wrap it to store. Use zip-top plastic bags or wrap in foil, turning the edges over several times to seal air out.

Tarragon Mustard Bread

Use country-style grainy Dijon, honey Dijon, or any other exotic mustard you like.

1 1/2-POUND	INGREDIENTS	2-POUND
1 cup + 2 tablespoons	**Warm water (80°F)**	1 1/4 cups
2 1/2 tablespoons	**Dijon mustard**	3 tablespoons
1 1/2 tablespoons	**Olive or vegetable oil**	2 tablespoons
1 1/2 tablespoons	**Sugar**	2 tablespoons
1 teaspoon	**Salt**	1 1/4 teaspoons
1/2 teaspoon	**Dried tarragon***	1/2 teaspoon
3 1/3 cups	**Bread flour, unsifted**	3 2/3 cups
2 1/2 teaspoons	**Active dry yeast or bread machine yeast***	2 1/2 teaspoons

*Use the same amount for either size loaf.

CYCLE BASIC
CRUST SETTING AS DESIRED

1 Measure ingredients into the bread pan according to the manufacturer's directions for your machine. Set the CYCLE, LOAF SIZE, and CRUST SETTING. Press START.

2 After about 5 minutes of kneading, check the consistency of your dough. If dough is not in a smooth round ball, open lid and with machine ON, add liquid a tablespoon at a time if too dry, or add flour a tablespoon at a time if too wet.

3 Remove the bread promptly from the pan when the machine beeps or on completing the cycle. Cool on rack before slicing

Green Onion-Poppyseed Loaf

This loaf won't last long—and it doesn't even need butter!

1 1/2-POUND	INGREDIENTS	2-POUND
1 cup + 2 tablespoons	**Milk**	1 1/3 cups
2 tablespoons	**Butter or margarine, softened**	3 tablespoons
1/2 cup	**Sliced green onions (scallions)**	2/3 cup
1 tablespoon	**Poppyseed**	4 teaspoons
1 1/2 tablespoons	**Sugar**	2 tablespoons
1 1/2 teaspoons	**Salt**	2 teaspoons
3 1/3 cups	**Bread flour, unsifted**	4 cups
2 1/4 teaspoons	**Active dry yeast or bread machine yeast**	2 1/2 teaspoons

CYCLE BASIC
CRUST SETTING AS DESIRED

1 If your machine does not have a preheat cycle, heat milk in microwave on HIGH power for 30 seconds (or heat in a saucepan for 1 minute to 80°F). Add to the bread pan with remaining ingredients according to the manufacturer's directions for your machine. Set the CYCLE, LOAF SIZE, and CRUST SETTING. Press START.

2 After about 5 minutes of kneading, check the consistency of your dough. If dough is not in a smooth round ball, open lid and with machine ON, add liquid a tablespoon at a time if too dry, or add flour a tablespoon at a time if too wet.

3 Remove the bread promptly from the pan when the machine beeps or on completing the cycle. Cool on rack before slicing.

CHAPTER

Sourdough Breads

MAKING SOURDOUGH BREADS IN THE BREAD MACHINE

BASIC SOURDOUGH STARTER

SAN FRANCISCO-STYLE SOURDOUGH BREAD

SOURDOUGH FRENCH BREAD

SOURDOUGH MILWAUKEE BEER BREAD

SOURDOUGH CHILE AND CHEESE BREAD

SOURDOUGH TOMATO AND BASIL LOAF

THAT'SA PIZZA SOURDOUGH LOAF

CHEESY CHIVE SOURDOUGH LOAF

BLUE CHEESE SOURDOUGH BREAD

ROSEMARY AND THYME SOURDOUGH

FRENCH ONION SOURDOUGH

HONEY AND NUTMEG SOURDOUGH LOAF

SOURDOUGH HONEY-RAISIN BREAD

APRICOT AND ALMOND SOURDOUGH BREAD

PUMPKIN AND GOLDEN RAISIN SOURDOUGH

GAIL'S CRANBERRY-LEMON SOURDOUGH LOAF

SOURDOUGH CINNAMON-OATMEAL LOAF

SOURDOUGH WHEAT BREAD WITH ORANGE AND CURRANTS

WHEAT AND SESAME SOURDOUGH BREAD

OLD WORLD SOURDOUGH BREAD

SOURDOUGH PUMPERNICKEL BREAD

SOURDOUGH JEWISH RYE BREAD

Making Sourdough Breads in the Bread Machine

In the mid-1800s, gold prospectors in the West who carried a crock of sourdough starter with their mining gear were called "sourdoughs." A starter is as easy to put together as pancake batter; you just have to make it several days before you need it. Once you've made the starter (see recipe on page 126), a weekly "feeding" will keep it going for years in the refrigerator—ready when you want to bake a sourdough bread.

Here are some tips for success with sourdough starter:

- The starter should have a warm, draft-free place to ferment, approximately 85°F.
- Metal utensils will detract from the flavor of the starter. Use a glass bowl or crock, along with wooden, not metal spoons, for mixing your starter. Make sure the container is large enough for the starter to double in bulk.
- The starter should be the consistency of thin pancake batter. Add a few tablespoons warm water to thin it, if necessary.
- Cover the container loosely during the fermentation period and when you refrigerate it. A tight cover could trap the accumulated gases, and the container could explode! Try cheesecloth secured with an elastic band, or waxed paper placed over the top, or vented plastic wrap.
- Label your starter container with a date, so you'll know when it needs to be fed.
- To get the most accurate measurement of starter for bread recipes, measure well-stirred refrigerated starter and allow it to stand at room temperature about 1 hour before using. The starter expands as it warms.
- Reserve at least 1 cup of the starter in the container to keep the starter going.

- If the starter develops a greenish or pinkish cast, mold appears, or you notice a truly unpleasant odor, discard it and start over.
- It's a good policy to wash out your starter container every few weeks with hot soapy water to remove any residue around the sides.
- All of the recipes in this chapter call for some yeast in addition to the starter, to ensure that the bread will rise sufficiently within the pre-set rising times for the bread machine. Sourdough breads usually need twice the amount of rising time when just the starter is used for leavening. The additional yeast does slightly affect some of the characteristic sourdough flavor. If you are the adventurous type, omit the additional yeast and extend the rising time by presetting a custom program on your machine, if it offers that option. Consult your machine's manual for tips on adding to the rising time.
- If you are not having any luck in making your own starter, don't be embarrassed—sourdough can be fickle! Just buy a commercially made starter, available in large markets and specialty stores, and no one will be the wiser.

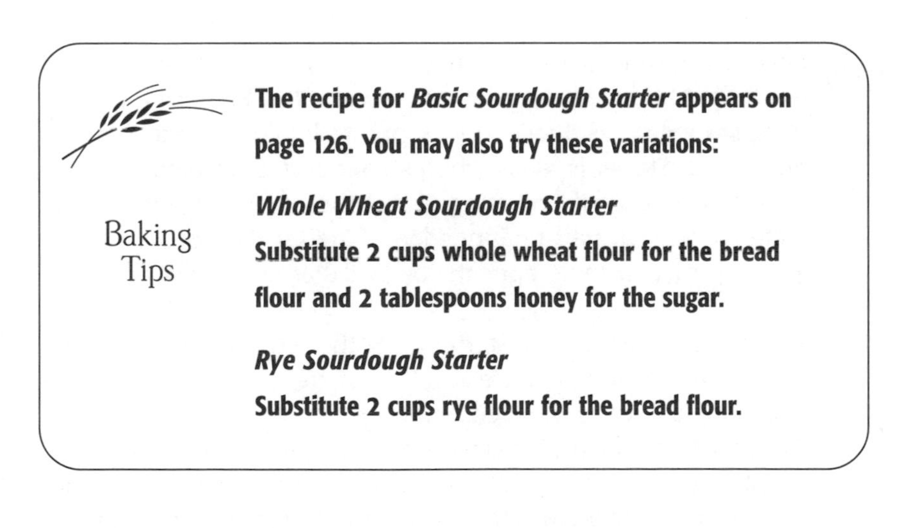

Baking Tips

The recipe for *Basic Sourdough Starter* appears on page 126. You may also try these variations:

Whole Wheat Sourdough Starter

Substitute 2 cups whole wheat flour for the bread flour and 2 tablespoons honey for the sugar.

Rye Sourdough Starter

Substitute 2 cups rye flour for the bread flour.

Basic Sourdough Starter

Allow two to three days for this starter to ferment.

INGREDIENTS	
2 cups	**Bread flour, unsifted**
2 tablespoons	**Sugar**
1 (1/4-oz.) package or 2 1/4 teaspoons	**Active dry yeast or bread machine yeast**
2 cups	**Warm (105-115°F) water or potato water** *

* Potato water is water in which potatoes have been cooked. It can be used for all or a portion of the water.

Note: Recipe can be doubled. Also, see Whole Wheat and Rye Sourdough Starters (page 125).

1 In a nonmetal, nonplastic container, combine flour, sugar, and yeast.

2 Gradually add the warm water and beat mixture with a wooden or non-metal spoon until nearly smooth.

3 Cover mixture loosely with cheesecloth or plastic wrap (do not use a tight-fitting lid). Let stand in a warm (85°F) place for 2 to 3 days, stirring occasionally to incorporate liquid that accumulates on the top. Starter is ready when a sour aroma develops and the mixture is bubbly. If not using starter the day it develops, refrigerate loosely covered until needed. If starter develops a pink or greenish cast, or mold appears, discard starter and start over.

To Use Starter: Measure starter from the refrigerator. Allow it to stand at room temperature for 1 hour before using. Replenish remaining starter as directed below.

To Replenish Starter: If starter is not used, replenish it every 7 to 10 days. Remove 1/2 cup of the mixture. Stir together 1/2 cup flour and 1/2 cup warm water. Stir mixture into the starter and let stand in a warm place overnight. Cover and refrigerate.

If a portion of starter has been used in a recipe, add a mixture of equal amounts flour and water. For example, if you used 1 cup starter, add a mixture of 1 cup flour and 1 cup warm water. Cover and let stand in a warm place overnight. Refrigerate, still covered.

San Francisco-Style Sourdough Bread

This produces a crusty loaf with an open texture. It is best the day it is made. If you are lucky enough to have leftovers, see Chapter 11 for some great recipes using day-old sourdough.

1 1/2-POUND	INGREDIENTS	2-POUND
1/2 cup + 2 tablespoons	**Warm water (80°F)**	3/4 cup
3/4 cup	**Basic Sourdough starter, room temperature**	1 cup
1 tablespoon	**Sugar**	4 teaspoons
1 1/4 teaspoons	**Salt**	1 1/2 teaspoons
3 1/4 cups	**Bread flour, unsifted**	3 3/4 cups
1 1/2 teaspoons	**Active dry yeast, or bread machine yeast**	1 3/4 teaspoons

CYCLE FRENCH (DELAY-BAKE CAN BE USED)
CRUST SETTING AS DESIRED

1. Measure ingredients into the bread pan according to the manufacturer's directions for your machine. Set the CYCLE, LOAF SIZE, and CRUST SETTING. Press START.

2. After about 5 minutes of kneading, check the consistency of your dough. If dough is not in a smooth round ball, open lid and with machine ON, add liquid a tablespoon at a time if too dry, or add flour a tablespoon at a time if too wet.

3. Remove the bread promptly from the pan when the machine beeps or on completing the cycle. Cool on rack before slicing.

Sourdough French Bread

This loaf is lighter in texture than the San Francisco version.

1 1/2-POUND	INGREDIENTS	2-POUND
1/2 cup	**Warm water (80°F)**	1/2 cup + 2 tablespoons
3/4 cup	**Basic Sourdough starter, room temperature**	1 cup
1 1/2 tablespoons	**Sugar**	2 tablespoons
1 1/4 teaspoons	**Salt**	1 1/2 teaspoons
3 cups	**Bread flour, unsifted**	3 2/3 cups
1 teaspoon	**Active dry yeast or bread machine yeast**	1 1/2 teaspoons

CYCLE FRENCH (DELAY-BAKE CAN BE USED)
CRUST SETTING AS DESIRED

1 Measure ingredients into the bread pan according to the manufacturer's directions for your machine. Set the CYCLE, LOAF SIZE, and CRUST SETTING. Press START.

2 After about 5 minutes of kneading, check the consistency of your dough. If dough is not in a smooth round ball, open lid and with machine ON, add liquid a tablespoon at a time if too dry, or add flour a tablespoon at a time if too wet.

3 Remove the bread promptly from the pan when the machine beeps or on completing the cycle. Cool on rack before slicing.

Baking Tips

This bread, when it's a day or two old, makes excellent croutons. Try the recipe for Italian-Style Croutons (page 245).

Sourdough Milwaukee Beer Bread

Sourdough lovers like to enhance the characteristic sour flavor by using beer for some or all of the liquid called for in the bread recipe. Beer also improves the volume.

1 1/2-POUND	INGREDIENTS	2-POUND
1/2 cup	**Beer, room temperature**	1/2 cup + 2 tablespoons
3/4 cup	**Basic Sourdough starter, room temperature**	1 cup
1 tablespoon	**Sugar**	2 tablespoons
1 1/4 teaspoons	**Salt**	1 1/2 teaspoons
3 cups	**Bread flour, unsifted**	3 3/4 cups
1 1/2 teaspoons	**Active dry yeast or bread machine yeast**	1 3/4 teaspoons

CYCLE FRENCH (DELAY-BAKE CAN BE USED)
CRUST SETTING AS DESIRED

1. Measure ingredients into the bread pan according to the manufacturer's directions for your machine. Set the CYCLE, LOAF SIZE, and CRUST SETTING. Press START.

2. After about 5 minutes of kneading, check the consistency of your dough. If dough is not in a smooth round ball, open lid and with machine ON, add liquid a tablespoon at a time if too dry, or add flour a tablespoon at a time if too wet.

3. Remove the bread promptly from the pan when the machine beeps or on completing the cycle. Cool on rack before slicing.

When you are feeding your sourdough starter, you can substitute room temperature beer for the water called for in the starter recipe.

Sourdough Chile and Cheese Bread

This bread is a great tribute to sourdough—it's crusty, spicy, and perfect with a steak or stew. Choose the spice level that suits you.

1 1/2-POUND	INGREDIENTS	2-POUND
1/2 cup	**Warm water (80°F)**	1/2 cup + 2 tablespoons
3/4 cup	**Basic Sourdough starter, room temperature**	1 cup
1/2 cup	**Shredded cheddar or Pepper jack cheese***	1/2 cup
1 1/2 tablespoons	**Sugar**	2 tablespoons
1- 1 1/2 teaspoons	**Ground chile powder**	2–2 1/2 teaspoons
1 1/4 teaspoons	**Salt**	1 1/2 teaspoons
1/4 teaspoon	**Onion powder**	1/2 teaspoon
3 cups	**Bread flour, unsifted**	3 3/4 cups
1 teaspoon	**Active dry yeast or bread machine yeast**	1 1/2 teaspoons

*Use the same amount for either size loaf.

CYCLE SWEET
CRUST SETTING AS DESIRED

1. Measure ingredients into the bread pan according to the manufacturer's directions for your machine. Set the CYCLE, LOAF SIZE, and CRUST SETTING. Press START.

2. After about 5 minutes of kneading, check the consistency of your dough. If dough is not in a smooth round ball, open lid and with machine ON, add liquid a tablespoon at a time if too dry, or add flour a tablespoon at a time if too wet.

3. Remove the bread promptly from the pan when the machine beeps or on completing the cycle. Cool on rack before slicing.

Sourdough Tomato and Basil Loaf

If you are watching calories, forgo the oil-packed tomatoes in favor of the dried ones you'll find in bags in the produce department. Just simmer them in water for a few minutes to plump them up. Drain well and chop.

1 1/2-POUND	INGREDIENTS	2-POUND
1/2 cup	Warm water (80°F)	3/4 cup
3/4 cup	Basic Sourdough starter, room temperature	1 cup
1/3 cup	Chopped fresh basil leaves	1/2 cup
1 1/2 tablespoons	Sugar	2 tablespoons
1 1/4 teaspoons	Salt	1 1/2 teaspoons
1/4 teaspoon	Ground black pepper*	1/4 teaspoon
3 1/4 cups	Bread flour, unsifted	3 2/3 cups
1 1/2 teaspoons	Active dry yeast or bread machine yeast	2 teaspoons
1/3 cup	Oil-packed sun-dried tomatoes, well drained and chopped	1/2 cup

*Use the same amount for either size loaf.

CYCLE SWEET
CRUST SETTING AS DESIRED

1 Measure all ingredients into the bread pan (except sun-dried tomatoes) according to the manufacturer's directions for your machine. Measure sun-dried tomatoes to add at the beep or when manufacturer directs. Set the CYCLE, LOAF SIZE, and CRUST SETTING. Press START.

2 After about 5 minutes of kneading, check the consistency of your dough. If dough is not in a smooth round ball, open lid and with machine ON, add liquid a tablespoon at a time if too dry, or add flour a tablespoon at a time if too wet.

3 Remove the bread promptly from the pan when the machine beeps or on completing the cycle. Cool on rack before slicing.

That'sa Pizza Sourdough Loaf

Here's a fun way to enjoy the great flavor of pizza while sidestepping some of the calories! Serve it with a main dish salad or soup.

1 1/2-POUND	INGREDIENTS	2-POUND
1/2 cup + 2 tablespoons	**Warm water (80°F)***	1/2 cup + 2 tablespoons
3/4 cup	**Basic Sourdough starter, room temperature**	1 cup
1/3 cup	**Chopped pepperoni**	1/2 cup
1/4 cup	**Grated Parmesan or Romano cheese**	1/3 cup
1 tablespoon	**Sugar**	1 1/2 tablespoons
1 teaspoon	**Dried Italian herbs or Italian seasoning**	1 1/4 teaspoons
3/4 teaspoon	**Salt**	3/4 teaspoon
3 1/4 cups	**Bread flour, unsifted**	3 3/4 cups
1 1/2 teaspoons	**Active dry yeast or bread machine yeast**	2 teaspoons

*Use the same amount for either size loaf.

CYCLE SWEET
CRUST SETTING AS DESIRED

1 Measure ingredients into the bread pan according to the manufacturer's directions for your machine. Set the CYCLE, LOAF SIZE, and CRUST SETTING. Press START.

2 After about 5 minutes of kneading, check the consistency of your dough. If dough is not in a smooth round ball, open lid and with machine ON, add liquid a tablespoon at a time if too dry, or add flour a tablespoon at a time if too wet.

3 Remove the bread promptly from the pan when the machine beeps or on completing the cycle. Cool on rack before slicing.

Cheesy Chive Sourdough Loaf

A little onion powder helps boost the delicate flavor of the chives in this loaf.

1 1/2-POUND	INGREDIENTS	2-POUND
1/2 cup + 2 tablespoons	**Warm water (80°F)**	3/4 cup
3/4 cup	**Basic Sourdough starter, room temperature**	1 cup
2/3 cup	**Shredded sharp cheddar cheese**	1 cup
2 tablespoons	**Fresh chopped chives**	3 tablespoons
1 tablespoon	**Sugar**	1 1/2 tablespoons
1 teaspoon	**Salt**	1 1/4 teaspoons
1/4 teaspoon	**Onion powder***	1/4 teaspoon
3 cups	**Bread flour, unsifted**	3 3/4 cups
1 1/2 teaspoons	**Active dry yeast or bread machine yeast**	2 teaspoons

*Use the same amount for either size loaf.

CYCLE SWEET
CRUST SETTING AS DESIRED

1 Measure ingredients into the bread pan according to the manufacturer's directions for your machine. Set the CYCLE, LOAF SIZE, and CRUST SETTING. Press START.

2 After about 5 minutes of kneading, check the consistency of your dough. If dough is not in a smooth round ball, open lid and with machine ON, add liquid a tablespoon at a time if too dry, or add flour a tablespoon at a time if too wet.

3 Remove the bread promptly from the pan when the machine beeps or on completing the cycle. Cool on rack before slicing.

Blue Cheese Sourdough Bread

After my friend Donna Skidmore commented to me about a delicious blue cheese sourdough she had sampled in her travels, I had to try one for myself. Now it ranks as one of my top 10 personal favorites in this book. Slice it while warm and savor it with a glass of red wine.

1 1/2-POUND	INGREDIENTS	2-POUND
1/2 cup + 2 tablespoons	**Warm water (80°F)**	3/4 cup
3/4 cup	**Basic Sourdough starter, room temperature**	1 cup
1/3 cup	**Crumbled blue cheese**	1/2 cup
1 1/2 tablespoons	**Nonfat dry milk**	2 tablespoons
1 1/2 tablespoons	**Sugar**	2 tablespoons
1 1/2 tablespoons	**Fresh chopped parsley**	2 tablespoons
1 teaspoon	**Salt**	1 1/4 teaspoons
3 1/4 cups	**Bread flour, unsifted**	3 3/4 cups
1 1/2 teaspoons	**Active dry yeast or bread machine yeast**	2 teaspoons

CYCLE SWEET
CRUST SETTING AS DESIRED

1. Measure ingredients into the bread pan according to the manufacturer's directions for your machine. Set the CYCLE, LOAF SIZE, and CRUST SETTING. Press START.

2. After about 5 minutes of kneading, check the consistency of your dough. If dough is not in a smooth round ball, open lid and with machine ON, add liquid a tablespoon at a time if too dry, or add flour a tablespoon at a time if too wet.

3. Remove the bread promptly from the pan when the machine beeps or on completing the cycle. Cool on rack before slicing.

Rosemary and Thyme Sourdough

You may find yourself speaking Italian after trying this one! Try dipping pieces of this bread in a garlic-flavored olive oil.

1 1/2-POUND	INGREDIENTS	2-POUND
1/2 cup + 2 tablespoons	**Milk**	3/4 cup
3/4 cup	**Basic Sourdough starter, room temperature**	1 cup
1 1/2 tablespoons	**Sugar**	2 tablespoons
1 teaspoon	**Salt**	1 1/4 teaspoons
1 teaspoon	**Dried rosemary**	1 1/4 teaspoons
1 teaspoon	**Dried thyme**	1 1/4 teaspoons
1/4 teaspoon	**Garlic salt**	1/2 teaspoon
3 cups	**Bread flour, unsifted**	3 1/2 cups
1 1/2 teaspoons	**Active dry yeast or bread machine yeast**	2 teaspoons

CYCLE FRENCH
CRUST SETTING AS DESIRED

1 If your machine does not have a preheat cycle, heat milk in microwave on HIGH power for 30 seconds (or heat in a saucepan for 1 minute to 80°F). Add to the bread pan with remaining ingredients according to the manufacturer's directions for your machine. Set the CYCLE, LOAF SIZE, and CRUST SETTING. Press START.

2 After about 5 minutes of kneading, check the consistency of your dough. If dough is not in a smooth round ball, open lid and with machine ON, add liquid a tablespoon at a time if too dry, or add flour a tablespoon at a time if too wet.

3 Remove the bread promptly from the pan when the machine beeps or on completing the cycle. Cool on rack before slicing.

French Onion Sourdough

No onions to chop for this one.
So easy and so delicious!

1 1/2-POUND	INGREDIENTS	2-POUND
1/2 cup + 2 tablespoons	**Warm water (80°F)**	3/4 cup
3/4 cup	**Basic Sourdough starter, room temperature**	1 cup
2 1/2 tablespoons	**Dry onion soup mix**	3 tablespoons
1 1/2 tablespoons	**Sugar**	2 tablespoons
1/2 teaspoon	**Salt**	3/4 teaspoon
3 cups	**Bread flour, unsifted**	3 2/3 cups
1 1/2 teaspoons	**Active dry yeast or bread machine yeast**	2 teaspoons

CYCLE FRENCH (DELAY-BAKE CAN BE USED)
CRUST SETTING AS DESIRED

1. Measure ingredients into the bread pan according to the manufacturer's directions for your machine. Set the CYCLE, LOAF SIZE, and CRUST SETTING. Press START.

2. After about 5 minutes of kneading, check the consistency of your dough. If dough is not in a smooth round ball, open lid and with machine ON, add liquid a tablespoon at a time if too dry, or add flour a tablespoon at a time if too wet.

3. Remove the bread promptly from the pan when the machine beeps or on completing the cycle. Cool on rack before slicing.

Baking Tips

If you are using the Delay-Bake feature on your bread machine, layer the ingredients carefully in the bread pan, according to the manufacturer's directions. It's very important that the yeast does not come in contact with either the liquids or the salt.

Honey and Nutmeg Sourdough Loaf

Honey tempers the sourdough flavor with a bit of sweetness, and the nutmeg adds just a hint of spice.

1 1/2-POUND	INGREDIENTS	2-POUND
1/2 cup	**Warm water (80°F)***	1/2 cup
3/4 cup	**Basic Sourdough starter, room temperature**	1 cup
2 1/2 tablespoons	**Honey**	3 tablespoons
1 1/4 teaspoons	**Salt***	1 1/4 teaspoons
1/4 teaspoon	**Ground nutmeg**	1/2 teaspoon
3 1/4 cups	**Bread flour, unsifted**	3 3/4 cups
1 1/2 teaspoons	**Active dry yeast or bread machine yeast**	1 3/4 teaspoons

*Use the same amount for either size loaf.

CYCLE FRENCH (DELAY-BAKE CAN BE USED)
CRUST SETTING AS DESIRED

1 Measure ingredients into the bread pan according to the manufacturer's directions for your machine. Set the CYCLE, LOAF SIZE, and CRUST SETTING. Press START.

2 After about 5 minutes of kneading, check the consistency of your dough. If dough is not in a smooth round ball, open lid and with machine ON, add liquid a tablespoon at a time if too dry, or add flour a tablespoon at a time if too wet.

3 Remove the bread promptly from the pan when the machine beeps or on completing the cycle. Cool on rack before slicing.

Sourdough Honey-Raisin Bread

Currants as well as raisins stud this loaf. Golden raisins are dried Thompson grapes, processed to retain the light golden color of the ripe fruit. The dried currants sold in markets are actually tiny seedless black corinth grapes.

1½-POUND	INGREDIENTS	2-POUND
½ cup + 2 tablespoons	**Warm water (80°F)**	¾ cup + 2 tablespoons
¾ cup	**Basic Sourdough starter, room temperature**	1 cup
2 tablespoons	**Honey**	3 tablespoons
1½ tablespoons	**Nonfat dry milk**	2 tablespoons
1 teaspoon	**Salt**	1¼ teaspoons
3¼ cups	**Bread flour, unsifted**	3⅔ cups
1½ teaspoons	**Active dry yeast or bread machine yeast**	2 teaspoons
¾ cup	**Golden raisins, currants, or dark raisins**	1 cup

CYCLE FRENCH OR RAISIN/NUT
(DELAY-BAKE CAN BE USED)
SETTING AS DESIRED

1. Measure ingredients into the bread pan (except raisins or currants) according to the manufacturer's directions for your machine. Measure raisins or currants to add at the beep or when manufacturer directs. Set the CYCLE, LOAF SIZE, and CRUST SETTING. Press START.

2. After about 5 minutes of kneading, check the consistency of your dough. If dough is not in a smooth round ball, open lid and with machine ON, add liquid a tablespoon at a time if too dry, or add flour a tablespoon at a time if too wet.

3. Remove the bread promptly from the pan when the machine beeps or on completing the cycle. Cool on rack before slicing.

Apricot and Almond Sourdough Bread

Here's a bread that is much more sophisticated, and much more fun, than a run-of-the-mill doughnut for breakfast!

1 1/2-POUND	INGREDIENTS	2-POUND
1/2 cup	**Warm water (80°F)**	1/2 cup + 2 tablespoons
3/4 cup	**Basic Sourdough starter, room temperature**	1 cup
2 tablespoons	**Sugar**	3 tablespoons
1 teaspoon	**Salt**	1 1/4 teaspoons
1 teaspoon	**Almond extract**	1 1/4 teaspoons
3 cups	**Bread flour, unsifted**	3 3/4 cups
1 1/2 teaspoons	**Active dry yeast or bread machine yeast**	2 teaspoons
2/3 cup	**Chopped dried apricots**	1 cup
1/2 cup	**Chopped almonds**	3/4 cup

CYCLE SWEET OR RAISIN/NUT
(DELAY-BAKE CAN BE USED)
SETTING AS DESIRED

1. Measure ingredients into the bread pan (except dried apricots and almonds) according to the manufacturer's directions for your machine. Measure dried apricots and chopped almonds to add at the beep or when manufacturer directs. Set the CYCLE, LOAF SIZE, and CRUST SETTING. Press START.

2. After about 5 minutes of kneading, check the consistency of your dough. If dough is not in a smooth round ball, open lid and with machine ON, add liquid a tablespoon at a time if too dry, or add flour a tablespoon at a time if too wet.

3. Remove the bread promptly from the pan when the machine beeps or on completing the cycle. Cool on rack before slicing.

Pumpkin and Golden Raisin Sourdough

A beautiful, lightly sweetened loaf that's destined to disappear quickly. Spread slices of this bread with soft cream cheese and marmalade.

1 1/2-POUND	INGREDIENTS	2-POUND
2/3 cup*	**Pumpkin or squash puree**	3/4 cup*
1/4 cup	**Milk**	1/3 cup
3/4 cup	**Basic Sourdough starter, room temperature**	1 cup
2 tablespoons	**Sugar**	3 tablespoons
1 teaspoon	**Salt**	1 1/4 teaspoons
1 teaspoon	**Ground cinnamon**	1 1/4 teaspoons
3 1/4 cups	**Bread flour, unsifted**	3 3/4 cups
1 1/2 teaspoons	**Active dry yeast or bread machine yeast**	2 teaspoons
1/2 cup	**Golden raisins or dark raisins**	2/3 cup

*Or 1 - 6 oz. jar baby food for 1 1/2-pound loaf; 1 - 6 oz. jar plus 1 heaping teaspoon for 2-pound loaf.

CYCLE BASIC OR RAISIN/NUT
CRUST SETTING AS DESIRED

1 If your machine does not have a preheat cycle, combine pumpkin puree with milk and heat in microwave on HIGH power for 30 seconds (or heat in a saucepan for 1 minute to 80°F). Add to the bread pan with remaining ingredients (except raisins) according to the manufacturer's directions for your machine. Measure raisins to add at the beep or when manufacturer directs. Set the CYCLE, LOAF SIZE, and CRUST SETTING. Press START.

2 After about 5 minutes of kneading, check the consistency of your dough. If dough is not in a smooth round ball, open lid and with machine ON, add liquid a tablespoon at a time if too dry, or add flour a tablespoon at a time if too wet.

3 Remove the bread promptly from the pan when the machine beeps or on completing the cycle. Cool on rack before slicing.

Gail's Cranberry-Lemon Sourdough Loaf

My sister, Gail Hudson, loves cranberries, so this recipe is my gift to her. You won't want to relegate this bread to the holidays. It's great for tuna or turkey sandwiches–or all by itself.

1 1/2-POUND	INGREDIENTS	2-POUND
1/2 cup + 2 tablespoons	**Warm water (80°F)**	3/4 cup
3/4 cup	**Basic Sourdough starter, room temperature**	1 cup
3 tablespoons	**Sugar**	1/4 cup
1 1/2 teaspoons	**Grated lemon peel**	2 teaspoons
1 teaspoon	**Salt**	1 1/4 teaspoons
3 cups	**Bread flour, unsifted**	3 2/3 cups
1 1/2 teaspoons	**Active dry yeast or bread machine yeast**	1 3/4 teaspoons
3/4 cup	**Dried cranberries or Craisins**	1 cup

CYCLE FRENCH OR RAISIN/NUT (DELAY-BAKE CAN BE USED)

CRUST SETTING MEDIUM TO DARK RECOMMENDED

1. Measure ingredients into the bread pan (except dried cranberries or Craisins) according to the manufacturer's directions for your machine. Measure cranberries or Craisins to add at the beep or when manufacturer directs. Set the CYCLE, LOAF SIZE, and CRUST SETTING. Press START.

2. After about 5 minutes of kneading, check the consistency of your dough. If dough is not in a smooth round ball, open lid and with machine ON, add liquid a tablespoon at a time if too dry, or add flour a tablespoon at a time if too wet.

3. Remove the bread promptly from the pan when the machine beeps or on completing the cycle. Cool on rack before slicing.

Sourdough Cinnamon-Oatmeal Loaf

Molasses and cinnamon flavor this delectable whole wheat sourdough.

1 1/2-POUND	INGREDIENTS	2-POUND
1/2 cup + 2 tablespoons	**Warm water (80°F)**	3/4 cup
3/4 cup	**Whole Wheat (page 125) or Basic Sourdough starter (page 126), room temperature**	1 cup
3 tablespoons	**Molasses**	1/4 cup
1 teaspoon	**Salt**	1 1/4 teaspoons
1 teaspoon	**Ground cinnamon**	1 1/2 teaspoons
1/2 cup	**Oatmeal, dry**	2/3 cup
1 1/2 cups	**Bread flour, unsifted**	2 cups
1 cup	**Whole wheat flour, unsifted***	1 cup
1 1/2 teaspoons	**Active dry yeast or bread machine yeast**	2 teaspoons

*Use the same amount for either size loaf.

CYCLE WHOLE WHEAT
CRUST SETTING AS DESIRED

1 Measure ingredients into the bread pan according to the manufacturer's directions for your machine. Set the CYCLE, LOAF SIZE, and CRUST SETTING. Press START.

2 After about 5 minutes of kneading, check the consistency of your dough. If dough is not in a smooth round ball, open lid and with machine ON, add liquid, a tablespoon at a time, or add flour, a tablespoon at a time if too wet.

3 Remove the bread promptly from the pan when the machine beeps or on completing the cycle. Cool on rack before slicing.

Sourdough Wheat Bread with Orange and Currants

This is another four-star favorite with my family.
It's just absolutely yummy!

1 1/2-POUND	INGREDIENTS	2-POUND
1/2 cup	**Warm water (80°F)**	3/4 cup
3/4 cup	**Whole Wheat (page 125) or Basic Sourdough starter (page 126), room temperature**	1 cup
2 tablespoons	**Honey**	3 tablespoons
1 tablespoon	**Grated orange peel**	4 teaspoons
1 teaspoon	**Salt**	1 1/4 teaspoons
2 cups	**Whole wheat flour, unsifted**	2 1/3 cups
1 cup	**Bread flour, unsifted**	1 1/3 cups
1 1/2 teaspoons	**Active dry yeast or bread machine yeast**	2 teaspoons
1/2 cup	**Currants or raisins**	2/3 cup

CYCLE WHOLE WHEAT OR RAISIN/NUT
(DELAY-BAKE CAN BE USED)
CRUST SETTING AS DESIRED

1 Measure ingredients into the bread pan (except currants or raisins) according to the manufacturer's directions for your machine. Measure currants or raisins to add at the beep or when manufacturer directs. Set the CYCLE, LOAF SIZE, and CRUST SETTING. Press START.

2 After about 5 minutes of kneading, check the consistency of your dough. If dough is not in a smooth round ball, open lid and with machine ON, add liquid a tablespoon at a time if too dry, or add flour a tablespoon at a time if too wet.

3 Remove the bread promptly from the pan when the machine beeps or on completing the cycle. Cool on rack before slicing.

Wheat and Sesame Sourdough Bread

Sesame seeds and wheat germ add texture to this bread. If you like, toast the sesame seeds first for a bit of extra flavor. Place them on a tray in your toaster oven, or brown them in a non-stick skillet, stirring frequently and watching carefully, until golden brown.

1 1/2-POUND	INGREDIENTS	2-POUND
1/2 cup + 2 tablespoons	**Warm water (80°F)***	1/2 cup + 2 tablespoons
3/4 cup	**Whole Wheat (page 125) or Basic Sourdough starter (page 126), room temperature**	1 cup
1/4 cup	**Wheat germ**	1/3 cup
1 1/2 tablespoons	**Sesame seed, toasted if desired**	2 tablespoons
1 tablespoon	**Sugar**	1 1/2 tablespoons
1 1/4 teaspoons	**Salt**	1 1/2 teaspoons
1 1/2 cups	**Whole wheat flour, unsifted**	1 3/4 cups
1 1/2 cups	**Bread flour, unsifted**	1 3/4 cups
1 1/2 teaspoons	**Active dry yeast or bread machine yeast**	2 teaspoons

*Use the same amount for either size loaf.

CYCLE WHOLE WHEAT
(DELAY-BAKE CAN BE USED)
CRUST SETTING AS DESIRED

1 Measure ingredients into the bread pan according to the manufacturer's directions for your machine. Set the CYCLE, LOAF SIZE, and CRUST SETTING. Press START.

2 After about 5 minutes of kneading, check the consistency of your dough. If dough is not in a smooth round ball, open lid and with machine ON, add liquid a tablespoon at a time if too dry, or add flour a tablespoon at a time if too wet.

3 Remove the bread promptly from the pan when the machine beeps or on completing the cycle. Cool on rack before slicing.

Old World Sourdough Bread

A perfect pairing for a roast beef sandwich, with horseradish on the side.

1 1/2-POUND	INGREDIENTS	2-POUND
1/2 cup + 2 tablespoons	**Beer or water, room temperature**	3/4 cup + 2 tablespoons
3/4 cup	**Whole Wheat (page 125) or Basic Sourdough starter (page 126), room temperature**	1 cup
2 teaspoons	**Sugar**	1 tablespoon
1 teaspoon	**Salt**	1 1/4 teaspoons
1/2 teaspoon	**Fennel seed**	1 teaspoon
1 1/2 cups	**Bread flour, unsifted**	2 cups
1 cup	**Whole wheat flour, unsifted***	1 cup
1/2 cup	**Rye flour, unsifted***	1/2 cup
1 1/2 teaspoons	**Active dry yeast or bread machine yeast**	2 teaspoons

*Use the same amount for either size loaf.

CYCLE WHOLE WHEAT
(DELAY-BAKE CAN BE USED)
CRUST SETTING AS DESIRED

1 Measure ingredients into the bread pan according to the manufacturer's directions for your machine. Set the CYCLE, LOAF SIZE, and CRUST SETTING. Press START.

2 After about 5 minutes of kneading, check the consistency of your dough. If dough is not in a smooth round ball, open lid and with machine ON, add liquid a tablespoon at a time if too dry, or add flour a tablespoon at a time if too wet.

3 Remove the bread promptly from the pan when the machine beeps or on completing the cycle. Cool on rack before slicing.

Sourdough Pumpernickel Bread

This pumpernickel loaf gets a boost from the sourdough starter—it makes a larger-than-normal loaf with unbeatable flavor. The darker the molasses, the stronger the flavor.

1 1/2-POUND	INGREDIENTS	2-POUND
3/4 cup + 1 tablespoon	**Warm water (80°F)**	3/4 cup + 2 tablespoons
3/4 cup	**Rye (page 125) or Basic Sourdough starter (page 126), room temperature**	1 cup
3 tablespoons	**Molasses**	1/4 cup
1/3 cup	**Instant mashed potato flakes**	1/2 cup
1 1/2 tablespoons	**Unsweetened cocoa powder**	2 tablespoons
1 1/2 teaspoons	**Instant coffee crystals**	2 teaspoons
1 teaspoon	**Salt**	1 1/4 teaspoons
1 teaspoon	**Caraway seed**	1 1/2 teaspoons
2 1/4 cups	**Bread flour, unsifted**	3 cups
1 cup	**Rye flour, unsifted***	1 cup
1 1/2 teaspoons	**Active dry yeast or bread machine yeast**	2 teaspoons

*Use the same amount for either size loaf.

CYCLE WHOLE WHEAT
(DELAY-BAKE CAN BE USED)
CRUST SETTING AS DESIRED

1 Measure ingredients into the bread pan according to the manufacturer's directions for your machine. Set the CYCLE, LOAF SIZE, and CRUST SETTING. Press START.

2 After about 5 minutes of kneading, check the consistency of your dough. If dough is not in a smooth round ball, open lid and with machine ON, add liquid a tablespoon at a time if too dry, or add flour a tablespoon at a time if too wet.

3 Remove the bread promptly from the pan when the machine beeps or on completing the cycle. Cool on rack before slicing.

Sourdough Jewish Rye Bread

Who needs a deli when you can produce a bread like this from your own machine? This one's a natural for meat or cheese sandwiches.

1 1/2-POUND	INGREDIENTS	2-POUND
1/2 cup	**Warm water (80°F)**	1/2 cup + 2 tablespoons
3/4 cup	**Rye (page 125) or Basic Sourdough starter (page 126), room temperature**	1 cup
2 tablespoons	**Molasses**	3 tablespoons
1/3 cup	**Finely minced onion**	1/2 cup
1 1/4 teaspoons	**Salt**	1 1/2 teaspoons
1 teaspoon	**Caraway seed**	1 1/2 teaspoons
2 cups	**Bread flour, unsifted**	2 1/4 cups
1 1/4 cups	**Rye flour, unsifted**	1 3/4 cups
1 1/2 teaspoons	**Active dry yeast or bread machine yeast**	2 teaspoons

CYCLE WHOLE WHEAT
CRUST SETTING AS DESIRED

1. Measure ingredients into the bread pan according to the manufacturer's directions for your machine. Set the CYCLE, LOAF SIZE, and CRUST SETTING. Press START.

2. After about 5 minutes of kneading, check the consistency of your dough. If dough is not in a smooth round ball, open lid and with machine ON, add liquid a tablespoon at a time if too dry, or add flour a tablespoon at a time if too wet.

3. Remove the bread promptly from the pan when the machine beeps or on completing the cycle. Cool on rack before slicing.

CHAPTER

7

Shaped Bread and Roll Doughs, Pizza, and Focaccia

FRENCH BREAD AND ROLL DOUGH

REFRIGERATOR ROLL DOUGH

PIZZA CRUST DOUGH

FOCACCIA BREAD DOUGH

SOFT PRETZEL DOUGH

POTATO BREAD, ROLL, AND COFFEECAKE DOUGH

WHOLE WHEAT BUTTERMILK DOUGH

SWEET BREAD AND COFFEECAKE DOUGH

FRUIT-FILLED KUCHEN DOUGH

French Bread and Roll Dough

You can make French baguettes, rolls, or breadsticks
with this versatile dough.

INGREDIENTS

(For 1½- and 2-pound Bread Machines)

1¼ cups	**Warm water (80°F)**
2 tablespoons	**Vegetable oil**
1½ tablespoons	**Sugar**
1½ teaspoons	**Salt**
4 cups	**Bread flour, unsifted**
2 teaspoons	**Active dry yeast or bread machine yeast**

VARIATION

For Whole Wheat French Bread and Roll Dough, you can substitute 2 cups whole wheat flour for 2 cups of the bread flour.

CYCLE DOUGH

1 Measure ingredients into the bread pan according to the manufacturer's directions for your machine. Set the DOUGH CYCLE and press the START button.

2 After about 5 minutes of kneading, check the consistency of your dough. If dough is not in a smooth round ball, open lid and with machine ON, add liquid a tablespoon at a time if too dry, or add flour a tablespoon at a time if too wet.

3 Remove the dough promptly from the machine at the end of the cycle. KNEAD dough about 10 times on a lightly floured surface. Choose one or two Shaping Variations below and continue as directed.

Baguettes

Use all of the dough for 2 baguettes or half the dough to make 1 baguette. Shape each half of dough into a 15- to17-inch-long rope. Place in a greased baguette pan or on a lightly greased baking sheet (4 inches apart for 2 loaves). Slash loaves diagonally across the top 3 or 4 times for a decorative effect, if desired. Cover with plastic wrap or a towel and let rise in a warm place until doubled, 30 to 45 minutes. Uncover; BAKE in a preheated 350°F oven for 25 to 30 minutes, or until loaves are golden brown and sound hollow when lightly tapped. (If using a baguette pan, brown bottoms of loaves if desired by removing them from the pans and baking loaves on oven rack for 5 minutes more.) Cool loaves on racks.

French Loaves

Follow directions for Baguettes, except shape each half of dough into a 12-inch loaf. Cover and let rise as for Baguettes. BAKE in a preheated 350°F oven for 25 to 30 minutes, or until loaves are golden brown and sound hollow when lightly tapped. Cool on racks.

Petite French Dinner Rolls

For 24 rolls, use all of the dough or use half the dough to make 12 rolls. On a lightly floured surface, divide dough into quarters. If making 24 rolls, divide each quarter into 6 pieces. If making 12 rolls, divide each quarter into 3 pieces. Shape each piece into a small ball; place balls 3 inches apart on greased baking sheets. Cover with plastic wrap or a towel and let rise in a warm place until doubled, 30 to 45 minutes. Uncover and BAKE in a preheated 350°F oven for 16 to 18 minutes, or until rolls are golden brown and sound hollow when lightly tapped. Serve warm, or cool on racks.

French Sandwich Rolls

Use all of the dough to make 12 rolls or half the dough to make 6 rolls. On a lightly floured surface, divide dough in half, then divide each half into 6 pieces if making 12 rolls or 3 pieces if making 6 rolls. Shape each piece of dough into an oval; continue as directed for Petite French Dinner Rolls. Uncover and BAKE in a preheated 350°F oven for 16 to 19 minutes, or until rolls are golden brown and sound hollow when lightly tapped. Serve warm or cool on racks.

Breadsticks

One batch of dough makes 18 large breadsticks or 24 thin breadsticks. On a lightly floured surface, roll dough to an 10x9-inch rectangle for 18 breadsticks, or a 12x12-inch rectangle for 24 breadsticks. Cut the 10-inch rectangle across the 9-inch side into eighteen ½-inch-wide strips; cut the 12-inch rectangle into twenty-four ½-inch-wide strips. Flour palms of hands; roll each piece of dough between palms to shape into breadsticks. Place 1 inch apart on greased baking sheets. Brush sticks with 1 *egg white,* beaten with 1 teaspoon *water*. Sprinkle with *sesame* or *poppy seed,* or *coarse salt,* if desired. Cover with plastic wrap or a towel and let rise in a warm place until doubled, about 30 minutes. Uncover and BAKE in a preheated 350°F oven for 18 to 20 minutes, or until golden brown. Serve warm or cool on racks.

Crust Tricks

Crust is very important to French bread-lovers–some like it thin and tender, others prefer their crust thick and chewy. For a thin, delicate crust, brush the dough with milk, cream, melted butter, or salted water after you've shaped the dough and again just before baking. For a thicker, chewier crust, do not apply any type of glaze. Instead, dust the dough with flour; it causes the dough to dry out on the surface and promotes a crisp-textured crust.

Refrigerator Roll Dough

This versatile roll dough lets you postpone baking your rolls for up to 24 hours. Just shape the dough into rolls, place them on baking sheets, and refrigerate them until you are ready for the last rise and baking steps.

INGREDIENTS

(For 1½- and 2-Pound Bread Machines)

½ cup	**Milk**
½ cup	**Water**
1½ tablespoons	**Butter or margarine, softened**
2 tablespoons	**Sugar**
1½ teaspoons	**Salt**
3¼ cups	**Bread flour, unsifted**
3 teaspoons	**Active dry yeast or bread machine yeast**

CYCLE DOUGH

1 If your machine does not have a preheat cycle, combine milk and water and heat in microwave on HIGH power for 30 seconds (or heat in a saucepan for 1 minute to 80°F).

2 Add to the bread pan with remaining ingredients according to the manufacturer's directions for your machine. Set the DOUGH CYCLE and press the START button.

3 After about 5 minutes of kneading, check the consistency of your dough. If dough is not in a smooth round ball, open lid and with machine ON, add liquid a tablespoon at a time if too dry, or add flour a tablespoon at a time if too wet.

4 Remove the dough promptly from the machine at the end of the cycle. KNEAD dough about 10 times on a lightly floured surface. Choose one or more Roll Variations and continue as directed.

(continues)

Classic Dinner Rolls

Divide dough into quarters, then quarter again. Shape each piece into a smooth, round ball. Place rolls in 2 greased 9-inch round or square pans. Brush rolls with melted *butter*. Cover and refrigerate rolls for 2 to 24 hours. Uncover; let stand 20 minutes at room temperature. BAKE in a preheated 400°F oven for 11 to 13 minutes, or until rolls are golden brown and sound hollow when lightly tapped. Serve warm. Makes 16 rolls.

French Dinner Buns

Divide dough into 12 pieces. Shape each piece into an oval; place rolls 2 inches apart on greased baking sheet. Brush with melted *butter;* cover and refrigerate for 2 to 24 hours. Uncover and slash each roll across the top with a sharp knife dipped in *flour*. Let stand at room temperature 20 minutes. BAKE in a preheated 400°F oven for 12 to 14 minutes. Serve warm. Makes 12 rolls.

Fan-Tan Rolls

Divide dough in half; roll each half to a 10x8-inch rectangle. Brush dough with 2 tablespoons melted *butter*. Cut each rectangle lengthwise into 6 strips. Stack strips from each rectangle to make 2 stacks. Cut each stack crosswise into ten 1-inch pieces. Place each cut stack cut side up in greased muffin cups. Brush rolls with 1 to 2 tablespoons additional melted *butter*. Cover and refrigerate for 2 to 24 hours. Uncover and let stand at room temperature for 20 minutes. BAKE in a preheated 400°F oven for 13 to 15 minutes, or until golden brown. Serve warm. Makes 20 rolls.

Easy Cloverleaf Rolls

Divide dough into quarters; quarter again. Shape each piece into a smooth ball; place each ball seam side down in a greased muffin cup. With floured kitchen shears, cut each ball in half across the top in 2 directions to make a cross, clipping almost to the bottom of each roll. Brush with 2 tablespoons melted *butter* or *margarine*. Cover and refrigerate for 2 to 24 hours. Uncover; let stand at room temperature 20 minutes. BAKE in a preheated 400°F oven for 13 to 15 minutes. Serve warm. Makes 16 rolls.

Pizza Crust Dough

There are three crust variations and four topping recipes following this recipe for a basic pizza crust dough. The Personal Pizza Topping lets you create your own pizza, with guidelines for your favorite topping ingredients.

INGREDIENTS

(For 1½- and 2-Pound Bread Machines)

1 cup	**Warm water (80°F)**
2 tablespoons	**Olive or vegetable oil**
1 tablespoon	**Sugar**
1½ teaspoons	**Salt**
3 cups	**Bread flour, unsifted**
2½ teaspoons	**Active dry yeast or bread machine yeast**

CYCLE DOUGH

1 Measure ingredients into the bread pan according to manufacturer's directions for your machine. Set the DOUGH CYCLE and press the START button.

2 After about 5 minutes of kneading, check the consistency of your dough. If dough is not in a smooth round ball, open lid and with machine ON, add liquid a tablespoon at a time if too dry, or add flour a tablespoon at a time if too wet.

3 Remove the dough promptly from the pan at the end of the cycle. KNEAD dough about 10 times on a lightly floured surface.

4 For thin crust, divide dough in half; roll each half to a 12-inch round or to a 13x9-inch rectangle. (If dough is difficult to roll, cover with plastic wrap or a towel and let rest 20 minutes, then roll out.) Place dough in a greased 12-inch round or 13x9x2-inch baking pan. Choose from the Pizza Topping Variations below and follow directions for baking. Makes 2 pizza crusts.

(continues)

5 For thick crust, follow directions for thin crust, except use all of the dough for 1 crust. Roll dough as directed above. Choose from the Pizza Topping Variations below and follow directions for baking. Makes 1 pizza crust.

Onion-Herb Crust

In a skillet, melt 1 tablespoon *butter* or *margarine*; sauté 1/2 cup finely chopped *onion* until tender but not brown. Stir in 1/2 teaspoon *celery seed* and 1/2 teaspoon *dried sage leaves*. Cool; add mixture to bread pan with remaining dough ingredients.

Cheddar Cheese Crust

Add 1 cup shredded *sharp cheddar cheese* and 1/3 cup thinly sliced *green onions* to remaining ingredients in bread pan.

Chili Crust

Add 1 teaspoon *chili powder* and 1/2 teaspoon *ground cumin* to remaining ingredients in bread pan.

Personal Pizza Topping: Top each crust with 1 cup *pizza* or *marinara sauce,* 1 cup cooked crumbled *meat* or 1 1/2 ounces sliced *pepperoni,* 1/4 cup sliced *green onions* or chopped *onion,* 1 cup sliced *bell peppers, onions, mushrooms,* or desired vegetables, and 2 cups shredded *cheddar* or *mozzarella cheese*. BAKE in a preheated 450°F oven for 15 to 17 minutes for a thin crust, or 16 to 18 minutes for a thick crust pizza, or until deep golden brown. Serve immediately.
Niçoise Pizza: Top each pizza crust with 1 cup *marinara sauce,* 1 cup sautéed *red* or *sweet yellow onions,* 1/2 cup sliced *pitted Kalamata, ripe,* or *green olives,* 1/4 cup chopped *fresh basil leaves,* one 2-ounce can *anchovies,* drained, rinsed and patted dry (optional), 2 minced *garlic cloves,* 1 cup shredded *mozzarella cheese,* and 1/3 cup shredded or grated *Parmesan* or *Romano cheese*. Bake as directed for Personal Pizza recipe above. Serve immediately.
Pizza New Mexico: Top each pizza crust with one 15-ounce can *black beans,* drained and mashed, 1/2 cup bottled *salsa,* 1/2 cup julienne-sliced *red* or *green bell pepper,* 1/2 cup *niblet corn*, 1/3 cup sliced *green onions*, 1 to 2 tablespoons chopped *chipotle chiles* in *adobo sauce,* and 1 1/2 cups shredded *Monterey jack* or *cheddar cheese*. BAKE as directed for Personal Pizza recipe above. Serve immediately topped

with sliced *avocado* and chopped *cilantro,* if desired. Serve with some additional salsa.

Tri-Pepper Pizza with Feta Cheese: For each crust, in a large skillet, sauté 2 cups julienne-sliced *red, green,* and *yellow bell peppers* with 1/2 cup sliced *red onion* and 1 cup sliced *mushrooms* in 2 tablespoons *olive* or *vegetable oil* for 3 to 5 minutes until tender. Stir in 2 minced *garlic cloves* and 2 teaspoons chopped *fresh basil, oregano,* or *rosemary.* Spread 1 cup *marinara* or *pizza sauce* over crust; top with sautéed vegetable mixture. Sprinkle with 1/2 cup crumbled *feta cheese,* 1 cup shredded *mozzarella cheese,* and 1/4 cup grated or shredded *Parmesan cheese.* BAKE as directed for Personal Pizza recipe above. Serve immediately.

Baking Tips

Making Pizza Like The Pros

Pizza aficionados use several different baking techniques to achieve the perfect crisp or chewy crust. Always bake your pizza on the bottom rack of the oven, and always preheat the oven to full temperature before baking. For a real pizza-oven texture and taste, buy a pizza stone, available at cookware shops and in gourmet food catalogs. You simply warm the stone in your oven and bake the pizza directly on it. Use a large pizza board (like a giant wooden spatula) to remove the pizza from the stone when it's baked. You can also use a heavy-gauge black steel pizza pan with a dull finish. It will quickly absorb the heat and create a browner, crisper crust than a shiny metal pizza pan.

Focaccia Bread Dough

Use these focaccia breads for your breadbasket or as a base for great sandwiches. The first three variations are hot bread ideas; the last is like a baked cheese sandwich. Focaccia is best served hot the day it is made.

INGREDIENTS

(For 1½- and 2-Pound Bread Machines)

1 cup	**Warm water (80°F)**
1½ tablespoons	**Olive or vegetable oil**
1½ tablespoons	**Sugar**
2 teaspoons	**Dried oregano or basil**
1¼ teaspoons	**Salt**
3¼ cups	**Bread flour, unsifted**
1½ teaspoons	**Active dry yeast or bread machine yeast**

CYCLE DOUGH

1. Measure ingredients into the bread pan according to the manufacturer's directions for your machine. Set the DOUGH CYCLE and press START.

2. After about 5 minutes of kneading, check the consistency of your dough. If dough is not in a smooth round ball, open lid and with machine ON, add liquid a tablespoon at a time if too dry, or add flour a tablespoon at a time if too wet

3. Remove the dough promptly from the machine at the end of the cycle.

4. KNEAD dough about 10 times on a lightly floured surface. Choose one of the Focaccia Variations that follows (on pages 159-160) and continue as directed.

Roasted Garlic Focaccia

Roll dough to a 15x10-inch rectangle. Place in a greased 15x10x2-inch baking pan. Poke your fingertips all over top of dough to make small indentations. Brush with 1 tablespoon *olive oil;* set aside. In a small skillet, sauté 4 *garlic cloves,* peeled and thinly sliced, with 3/4 cup coarsely chopped *red* or *yellow onion* in 2 tablespoons *olive* or *vegetable oil* over medium-low heat until tender, stirring frequently. Spread garlic-onion mixture over dough. Sprinkle 2 tablespoons chopped *fresh basil* and 1/2 teaspoon *cracked black peppercorns* over dough. Cover with plastic wrap or a towel and let rise in a warm place until nearly doubled, 20 to 30 minutes. BAKE in a preheated 375°F oven for 20 to 25 minutes, or until light golden brown. Cut into approximately fifteen 3-inch squares or 2 1/2 dozen 3x1 1/2-inch sticks. Serve hot.

Herb and Onion Focaccia

Roll dough to a 13x9-inch rectangle; place in a greased 13x9x2-inch baking pan. Poke your fingertips all over top of dough to make small indentations. Brush with 1 tablespoon *olive* or *vegetable oil*. Sprinkle with 2/3 cup thinly sliced *red* or *yellow onion,* 1/2 cup slivered *pitted olives (any type),* and 2 teaspoons chopped *fresh rosemary* or 1/2 teaspoon crushed *dried rosemary*. Gently press vegetables into dough. Cover with plastic wrap or a towel and let rise in a warm place until nearly doubled, 20 to 30 minutes. BAKE in a preheated 375°F oven for 30 to 35 minutes, until golden brown at the edges and light golden on the top. Cut into approximately twelve 3-inch square or 2 dozen 3x1 1/2-inch sticks. Serve hot.

Parmesan and Tomato Focaccia

Roll dough to a 15x10-inch rectangle; place in a greased 15x10x1-inch baking pan with sides. Poke your fingertips all over top of dough to make small indentations. Brush with 1 tablespoon *olive* or *vegetable oil*. Arrange 1 thinly sliced *large tomato,* over dough. Sprinkle with 1/4 cup shredded or grated *Parmesan* or *Romano cheese*, 2 tablespoons chopped *fresh basil leaves,* and 1/4 teaspoon *salt*. Cover with plastic wrap or a towel and let rise in a warm place until nearly doubled, 20 to 30 minutes. BAKE in a preheated 375°F oven for 20 to 25 minutes, until golden brown at the edges. Cut into approximately fifteen 3-inch squares or 2 1/2 dozen 3 1/2-inch sticks. Serve hot.

Four-Cheese Stuffed Focaccia

Cut dough in half; roll each half to a 13x9-inch rectangle. Place 1 rectangle in a greased 13x9x2-inch baking pan. In a bowl, stir together 1 1/2 cups shredded *sharp cheddar* or *Swiss cheese,* 1/2 cup shredded *mozzarella cheese,* 1/2 cup crumbled *blue cheese,* and 1/4 cup shredded or grated *Parmesan cheese*. Sprinkle cheese mixture over dough. Top with second rectangle of dough. Poke your fingertips all over top of dough to make small indentations. Brush with 1 tablespoon *olive* or *vegetable oil*. Sprinkle with 1 tablespoon grated *Parmesan cheese* and 2 tablespoons chopped *fresh parsley*. Cover with plastic wrap or a towel and let rise in a warm place until nearly doubled, about 30 minutes. BAKE in a preheated 375°F oven for 35 to 40 minutes, or until deep golden brown. Serve hot, cut into squares. Makes 9 sandwiches.

Baking Tips

Uses for Day-Old Focaccia

Although focaccia is best served the same day, the recipes here make a large pan of it, and you won't want to discard the leftovers on the second day. Try these simple ideas for day-old focaccia: Homemade Croutons (page 244); Italian-Style Croutons (page 245); or Toasted Baguette Nicoise (page 251). Or, you might plan a brunch for the next day and use your leftover focaccia in a fine strata (pages 254-256), which you can prepare the night before.

Soft Pretzel Dough

You can make the Traditional Pretzels that are boiled and then baked, or you can make the Easy Baked Pretzels in just one step. Baked pretzels are not quite as chewy as those that have been boiled first. You'll find coarse or kosher salt in the baking section of larger markets.

INGREDIENTS

(For 1½- and 2-Pound Bread Machines)

1 cup	**Warm water (80°F)**
1½ tablespoons	**Vegetable oil**
1½ tablespoons	**Nonfat dry milk**
1½ tablespoons	**Sugar**
1½ teaspoons	**Salt**
3 cups	**Bread flour, unsifted**
1½ teaspoons	**Active dry yeast or bread machine yeast**

CYCLE DOUGH

1 Measure ingredients into the bread pan according to manufacturer's directions for your machine. Set the DOUGH CYCLE and press START.

2 After about 5 minutes of kneading, check the consistency of your dough. If dough is not in a smooth round ball, open lid and with machine ON, add liquid a tablespoon at a time if too dry, or add flour a tablespoon at a time if too wet.

3 Remove the dough promptly from the pan at the end of the cycle. KNEAD dough about 10 times on a lightly floured surface. Choose one of the Pretzel Variations that follows (on page 162) and continue as directed.

Traditional Pretzels

Roll dough to an 18x6-inch square. Cut into 12 strips that are 18 inches long by ½ inch wide. Shape each strip into an 18-inch rope by rolling dough between your palms. Shape into pretzels by forming a simple knot and gently looping the ends through. Place pretzels on lightly greased baking sheets; cover with plastic wrap or a towel and let rise in a warm place for 20 minutes. Meanwhile, preheat oven to 350°F. In a large saucepan or Dutch oven, bring 3 quarts *water* to a boil. Stir in 3 tablespoons *salt*. Using a slotted spoon, place 1 or 2 pretzels at a time into boiling *water*. Boil pretzels for 1 minute on each side, turning once with tongs. Transfer pretzels to paper towels; pat dry. Arrange on lightly greased baking sheets. Brush with a mixture of 1 beaten *egg white* and 1 tablespoon *water*. Sprinkle with *coarse* or *kosher salt,* if desired. Immediately BAKE the boiled pretzels in preheated oven for 25 to 30 minutes, or until golden brown. Makes 12 pretzels.

Whole Wheat Pretzels

Prepare dough as directed for bread machine above, except use 1½ cups *bread flour* and 1½ cups *whole wheat flour*. On a lightly floured surface, roll dough to a 12-inch square. Cut dough into twelve 1-inch-wide strips. Shape each strip into a rope, rolling it between your palms, to a rope that is 16 to 18 inches long. Shape into pretzels by forming a simple knot and gently looping the ends through. Continue as directed for Traditional Pretzels or Baked Pretzels. Makes 12 pretzels.

Easy Baked Pretzels

Roll and shape pretzels as directed for Traditional Pretzels. Place on lightly greased baking sheets. Cover with plastic wrap or a towel and let rise in a warm place for 20 minutes. Stir together 1 beaten *egg yolk* and 1 tablespoon *water*; brush mixture over pretzels. Sprinkle with *coarse* or *kosher salt*, if desired. BAKE in a preheated 350°F oven for 20 to 25 minutes, or until golden brown. Cool on rack. Makes 12 pretzels.

Potato Bread, Roll, and Coffeecake Dough

For the mashed potatoes in this recipe, cook potatoes in water to cover, then mash the potatoes with milk and butter as you normally do. Save the potato cooking water to use for the liquid in this recipe. If you would like to make the Lemon-Glazed Savarin (page 165), you'll need to add grated lemon peel and raisins to the remaining ingredients in the bread machine before you begin the dough cycle.

INGREDIENTS

(For 1½- and 2-Pound Bread Machines)

¾ cup	**Potato water or warm water (80°F)**
½ cup	**Prepared mashed potatoes, room temperature**
2 tablespoons	**Butter or margarine, softened**
3 tablespoons	**Sugar**
1 teaspoon	**Salt**
3¼ cups	**Bread flour, unsifted**
2 teaspoons	**Active dry yeast or bread machine yeast**

CYCLE DOUGH

1 If your machine does not have a preheat cycle, combine potato water or water and mashed potatoes and heat in microwave on HIGH power for 30 seconds (or heat in a saucepan for 1 minute to 80°F). Add to the bread pan with remaining ingredients according to the manufacturer's directions for your machine. Set the DOUGH CYCLE and press START.

2 After about 5 minutes of kneading, check the consistency of your dough. If your dough is not in a smooth round ball, open lid and with machine ON, add liquid a tablespoon at a time if too dry, or add flour a tablespoon at a time if too wet.

(continues)

3 Remove the dough promptly from the machine at the end of the cycle.

4 KNEAD dough about 10 times on a lightly floured surface. Choose one of the Shaping Variations below and continue as directed.

Potato-Rosemary-Chive Spirals

Roll dough to a 12x10-inch rectangle. Brush dough with 1 tablespoon melted *butter* or *margarine*. Sprinkle the dough with 1 tablespoon chopped *fresh rosemary* and 2 tablespoons minced *chives*. Roll up the dough from the long side, as for cinnamon rolls. Cut the dough crosswise into 1-inch slices; arrange the slices cut side down in a greased 13x9x2-inch baking pan. Brush rolls with an additional 1 to 2 tablespoons melted *butter*. Cover rolls with plastic wrap or a towel and let rise in a warm place until doubled, 30 to 45 minutes. Uncover and BAKE in a preheated 375°F oven for 24 to 27 minutes, or until golden brown. Serve warm. Makes 12 rolls.

Cheese and Olive-Filled Bread

Roll dough to a 13x9-inch rectangle. Brush dough with 1 tablespoon melted *butter* or *margarine*. Sprinkle 1½ cups shredded *cheddar cheese,* ½ cup chopped drained *pitted olives (any type),* and 1 tablespoon chopped drained *pimiento* over dough. Roll dough up tightly from the 9-inch side, rolling tightly and pinching all edges together to seal. Place roll seam side down in a greased 9x5x3-inch loaf pan. Brush with 1 tablespoon additional melted *butter*. Cover with plastic wrap or a towel and let rise in a warm place until doubled, 40 to 50 minutes. BAKE in a preheated 375°F oven for 30 to 35 minutes, until deep golden brown. Cool loaf for 15 minutes before slicing. Serve warm. Makes one 9-inch loaf.

Twisted Herb Bread

Roll dough to a 14x10-inch rectangle. Place on a large greased baking sheet. Cut dough in half lengthwise to make two 14x5-inch rectangles. In a small bowl, stir together ¼ cup melted *butter* or *margarine,* ½ cup chopped *fresh basil,* 2 tablespoons desired chopped *fresh herbs* (such as chives, chervil, rosemary, marjoram, oregano, thyme, or dill), and 2 finely chopped *garlic cloves*. Spread mixture generously on both pieces of dough, to within 1 inch of edges. Starting from the long side, roll up each piece of dough, pinching all edges together, to make 2 cylinders. Arrange dough cylinders side by side. Twist the 2 rolls together, sealing at both ends, to make 1 loaf. Cover with plastic wrap or a towel and let rise in a warm place until doubled, about 30 minutes. Brush loaf with any remaining butter-herb mixture or *olive oil*. Sprinkle with 1 tablespoon grated *Parmesan cheese*. BAKE in a preheated 375°F oven for 30 to 35 minutes, or until deep golden brown and loaf sounds hollow when lightly tapped. Cool on rack 15 minutes before slicing. Serve warm. Makes one loaf.

Lemon-Glazed Savarin

Add 1 tablespoon grated *lemon peel* and 1/2 cup *raisins* to ingredients in bread pan. After cycle is completed, KNEAD dough several times on lightly floured surface. Roll dough to a 17x4-inch rectangle; shape dough into a 17-inch rope. Shape rope into a ring by sealing ends together; place in a greased 9-inch fluted tube pan. Brush with 1 tablespoon melted *butter* or *margarine*. Cover with plastic wrap or a towel and let rise in a warm place until doubled, 30 to 45 minutes. BAKE in a preheated 375°F oven for 23 to 26 minutes, or until golden brown. Meanwhile, prepare glaze: In a saucepan combine half of a 6-ounce can *frozen lemonade concentrate,* 1/4 cup *confectioners' sugar,* and 1 tablespoon *butter* or *margarine*. Cook and stir until mixture is smooth; remove from heat. When cake is done, immediately turn it out onto a cooling rack set in a shallow baking pan. Poke surface of cake all over with tines of a fork. Spoon warm glaze all over top and sides of cake. Serve warm or cool. Makes one 9-inch coffeecake.

Whole Wheat Buttermilk Dough

You can make burger or hot dog buns, breadsticks, caramel rolls, or monkey bread with this versatile dough. Dough made with whole wheat flour can sometimes be a bit sticky—knead on a floured surface.

INGREDIENTS

(For 1½- and 2-Pound Bread Machines)

1 cup + 2 tablespoons	**Buttermilk**
⅓ cup	**Butter or margarine, softened and cut up**
1	**Egg**
⅓ cup	**Packed brown sugar**
1 teaspoon	**Salt**
1⅔ cups	**Whole wheat flour, unsifted**
⅔ cups	**Bread flour, unsifted**
2½ teaspoons	**Active dry yeast or bread machine yeast**

CYCLE DOUGH

1. If your machine does not have a preheat cycle, heat buttermilk in microwave on HIGH power for 30 seconds (or heat in a saucepan for 1 minute to 80°F). Add to the bread pan with remaining ingredients according to the manufacturer's directions for your machine. Set the DOUGH CYCLE and press START.

2. After about 5 minutes of kneading, check the consistency of your dough. If dough is not in a smooth round ball, open lid and with machine ON, add liquid a tablespoon at a time if dry, or add flour a tablespoon at a time if too wet.

3. Remove the dough promptly from the machine at the end of the cycle.

4. KNEAD dough about 10 times on a lightly floured surface. Choose one of the Shaping Variations that follows and continue as directed.

Whole Wheat Burger Buns

Divide dough in half; cut each half into 5 pieces. Shape each piece into a ball; place 3 inches apart on a greased baking sheet. Flatten balls slightly. Brush dough with a mixture of 1 beaten *egg white* and 1 tablespoon *water*. Sprinkle with *sesame* or *poppy seeds,* if desired. Cover with plastic wrap or a towel and let rise in a warm place until doubled, 30 to 45 minutes. BAKE in a preheated 400°F oven for 12 to 15 minutes, or until golden brown and rolls sound hollow when lightly tapped. Cool on rack. Makes 10 buns.

Whole Wheat Hot Dog Buns

Divide dough in half; cut each half into 4 pieces. Shape each piece into a 6-inch rope. Place 3 inches apart on greased baking sheet. Brush rolls with a mixture of 1 beaten *egg white* and 1 tablespoon *water;* sprinkle with *sesame* or *poppy seeds,* if desired. Let rise and BAKE as directed for Whole Wheat Burger Buns above. Makes 8 buns.

Whole Wheat Breadsticks

Roll dough to a 10x10-inch square. Cut into twenty ½-inch-wide strips. Shape each strip into a 12-inch rope. Place ropes 2 inches apart on greased baking sheets. Brush sticks with a mixture of 1 lightly beaten *egg white* and 1 tablespoon *water*. Sprinkle sticks with *coarse salt, sesame seed,* or *poppy seed* if desired. Cover with plastic wrap or a towel and let rise in a warm place until doubled, 30 to 45 minutes. Uncover and BAKE in a preheated 350°F oven for 18 to 20 minutes, or until golden brown. Serve warm. Makes 20 breadsticks.

Caramel-Pecan Wheat Rolls

In a medium saucepan, stir together 1 cup chopped *pecans* or *walnuts,* ⅔ cup packed *brown sugar,* ⅔ cup cut-up *butter* or *margarine,* 1½ teaspoons *ground cinnamon,* and 3 tablespoons *maple syrup* or *honey*. Cook and stir over medium heat until butter is melted. Grease two 9-inch round cake pans. Spread half of the pecan mixture in the bottom of each prepared pan. Set aside. Divide dough into quarters; divide each quarter into 4 pieces. Shape each piece into a ball. Arrange 8 rolls, seam side down, over topping in each pan. Cover with plastic wrap or a towel and let rise in a warm place until doubled, 30 to 45 minutes. BAKE in a preheated 375°F oven for 18 to 20 minutes, or until rolls are golden brown. Cool rolls in pans for 1 minute; invert rolls onto platter. Allow pan to remain on platter for 2 minutes; carefully remove pans. Scrape any topping left in pans over rolls. Cool slightly; serve warm. Makes 16 rolls.

Whole Wheat Monkey Bread

In a saucepan, melt 1/4 cup *butter* or *margarine*. Stir in 3 tablespoons *granulated sugar,* 3 tablespoons *brown sugar,* 2 teaspoons grated *lemon peel,* 1 teaspoon *ground cinnamon,* and 1/3 cup coarsely ground *walnuts* or *pecans*. Remove from heat; set aside. Divide dough into quarters; divide each quarter into 5 pieces. Shape each piece of dough into a ball. Grease a 9-inch tube or fluted tube pan. Dip each dough ball into butter mixture until well coated; arrange coated dough balls evenly inside the tube pan. Cover with plastic wrap or a towel and let rise in a warm place until doubled, about 45 minutes. BAKE in a preheated 350°F oven for 30 to 35 minutes, or until golden brown. Cool in pan 2 minutes; invert bread ring onto a serving plate. Serve warm by pulling apart balls of dough. Makes one 9-inch coffeecake.

Baking Tips

Tool Time

The right tools make your time in the kitchen easier and that much more fun. One of my favorite tools is a good pair of kitchen shears. I use them for snipping fresh herbs, cutting dried fruits, opening packages of yeast, and for snipping the tops of rolls before the last rise. Be sure to buy kitchen shears that won't rust, and you can run them through the dishwasher at the end of your baking session.

Sweet Bread and Coffeecake Dough

This sweet dough is very easy to handle. It's the perfect base for old-fashioned cinnamon rolls, a braided coffeecake with a peach filling, or a spiral-shaped honey and pinenut coffee bread.

INGREDIENTS
(For 1½- and 2-Pound Bread Machines)

½ cup	**Milk**
2	**Eggs**
¼ cup	**Butter or margarine, softened and cut up**
⅓ cup	**Sugar**
1 tablespoon	**Grated orange or lemon peel**
1 teaspoon	**Salt**
½ teaspoon	**Ground nutmeg**
3⅓ cups	**Bread flour, unsifted**
2½ teaspoons	**Active dry yeast or bread machine yeast**

CYCLE DOUGH

1 If your machine does not have a preheat cycle, heat milk in microwave on HIGH power for 30 seconds (or heat in a saucepan for 1 minute to 80°F). Add to the bread pan with remaining ingredients according to the manufacturer's directions for your machine. Set the DOUGH CYCLE and press START.

2 After about 5 minutes of kneading, check the consistency of your dough. If dough is not in a smooth round ball, open lid and with machine ON, add liquid a tablespoon at a time if too dry, or add flour a tablespoon at a time if too wet.

3 Remove the dough promptly from the machine at the end of the cycle.

(continues)

4 KNEAD dough about 10 times on a lightly floured surface. Choose one of the Sweet Bread Variations below and continue as directed.

Old-Fashioned Cinnamon Rolls

Combine ½ cup packed *brown sugar,* ½ cup chopped *pecans* or *walnuts,* ½ cup *raisins,* and ½ teaspoon *ground cinnamon*. Roll dough to a 12x10-inch rectangle. Brush dough with 1 tablespoon melted *butter*. Sprinkle brown sugar mixture evenly over dough. Roll up dough from the long side, pinching all edges together to seal. Cut roll crosswise into twelve 1-inch slices. Place rolls cut side down in a greased 13x9x2-inch baking pan. Brush rolls with 2 tablespoons melted *butter*. Cover with plastic wrap or a towel and let rise in a warm place until doubled, 30 to 45 minutes. Uncover and BAKE in a preheated 400°F oven for 20 to 25 minutes, or until deep golden brown. Invert rolls onto a rack; invert again onto a serving platter. Glaze with *Powdered Sugar Glaze* (page 205). Cool slightly; serve warm. Makes 12 rolls.

Peach Braid Coffeecake

Roll dough to a 13x9-inch rectangle. Transfer dough to a large greased baking sheet. Spoon 1 cup *peach* or *apricot preserves* lengthwise over the center third of rectangle, to within ½ inch of each short end. With a sharp knife, cut 1-inch-wide strips along both sides of filling, cutting from filling to outside edges of dough. Starting at the top of the dough, fold strips over filling at an angle, alternating from side to side to enclose filling, for a "braided" effect. Combine 2 tablespoons *granulated sugar* and ½ teaspoon *ground cinnamon*. Brush braid with 1½ tablespoons melted *butter;* sprinkle with cinnamon-sugar mixture. Cover with plastic wrap or a towel and let rise in a warm place until doubled, 30 to 45 minutes. Uncover and BAKE in a preheated 375°F oven for 22 to 25 minutes, or until deep golden brown and filling is bubbly. Cool on a rack at least 20 minutes before serving. Makes 1 coffeecake.

Honey and Pinenut Spiral Coffeecake

Combine 1/4 cup *granulated sugar,* 1 teaspoon *ground cinnamon,* and 1/4 teaspoon *ground nutmeg*. Roll dough to a 25x6-inch rectangle. Brush with 1 1/2 tablespoons melted *butter* or *margarine*. Sprinkle with sugar-spice mixture. Starting with longer side, roll dough up tightly, pinching all edges with fingers to seal. Coil roll tightly into a snail shape. Place on a large greased baking sheet. Brush with 1 tablespoon melted *butter*. Cover with plastic wrap or a towel and let rise in a warm place until doubled, 30 to 45 minutes. Uncover and BAKE in a preheated 350°F oven for 25 to 30 minutes, or until deep golden brown and loaf sounds hollow when lightly tapped. Meanwhile, prepare glaze: In a saucepan, combine 1 tablespoon *butter* or *margarine,* 2 tablespoons *sugar,* and 2 tablespoons *honey*. Bring mixture to boiling, stirring constantly. When loaf is done, immediately transfer it to a cooling rack placed over a baking sheet. Spoon warm glaze over hot coffeecake to cover completely. Sprinkle with 2 to 3 tablespoons *pinenuts* or *slivered almonds*. Makes 1 coffeecake.

Baking Tips

Covering Your Dough

Both plastic wrap and cotton kitchen towels (not terry towels) are perfect for covering your shaped dough for its final rise. To use plastic wrap, spray the dough lightly with aerosol cooking spray or rub a light coating of oil over it (if you haven't already brushed the dough with butter or a glaze that's part of your recipe). If you use a cotton towel, dampen it before placing it over your dough.

Fruit-Filled Kuchen Dough

Kuchen is just the German word for "cake." Try one from this duo of sweet coffee cakes, each with its own unique filling—rhubarb streusel or fragrant Dutch apple. Why not make both?

INGREDIENTS

(For 1½- and 2-Pound Bread Machines)

1 cup	**Milk**
⅓ cup	**Butter or margarine, softened and cut up**
1	**Egg**
⅓ cup	**Sugar**
1½ teaspoons	**Salt**
3¾ cups	**Bread flour, unsifted**
2¼ teaspoons	**Active dry yeast or bread machine yeast**

CYCLE DOUGH

1. If your machine does not have a preheat cycle, heat milk in microwave on HIGH power for 30 seconds (or heat in a saucepan for 1 minute to 80°F). Add to the bread pan with remaining ingredients according to the manufacturer's directions for your machine. Set the DOUGH CYCLE and press START.

2. After about 5 minutes of kneading, check the consistency of your dough. If dough is not in a smooth round ball, open lid and with machine ON, add liquid a tablespoon at a time if too dry, or add flour a tablespoon at a time if too wet.

3. Remove the dough promptly from the machine at the end of the cycle.

4. KNEAD dough about 10 times on a lightly floured surface. Choose one of the Fruit Kuchen Variations that follows and continue as directed.

Rhubarb Streusel Kuchen

In a saucepan, combine 4 cups sliced fresh or frozen thawed *rhubarb,* 1/4 cup *orange juice,* and 1 tablespoon *lemon juice*. Bring mixture to a boil, reduce heat, and simmer, stirring occasionally, for 5 minutes. Stir together 2/3 cup *granulated sugar* and 1/4 cup *cornstarch;* add to saucepan. Cook and stir mixture until it begins to thicken; simmer 2 minutes more. Remove from heat. Roll dough to a 13x9-inch rectangle; transfer to a greased 13x9x2-inch baking pan. Spread rhubarb mixture over the top of dough. For streusel topping, stir together 1/2 cup chopped *pecans* or *walnuts,* 1/3 cup *all-purpose flour,* 1/3 cup *dry oatmeal,* 1/4 cup packed *brown sugar,* 1 teaspoon *ground cinnamon,* and 1/2 teaspoon *ground nutmeg*. Cut in 1/4 cup *butter* or *margarine* until mixture is the size of small peas. Sprinkle streusel evenly over filling. Cover with plastic wrap or a towel and let rise in a warm place until doubled, 30 to 45 minutes. BAKE in a preheated 375°F oven for 30 to 35 minutes, or until top is deep golden brown and filling is bubbly. Makes one 13x9-inch coffeecake.

Dutch Apple Kuchen

Roll dough to a 15x10-inch rectangle. Place dough in a greased 15x10x1-inch baking pan. Brush dough with 2 tablespoons melted *butter* or *margarine*. Arrange 3 cups thinly sliced *apples* in rows over dough. Brush apples with additional melted butter. Stir together 3/4 cup *all-purpose flour,* 1/2 cup packed *brown sugar,* 1 1/2 teaspoons *ground cinnamon,* and 1/2 teaspoon *ground nutmeg*. Cut in 1/2 cup chilled *butter* or *margarine* until mixture is crumbly. Sprinkle mixture evenly over apples. Cover with plastic wrap or a towel and let rise in a warm place until doubled, 30 to 45 minutes. BAKE in a preheated 375°F oven for 30 to 35 minutes, or until deep golden brown.

CHAPTER

8

Special Holiday Breads

NEW YEAR'S DAY

ORANGE CURRANT LOAF

VALENTINE'S DAY

DRIED CHERRY AND PORT WINE LOAF

ST. JOSEPH'S DAY

PANE DI SAN GIUSEPPE (ST. JOSEPH'S DAY BREAD)

GOOD FRIDAY

ENGLISH GOOD FRIDAY BREAD

EASTER

GREEK EASTER BREAD

HOT CROSS LOAF

PANETTONE

GOLDEN EASTER LOAF

FOURTH OF JULY

INDEPENDENCE DAY BREAD

COLUMBUS DAY

ITALIAN PEPPER BREAD

THANKSGIVING

THANKSGIVING HARVEST LOAF

TURKEY STUFFING BREAD

FESTIVE FIG AND DATE BREAD

CHRISTMAS

CRANBERRY CHEESE LOAF

RUSSIAN KULICH WITH LEMON ICING

AMARETTO CHRISTMAS BREAD

MARASCHINO CHERRY EGGNOG BREAD

GERMAN CHRISTMAS STOLLEN

SAFFRON CHRISTMAS BREAD

SCOTTISH HOLIDAY

SCOTCH OATMEAL BANNOCK

Orange Currant Loaf

Bring in the New Year with this loaf. It's not too heavy, nor too sweet.

1 1/2-POUND	INGREDIENTS	2-POUND
1/2 cup + 2 tablespoons	**Milk**	2/3 cup
1 tablespoon	**Butter or margarine, softened**	1 1/2 tablespoons
1	**Egg(s)**	2
1/4 cup	**Sugar***	1/4 cup
1 1/2 teaspoons	**Grated orange peel**	2 teaspoons
1 teaspoon	**Salt**	1 1/4 teaspoons
1/8 teaspoon	**Ground nutmeg**	1/4 teaspoon
2 3/4 cups	**Bread flour, unsifted**	3 1/3 cups
1 1/2 teaspoons	**Active dry yeast or bread machine yeast**	2 1/4 teaspoons
1/2 cup	**Currants or raisins***	1/2 cup

*Use the same amount for either size loaf.

GARNISH

Orange Glaze (page 205)

CYCLE SWEET OR RAISIN/NUT

CRUST SETTING AS DESIRED

1. If your machine does not have a preheat cycle, heat milk in microwave on HIGH power for 30 seconds (or heat in a saucepan for 1 minute to 80°F). Add to the bread pan with remaining ingredients (except raisins and Garnish) according to the manufacturer's directions for your machine. Measure raisins to add at the beep or when manufacturer directs. Set the CYCLE, LOAF SIZE, and CRUST SETTING. Press START.

2. After about 5 minutes of kneading, check the consistency of your dough. If dough is not in a smooth round ball, open lid and with machine ON, add liquid a tablespoon at a time if too dry, or add flour a tablespoon at a time if too wet.

3. Remove the bread promptly from the pan when the machine beeps or on completing the cycle. Cool on rack before slicing. If desired, glaze bread with Orange Glaze.

Dried Cherry and Port Wine Loaf

A great selection for Valentine's Day. If you don't have port, you can substitute a fruity red wine. You'll find dried cherries in the dried fruit section of larger markets. Allow extra time to soak the cherries in the wine first.

1 1/2-POUND	INGREDIENTS	2-POUND
2/3 cup	**Dried cherries**	1 cup
1/4 cup	**Port wine or sweet red wine**	1/3 cup
3/4 cup	**Milk***	3/4 cup
2 tablespoons	**Butter or margarine, softened**	3 tablespoons
1	**Egg***	1
1/2 teaspoon	**Vanilla extract**	1 teaspoon
3 tablespoons	**Sugar**	1/4 cup
1 teaspoon	**Salt**	1 1/4 teaspoons
3 1/3 cups	**Bread flour, unsifted**	4 cups
1 1/2 teaspoons	**Active dry yeast or bread machine yeast**	2 teaspoons

*Use the same amount for either size loaf.

CYCLE SWEET OR RAISIN/NUT
CRUST SETTING LIGHT RECOMMENDED

1. Place cherries and wine in a small saucepan. Bring mixture to boiling; remove from heat. Let mixture stand until it has cooled to 80°F or room temperature. Drain cherries, reserving cherries and liquid.

2. If your machine does not have a preheat cycle, heat milk in microwave on HIGH power for 30 seconds (or heat in a saucepan for 1 minute to 80°F). Add to the bread pan with reserved wine and remaining ingredients (except cherries) according to the manufacturer's directions for your machine. Add cherries at the beep or when manufacturer directs. Set the CYCLE, LOAF SIZE, and CRUST SETTING. Press START.

(continues)

3 After about 5 minutes of kneading, check the consistency of your dough. If dough is not in a smooth round ball, open lid and with machine ON, add liquid a tablespoon at a time if too dry, or add flour a tablespoon at a time if too wet.

4 Remove the bread promptly from the pan when the machine beeps or on completing the cycle. Cool on rack before slicing.

Baking Tips

High Altitude Tips

If you live at a high altitude (more than 1000 feet above sea level), you have probably discovered that baking under these conditions can produce results that are different from the norm. When it comes to baking with your bread machine, your manufacturer's instruction book is the best guide for using your bread machine at high altitudes. As always, observe the condition of the dough during the first kneading cycle. The main problem you'll encounter is the fact that flour often dries out faster at high altitudes. To compensate, you can reduce the amount of flour by a few tablespoons, or add a bit more liquid. Also, bread tends to rise higher and faster at high altitudes, so it's wise to cut the amount of yeast by 1/4 teaspoon. You can also try the Rapid-Bake cycle to accommodate the faster rising. Make note of the changes you've made for the next time you prepare the same recipe. With a little patience and some trial and error, you'll be rewarded with great loaves of bread!

Pane di San Giuseppe (St. Joseph's Day Bread)

St. Joseph's Day (March 19th), the feast day of St. Joseph, is a day when many Catholic churches and restaurants in Italy and the United States open their doors to feed the poor and unfortunate. Breads like this one are often made to commemorate the day.

1 1/2-POUND	INGREDIENTS	2-POUND
3/4 cup	**Milk**	3/4 cup + 2 tablespoons
1 1/2 tablespoons	**Butter or margarine, softened**	2 tablespoons
1	**Egg(s)**	1 egg + 1 yolk
2 tablespoons	**Honey**	3 tablespoons
2 teaspoons	**Aniseed**	3 teaspoons
1 1/2 teaspoons	**Salt**	2 teaspoons
3 1/3 cups	**Bread flour, unsifted**	4 cups
2 1/2 teaspoons	**Active dry yeast or bread machine yeast**	3 teaspoons
3/4 cup	**Golden raisins or currants**	1 cup

CYCLE BASIC OR RAISIN/NUT
CRUST SETTING AS DESIRED

1. If your machine does not have a preheat cycle, heat milk in microwave on HIGH power for 30 seconds (or heat in a saucepan for 1 minute to 80°F). Add to the bread pan with remaining ingredients (except golden raisins or currants) according to the manufacturer's directions for your machine. Measure raisins or currants to add at the beep or when manufacturer directs. Set the CYCLE, LOAF SIZE, and CRUST SETTING. Press START.

2. After about 5 minutes of kneading, check the consistency of your dough. If dough is not in a smooth round ball, open lid and with machine ON, add liquid a tablespoon at a time if too dry, or add flour a tablespoon at a time if too wet.

3. Remove the bread promptly from the pan when the machine beeps or on completing the cycle. Cool on rack before slicing.

English Good Friday Bread

This simple bread is a Good Friday tradition in southern England. It's unusual to flavor white bread with caraway seed, but the flavor and texture are wonderful.

1½-POUND	INGREDIENTS	2-POUND
1 cup + 2 tablespoons	**Warm water (80°F)**	1⅓ cups
1½ tablespoons	**Butter or margarine, softened**	2 tablespoons
1½ tablespoons	**Sugar**	3 tablespoons
1½ teaspoons	**Salt**	2 teaspoons
1½ teaspoons	**Caraway seed**	2 teaspoons
3¼ cups	**Bread flour, unsifted**	4 cups
2 teaspoons	**Active dry yeast or bread machine yeast**	2½ teaspoons

CYCLE BASIC (DELAY-BAKE CAN BE USED)
CRUST SETTING AS DESIRED

1 Measure ingredients into the bread pan according to the manufacturer's directions for your machine. Set the CYCLE, LOAF SIZE, and CRUST SETTING. Press START.

2 After about 5 minutes of kneading, check the consistency of your dough. If dough is not in a smooth round ball, open lid and with machine ON, add liquid a tablespoon at a time if too dry, or add flour a tablespoon at a time if too wet.

3 Remove the bread promptly from the pan when the machine beeps or on completing the cycle. Cool on rack before slicing.

Baking Tips

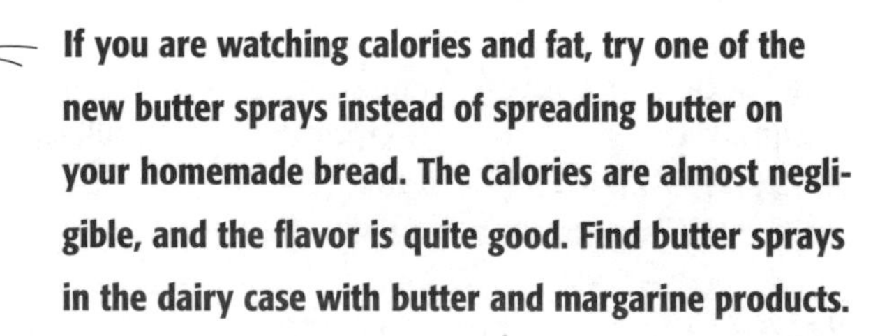

If you are watching calories and fat, try one of the new butter sprays instead of spreading butter on your homemade bread. The calories are almost negligible, and the flavor is quite good. Find butter sprays in the dairy case with butter and margarine products.

Greek Easter Bread

For Greek Easter, breads like this are often shaped into figure eights and decorated with eggs dyed in brilliant colors, or they are iced and decorated with almonds and cherries.

1 1/2-POUND	INGREDIENTS	2-POUND
1 cup	**Lemon yogurt**	1 cup + 2 tablespoons
1/4 cup	**Water***	1/4 cup
2 tablespoons	**Butter or margarine, softened**	3 tablespoons
3 tablespoons	**Sugar**	1/4 cup
1 teaspoon	**Salt**	1 1/2 teaspoons
1 teaspoon	**Grated lemon peel**	1 1/4 teaspoons
3 1/3 cups	**Bread flour, unsifted**	4 cups
2 teaspoons	**Active dry yeast or bread machine yeast**	2 1/2 teaspoons

*Use the same amount for either size loaf.

GARNISH
Lemon Glaze (page 205),
whole blanched almonds, and maraschino cherries

CYCLE SWEET
CRUST SETTING LIGHT RECOMMENDED

1 If your machine does not have a preheat cycle, combine yogurt and water and heat in microwave on HIGH power for 30 seconds (or heat in a saucepan for 1 minute to 80°F). Add to the bread pan with remaining ingredients (except Garnish) according to the manufacturer's directions for your machine. Set the CYCLE, LOAF SIZE, and CRUST SETTING. Press START.

2 After about 5 minutes of kneading, check the consistency of your dough. If dough is not in a smooth round ball, open lid and with machine ON, add liquid a tablespoon at a time if too dry, or add flour a tablespoon at a time if too wet.

3 Remove the bread promptly from the pan when the machine beeps or on completing the cycle. Cool on rack. Glaze with Lemon Glaze; decorate with whole blanched almonds and maraschino cherries.

Hot Cross Loaf

This is a wonderful sweet Easter bread.

1 1/2-POUND	INGREDIENTS	2-POUND
3/4 cup	**Milk**	1 cup
1/4 cup	**Butter or margarine, softened and cut up**	1/3 cup
1	**Egg(s)**	2
1/4 cup	**Sugar**	1/3 cup
2 teaspoons	**Grated orange peel**	1 tablespoon
1 1/4 teaspoons	**Salt**	1 1/2 teaspoons
1/2 teaspoon	**Ground nutmeg**	3/4 teaspoon
1/4 teaspoon	**Ground cloves**	1/2 teaspoon
3 cups	**Bread flour, unsifted**	3 3/4 cups
2 teaspoons	**Active dry yeast or bread machine yeast**	2 1/4 teaspoons
1/2 cup	**Golden raisins**	2/3 cup
1/2 cup	**Currants or chopped citron**	2/3 cup

GARNISH

Powdered Sugar Glaze (page 205)

CYCLE SWEET OR RAISIN/NUT

CRUST SETTING AS DESIRED

1 If your machine does not have a preheat cycle, heat milk in microwave on HIGH power for 30 seconds (or heat in a saucepan for 1 minute to 80°F). Add to the bread pan with remaining ingredients (except raisins, currants, or citron) according to the manufacturer's directions for your machine. Measure raisins, currants, or citron to add at the beep or when the manufacturer directs. Set the CYCLE, LOAF SIZE, and CRUST SETTING. Press START.

2 After about 5 minutes of kneading, check the consistency of your dough. If dough is not in a smooth round ball, open lid and with machine ON, add liquid a tablespoon at a time if too dry, or add flour a tablespoon at a time if too wet.

3 Remove the bread promptly from the pan when the machine beeps or on completing the cycle. Cool on rack. Glaze with Powdered Sugar Glaze, drizzling over top of loaf in a cross shape.

Panettone

This Italian bread is especially popular at Easter and Christmas.

1 1/2-POUND	INGREDIENTS	2-POUND
3/4 cup	**Milk**	3/4 cup + 2 tablespoons
1 1/2 tablespoons	**Butter or margarine, softened**	2 tablespoons
1 + 1 yolk	**Egg(s)**	2
3 tablespoons	**Sugar**	1/4 cup
1 1/2 teaspoons	**Grated orange peel**	2 teaspoons
1 teaspoon	**Salt**	1 1/2 teaspoons
1 teaspoon	**Vanilla extract**	1 1/2 teaspoons
3/4 teaspoon	**Aniseed**	1 teaspoon
3 1/4 cups	**Bread flour, unsifted**	4 cups
2 1/4 teaspoons	**Active dry yeast or bread machine yeast**	2 1/2 teaspoons
3/4 cup	**Chopped mixed candied fruit or citron**	1 cup
1/4 cup	**Sliced almonds**	1/3 cup

CYCLE SWEET OR RAISIN/NUT
CRUST SETTING LIGHT RECOMMENDED

1 If your machine does not have a preheat cycle, heat milk in microwave on HIGH power for 30 seconds (or heat in a saucepan for 1 minute to 80°F). Add to the bread pan with remaining ingredients (except candied fruit and almonds) according to the manufacturer's directions for your machine. Measure candied fruit and almonds to add at the beep or when manufacturer directs. Set the CYCLE, LOAF SIZE, and CRUST SETTING. Press START.

2 After about 5 minutes of kneading, check the consistency of your dough. If dough is not in a smooth round ball, open lid and with machine ON, add liquid a tablespoon at a time if too dry, or add flour a tablespoon at a time if too wet.

3 Remove the bread promptly from the pan when the machine beeps or on completing the cycle. Cool on rack before slicing.

Golden Easter Loaf

This lovely bread is a great way to start an Easter tradition!

1 1/2-POUND	INGREDIENTS	2-POUND
2/3 cup	**Milk**	3/4 cup
2 tablespoons	**Rum or orange juice**	3 tablespoons
1 1/2 tablespoons	**Butter or margarine, softened**	2 tablespoons
1 egg + 1 yolk	**Egg(s)**	2
3 tablespoons	**Sugar**	1/4 cup
1 teaspoon	**Salt**	1 1/2 teaspoons
1 teaspoon	**Grated lemon peel**	1 1/2 teaspoons
3 1/4 cups	**Bread flour, unsifted**	3 2/3 cups
2 teaspoons	**Active dry yeast or bread machine yeast**	2 1/4 teaspoons
1/2 cup	**Raisins**	2/3 cup
1/4 cup	**Chopped almonds**	1/3 cup

CYCLE SWEET OR RAISIN/NUT
CRUST SETTING LIGHT RECOMMENDED

1 If your machine does not have a preheat cycle, heat milk in microwave on HIGH power for 30 seconds (or heat in a saucepan for 1 minute to 80°F). Add to the bread pan with remaining ingredients (except raisins and almonds) according to the manufacturer's directions for your machine. Measure raisins and almonds to add at the beep or when manufacturer directs. Set the CYCLE, LOAF SIZE, and CRUST SETTING. Press START.

2 After about 5 minutes of kneading, check the consistency of your dough. If dough is not in a smooth round ball, open lid and with machine ON, add liquid a tablespoon at a time if too dry, or add flour a tablespoon at a time if too wet.

3 Remove the bread promptly from the pan when the machine beeps or on completing the cycle. Cool on rack before slicing.

Independence Day Bread

This Fourth of July bread was invented by a Philadelphia baker.

1½-POUND	INGREDIENTS	2-POUND
⅓ cup	**Milk**	½ cup
⅓ cup	**Water**	½ cup
3 tablespoons	**Butter or margarine, softened and cut up**	¼ cup
1 yolk	**Egg**	1 whole
3 tablespoons	**Sugar**	¼ cup
1 teaspoon	**Grated lemon peel***	1 teaspoon
¾ teaspoon	**Salt**	1 teaspoon
½ teaspoon	**Ground cinnamon***	½ teaspoon
¼ teaspoon	**Ground cloves**	½ teaspoon
¼ teaspoon	**Ground nutmeg***	¼ teaspoon
¼ teaspoon	**Ground allspice***	¼ teaspoon
2⅔ cups	**Bread flour, unsifted**	3⅓ cups
1½ teaspoons	**Active dry yeast or bread machine yeast**	2 teaspoons
¼ cup	**Currants**	⅓ cup
¼ cup	**Raisins**	⅓ cup

*Use the same amount for either size loaf.

GARNISH

Powdered Sugar Glaze (page 205)

CYCLE SWEET OR RAISIN/NUT
CRUST SETTING AS DESIRED

1 If your machine does not have a preheat cycle, combine milk and water and heat in microwave on HIGH power for 30 seconds (or heat in a saucepan for 1 minute to 80°F). Add to the bread pan with remaining ingredients (except currants and raisins) according to the manufacturer's directions for your machine. Measure currants and raisins to add at the beep or when manufacturer directs. Set the CYCLE, LOAF SIZE, and CRUST SETTING. Press START.

(continues)

2 After about 5 minutes of kneading, check the consistency of your dough. If dough is not in a smooth round ball, open lid and with machine ON, add liquid a tablespoon at a time if too dry, or add flour a tablespoon at a time if too wet.

3 Remove the bread promptly from the pan when the machine beeps or on completing the cycle. Cool on rack. Glaze with Powdered Sugar Glaze.

Baking Tips

Timeline for Herbs and Spices

When you buy packaged herbs and spices, always buy them in the smallest possible quantity. Since they are used in small amounts, a small container of a dried herb or spice goes a long way. Whole spices last longer than ground ones. Store these flavor-makers away from light and heat–the two greatest enemies of flavor and freshness. Date your packages when you purchase them, so you know how old they are. Most spices lose their flavor after 3 to 6 months of storage. Some spices are expensive, so consider splitting each package with a neighbor or friend–chances are, a half-quantity may be all you need for the next several months.

Italian Pepper Bread

This Columbus Day bread has a festive chocolate flavor.

1 1/2-POUND	INGREDIENTS	2-POUND
1/2 cup	**Milk**	3/4 cup
1/2 cup	**Water***	1/2 cup
1 1/2 tablespoons	**Olive or vegetable oil**	2 tablespoons
1/4 cup	**Sugar**	1/3 cup
1 1/4 teaspoons	**Salt**	1 1/2 teaspoons
1 teaspoon	**Ground cinnamon**	1 1/2 teaspoons
1/4 teaspoon	**Ground black pepper**	1/2 teaspoon
3 cups	**Bread flour, unsifted**	3 2/3 cups
2 teaspoons	**Active dry yeast or bread machine yeast**	2 1/4 teaspoons
1/3 cup	**Raisins**	1/2 cup
1/3 cup	**Chopped dates**	1/2 cup
1/4 cup	**Chocolate chips**	1/3 cup

*Use the same amount for either size loaf.

CYCLE SWEET OR RAISIN/NUT
CRUST SETTING AS DESIRED

1 If your machine does not have a preheat cycle, heat milk and water in microwave on HIGH power for 30 seconds (or heat in a saucepan for 1 minute to 80°F). Add to the bread pan with remaining ingredients (except raisins, dates, and chocolate chips) according to the manufacturer's directions for your machine. Measure raisins, dates, and chocolate chips to add at the beep or when manufacturer directs. Set the CYCLE, LOAF SIZE, and CRUST SETTING. Press START.

2 After about 5 minutes of kneading, check the consistency of your dough. If dough is not in a smooth round ball, open lid and with machine ON, add liquid a tablespoon at a time if too dry, or add flour a tablespoon at a time if too wet.

3 Remove the bread promptly from the pan when the machine beeps or on completing the cycle. Cool on rack before slicing.

Thanksgiving Harvest Loaf

This bread blends pumpkin, orange, and brown sugar flavors.

1 1/2-POUND	INGREDIENTS	2-POUND
3/4 cup	**Pumpkin puree**	3/4 cup + 2 tablespoons
1/2 cup	**Milk***	1/2 cup
3 tablespoons	**Orange liqueur or orange juice**	1/4 cup
1 1/2 tablespoons	**Butter or margarine, softened**	2 tablespoons
1/4 cup	**Brown sugar, packed**	1/3 cup
1 teaspoon	**Grated orange peel**	1 1/2 teaspoons
1 teaspoon	**Salt**	1 1/4 teaspoons
1 teaspoon	**Vanilla extract**	1 1/2 teaspoons
3 1/3 cups	**Bread flour, unsifted**	3 3/4 cups
1 1/2 teaspoons	**Active dry yeast or bread machine yeast**	2 teaspoons

*Use the same amount for either size loaf.

GARNISH

Lemon Glaze (page 205), candied orange peel strips, or shredded orange peel (optional)

CYCLE SWEET
CRUST SETTING AS DESIRED

1 If your machine does not have a preheat cycle, heat pumpkin puree and milk in microwave on HIGH power for 30 seconds (or heat in a saucepan for 1 minute to 80°F). Add to the bread pan with remaining ingredients (except Garnish) according to the manufacturer's directions for your machine. Set the CYCLE, LOAF SIZE, and CRUST SETTING. Press START.

2 After about 5 minutes of kneading, check the consistency of your dough. If dough is not in a smooth round ball, open lid and with machine ON, add liquid a tablespoon at a time if too dry, or add flour a tablespoon at a time if too wet.

3 Remove the bread promptly from the pan when the machine beeps or on completing the cycle. Cool on rack. Glaze with Lemon Glaze and decorate with candied orange peel, or thinly shredded fresh orange peel, if desired.

Turkey Stuffing Bread

This bread has been specially developed for use in stuffing recipes. It has a somewhat dry, coarse, corn bread-like texture with traditional stuffing seasonings. The 1½-pound recipe makes 12 to 13 cups of ½-inch bread cubes; the 2-pound recipe makes about 14 cups of bread cubes. This bread is ideal for stuffing recipes (pages 247 and 250).

1½-POUND	INGREDIENTS	2-POUND
1 cup	**Warm water (80°F)**	1 cup + 2 tablespoons
2 tablespoons	**Honey**	3 tablespoons
1½ tablespoons	**Vegetable oil**	2 tablespoons
1½ teaspoons	**Salt**	2 teaspoons
1 teaspoon	**Celery seed**	1¼ teaspoons
¼ teaspoon	**Dried basil**	½ teaspoon
¼ teaspoon	**Dried thyme**	½ teaspoon
¼ teaspoon	**Dried sage leaves (not ground)***	¼ teaspoon
2½ cups	**Bread flour, unsifted**	4 cups
½ cup	**Yellow cornmeal***	½ cup
2 teaspoons	**Active dry yeast or bread machine yeast**	2¼ teaspoons

*Use the same amount for either size loaf.

CYCLE WHOLE WHEAT
CRUST SETTING AS DESIRED

1 Measure ingredients into the bread pan according to the manufacturer's directions for your machine. Set the CYCLE, LOAF SIZE, and CRUST SETTING. Press START.

2 After about 5 minutes of kneading, check the consistency of your dough. If dough is not in a smooth round ball, open lid and with machine ON, add liquid a tablespoon at a time if too dry, or add flour a tablespoon at a time if too wet.

3 Remove the bread promptly from the pan when the machine beeps or on completing the cycle. Cool on rack for several hours before using. Recommended only for stuffings, croutons, or bread crumbs.

Festive Fig and Date Bread

Figs and dates always seem like special holiday treats. Enjoy this bread at the year-end holidays, or any time, paired with sliced mild cheeses and red wine.

1 1/2-POUND	INGREDIENTS	2-POUND
1 cup	**Boiling water**	1 cup + 2 tablespoons
1/3 cup	**Chopped pitted dates**	1/2 cup
1/3 cup	**Chopped dried figs**	1/2 cup
3 tablespoons	**Butter or margarine, softened and cut up**	1/4 cup
1/4 cup	**Brown sugar, packed**	1/3 cup
1 1/4 teaspoons	**Salt**	1 1/2 teaspoons
1 teaspoon	**Vanilla extract**	1 1/2 teaspoons
3 1/3 cups	**Bread flour, unsifted**	3 3/4 cups
2 teaspoons	**Active dry yeast or bread machine yeast**	2 1/4 teaspoons
1/3 cup	**Chopped pecans**	1/2 cup

CYCLE SWEET OR RAISIN/NUT
CRUST SETTING AS DESIRED

1 Pour water over dates and figs. Let mixture stand until it has cooled to 80°F or room temperature. Do not drain.

2 Measure ingredients into the bread pan, including the undrained date-fig mixture, (except pecans) according to the manufacturer's directions for your machine. Measure pecans to add at the beep or when manufacturer directs. Set the CYCLE, LOAF SIZE, and CRUST SETTING. Press START.

3 After about 5 minutes of kneading, check the consistency of your dough. If dough is not in a smooth round ball, open lid and with machine ON, add liquid a tablespoon at a time if too dry, or add flour a tablespoon at a time if too wet.

4 Remove the bread promptly from the pan when the machine beeps or on completing the cycle. Cool on rack before slicing.

Cranberry-Cheese Loaf

This loaf is great for holiday gifts.

1 1/2-POUND	INGREDIENTS	2-POUND
1/2 cup + 2 tablespoons	**Milk**	2/3 cup
1/3 cup	**Orange juice***	1/3 cup
1/2 cup	**Soft cream cheese, cut up***	1/2 cup
3 tablespoons	**Sugar**	1/4 cup
1 1/2 teaspoons	**Grated orange or lemon peel**	2 teaspoons
1 1/4 teaspoons	**Salt**	1 1/2 teaspoons
3 1/4 cups	**Bread flour, unsifted**	3 2/3 cups
1 1/2 teaspoons	**Active dry yeast or bread machine yeast**	2 teaspoons
1/2 cup	**Dried cranberries or Craisins**	2/3 cup
1/3 cup	**Chopped pecans or walnuts**	1/2 cup

*Use the same amount for either size loaf.

GARNISH

2 tablespoons orange marmalade, melted (optional)

CYCLE SWEET OR RAISIN/NUT

CRUST SETTING AS DESIRED

1. If your machine does not have a preheat cycle, combine milk, orange juice, and cream cheese and heat in microwave on HIGH power for 30 seconds (or heat in a saucepan for 1 minute to 80°F). Add to the bread pan with remaining ingredients (except cranberries and pecans) according to the manufacturer's directions for your machine. Measure cranberries and pecans to add at the beep or when manufacturer directs. Set the CYCLE, LOAF SIZE, and CRUST SETTING. Press START.

2. After about 5 minutes of kneading, check the consistency of your dough. If dough is not in a smooth round ball, open lid and with machine ON, add liquid a tablespoon at a time if too dry, or add flour a tablespoon at a time if too wet.

3. Remove the bread promptly from the pan when the machine beeps or on completing the cycle. Brush with melted orange marmalade, if desired. Cool on rack before slicing.

Russian Kulich with Lemon Icing

In Russia, this is a traditional holiday bread enjoyed on both Christmas and Easter. Bread machines, especially those that produce a vertical loaf, are perfect for making kulich because the traditional shape of this bread is the tall coffee-can shape. The top is traditionally glazed and decorated, representing the onion-shaped domes of the Orthodox churches with snow on them.

1½-POUND	INGREDIENTS	2-POUND
½ cup	**Milk**	¾ cup + 2 tablespoons
1½ tablespoons	**Butter or margarine, softened**	2 tablespoons
1	**Egg**	1 + 1 egg yolk
3 tablespoons	**Sugar**	¼ cup
1 teaspoon	**Salt**	1¼ teaspoons
1 teaspoon	**Grated orange or lemon peel***	1 teaspoon
2½ cups	**Bread flour, unsifted**	3⅓ cups
1½ teaspoons	**Active dry yeast or bread machine yeast**	2 teaspoons
⅓ cup	**Raisins**	½ cup
⅓ cup	**Chopped almonds**	½ cup

*Use the same amount for either size loaf.

GARNISH

Lemon Glaze (page 205); chopped candied fruit (optional)

CYCLE SWEET OR RAISIN/NUT
CRUST SETTING LIGHT RECOMMENDED

1 If your machine does not have a preheat cycle, heat milk in microwave on HIGH power for 30 seconds (or heat in a saucepan for 1 minute to 80°F). Add to the bread pan with remaining ingredients (except raisins and almonds) according to the manufacturer's directions for your machine. Measure raisins and almonds to add at the beep or when manufacturer directs. Set the CYCLE, LOAF SIZE, and CRUST SETTING. Press START.

2 After about 5 minutes of kneading, check the consistency of your dough. If dough is not in a smooth round ball, open lid and with machine ON, add liquid a tablespoon at a time if too dry, or add flour a tablespoon at a time if too wet.

3 Remove the bread promptly from the pan when the machine beeps or on completing the cycle. Cool on rack before slicing. Garnish with Lemon Glaze and candied fruit if desired.

Baking Tips

Bread Machine Strategy

After you have used your bread machine a few times, I hope that you, as I did, find it one of those indispensable appliances that you'll want to keep out on your countertop. Actually, a good strategy is to remind yourself that the time you spend waiting for your dinner to finish cooking or doing chores around the house is a good time to start a fresh loaf of bread going in your bread machine. Here are some of the tricks I have used to make the whole process simple, quick and easy. First, store all of your bread-making ingredients in a single area, cabinet, or drawer. Then you can set out all the ingredients you'll need and there will be no chance of forgetting to add a specific ingredient to the bread pan. It's a good idea to put those ingredients into small containers, which also makes measuring a lot easier. Also nearby, keep your liquid and dry measuring cups and measuring spoons handy. Finally, store ingredients like flours, dry yeast, nuts, bran, and seeds in containers in the refrigerator or freezer, where they will stay fresh, free of bugs, and ready to use.

Amaretto Christmas Bread

Allow some extra time for soaking the raisins in the almond liqueur. If you don't have the time, just add them to the ingredients in the bread machine right away—you'll still enjoy a great flavor.

1 1/2-POUND	INGREDIENTS	2-POUND
2/3 cup	**Golden or dark raisins**	1 cup
3 tablespoons	**Amaretto (almond liqueur) or brandy**	1/4 cup
3/4 cup	**Milk**	3/4 cup + 2 tablespoons
1/4 cup	**Butter or margarine, softened and cut up**	1/3 cup
1	**Egg yolk(s)**	2
1/4 cup	**Sugar**	1/3 cup
1 1/4 teaspoons	**Salt**	1 1/2 teaspoons
1 teaspoon	**Grated lemon peel**	1 1/2 teaspoons
1/2 teaspoon	**Ground cardamom**	3/4 teaspoon
3 cups	**Bread flour, unsifted**	3 3/4 cups
2 teaspoons	**Active dry yeast or bread machine yeast**	2 1/2 teaspoons
1/4 cup	**Chopped almonds**	1/3 cup

CYCLE SWEET OR RAISIN/NUT
CRUST SETTING AS DESIRED

1 Soak raisins in Amaretto or brandy for 1 hour. Drain off liquid, reserving it along with the raisins.

2 If your machine does not have a preheat cycle, combine milk and reserved soaking liquid and heat in microwave on HIGH power for 30 seconds (or heat in a saucepan for 1 minute to 80°F). Add to the bread pan with remaining ingredients (except almonds) and reserved raisins according to the manufacturer's directions for your machine. Measure almonds to add at the beep or when manufacturer directs. Set the CYCLE, LOAF SIZE, and CRUST SETTING. Press START.

3 After about 5 minutes of kneading, check the consistency of your dough. If dough is not in a smooth round ball, open lid and with machine ON, add liquid a tablespoon at a time if too dry, or add flour a tablespoon at a time if too wet.

4 Remove the bread promptly from the pan when the machine beeps or on completing the cycle. Cool on rack before slicing.

Baking Tips

Almost any bread recipe can be made special by adding a few tablespoons of a favorite liqueur. Consider using an orange liqueur, such as Grand Marnier or triple sec, a cranberry liqueur, a coffee liqueur or Kahlua, or a flavored brandy such as peach, apricot, cherry, or apple. The liqueur adds a spark of exotic flavor, and also aids in the rising of the dough. Simply substitute your favorite flavored liqueur or brandy for 3 or 4 tablespoons of the liquid called for in the recipe. As was done in this recipe, you can also use the liqueur to soak any raisins or other dried fruit called for in the recipe, to take advantage of the flavor even more. Cheers!

Maraschino Cherry Eggnog Bread

If you don't want a pink loaf, be sure to add the cherries on the Raisin/Nut cycle, or check your manual for information on when you can add them later in the kneading cycle. This loaf bakes up very light in color, so the Dark crust setting is recommended.

1 1/2-POUND	INGREDIENTS	2-POUND
1/2 cup	**Eggnog***	1/2 cup
1/3 cup	**Water**	1/2 cup
3 tablespoons	**Butter or margarine, softened and cut up**	1/4 cup
1/4 cup	**Sugar***	1/4 cup
1 1/4 teaspoons	**Salt**	1 1/2 teaspoons
1 teaspoon	**Almond extract**	1 1/2 teaspoons
1/8 teaspoon	**Ground nutmeg**	1/4 teaspoon
3 1/3 cups	**Bread flour, unsifted**	4 cups
2 teaspoons	**Active dry yeast or bread machine yeast**	2 1/2 teaspoons
2/3 cup	**Maraschino cherries, quartered and well-drained**	3/4 cup

*Use the same amount for either size loaf.

CYCLE SWEET OR RAISIN/NUT
CRUST SETTING DARK RECOMMENDED

1 If your machine does not have a preheat cycle, combine eggnog and water and heat in microwave on HIGH power for 30 seconds (or heat in a saucepan for 1 minute to 80°F). Add to the bread pan with remaining ingredients (except maraschino cherries) according to the manufacturer's directions for your machine. Measure maraschino cherries to add at the beep or when manufacturer directs. Set the CYCLE, LOAF SIZE, and CRUST SETTING. Press START.

2 After about 5 minutes of kneading, check the consistency of your dough. If dough is not in a smooth round ball, open lid and with machine ON, add liquid a tablespoon at a time if too dry, or add flour a tablespoon at a time if too wet.

3 Remove the bread promptly from the pan when the machine beeps or on completing the cycle. Cool on rack at least 1 hour before slicing (loaf will be very tender).

Baking Tips

Gift Wraps for Bread

Holiday breads like those featured in this chapter make wonderful gifts—especially for the person who seems to have everything! Once your bread is baked and cooled, there are several ways you can wrap it attractively. Purchase a large, inexpensive cotton tea towel or a tea towel with a holiday pattern, and wrap your bread in it, tying the corners together with a bow. Then place the loaf in a basket with a jar of gourmet bread spread or fruit jam (Chapters 9 and 10). Or, buy a roll of the colored plastic wrap; you'll find a choice of colored wraps right next to the regular plastic wrap on the supermarket shelf, or you can find more exotic cellophane wraps in arts and crafts stores. Cut the wrap into a large square, big enough so that when you wrap the bread in it, you'll wind up with a large ponytail end of wrap at the top. Tie it with a beautiful piece of wide ribbon. Then fluff out the excess wrap at the top for a festive effect.

German Christmas Stollen

Stollen, or fruit bread, is made in abundance in Germany at Christmas time. It is always well flavored with spices, glazed with a sweet icing and decorated. Although this loaf won't have the traditional stollen shape, you'll enjoy its rich, sweet flavor. Allow time to soak the raisins and currants first.

1 1/2-POUND	INGREDIENTS	2-POUND
1/4 cup	**Raisins**	1/3 cup
1/4 cup	**Currants**	1/3 cup
1/2 cup + 2 tablespoons	**Milk**	3/4 cup
1/2 cup	**Water***	1/2 cup
1 1/2 tablespoons	**Butter or margarine, softened**	2 tablespoons
2 1/2 tablespoons	**Sugar**	3 tablespoons
1 1/4 teaspoons	**Salt**	1 1/2 teaspoons
1 teaspoon	**Grated lemon or orange peel**	1 1/2 teaspoons
1/4 teaspoon	**Ground cinnamon**	1/2 teaspoon
1/4 teaspoon	**Ground cardamom***	1/4 teaspoon
1/8 teaspoon	**Ground cloves**	1/4 teaspoon
3 1/3 cups	**Bread flour, unsifted**	3 3/4 cups
2 1/4 teaspoons	**Active dry yeast or bread machine yeast**	2 1/2 teaspoons
1/2 cup	**Candied citrus peel or citron***	1/2 cup

*Use the same amount for either size loaf.

GARNISHES

Powdered Sugar Glaze (page 205) and candied cherries, halved

CYCLE SWEET OR RAISIN/NUT
CRUST SETTING LIGHT RECOMMENDED

1 Place raisins, currants, and water in a saucepan. Bring mixture to boiling; remove from heat. Let mixture stand until it has cooled to 80°F or room temperature. Drain off liquid and reserve with fruit.

2 If your machine does not have a preheat cycle, heat milk in microwave on HIGH power for 30 seconds (or heat in a saucepan for 1 minute to 80°F). Add to the bread pan with fruit mixture, reserved liquid and remaining ingredients (except candied citrus peel) according to the manufacturer's directions for your machine. Measure candied citrus peel to add at the beep or when manufacturer directs. Set the CYCLE, LOAF SIZE, and CRUST SETTING. Press START.

3 After about 5 minutes of kneading, check the consistency of your dough. If dough is not in a smooth round ball, open lid and with machine ON, add liquid a tablespoon at a time if too dry, or add flour a tablespoon at a time if too wet.

4 Remove the bread promptly from the pan when the machine beeps or on completing the cycle. Cool on rack. Glaze with Powdered Sugar Glaze and decorate with candied cherries as desired.

Baking Tips

Salt of the Earth

Salt is an important ingredient in bread—never eliminate it, unless you are using a salt-free bread recipe (page 28). Salt adds flavor, enables the browning of the crust, acts as a growth inhibitor for the yeast (so the dough doesn't rise out of control) and strengthens the gluten structure of the dough. Never use salt substitutes, since they will impart an off flavor to the bread.

Saffron Christmas Bread

Saffron comes ground or in thread form. Be certain it's well crushed or dissolved in liquid before adding it to the bread machine, for best results.

1 1/2-POUND	INGREDIENTS	2-POUND
1/4 teaspoon	**Saffron or turmeric***	1/4 teaspoon
3/4 cup + 2 tablespoons	**Milk**	1 cup
2 tablespoons	**Butter or margarine, softened**	3 tablespoons
1	**Egg***	1
1/4 cup	**Sugar**	1/3 cup
1 teaspoon	**Salt**	1 1/4 teaspoons
3 1/3 cups	**Bread flour, unsifted**	3 2/3 cups
2 teaspoons	**Active dry yeast or bread machine yeast**	2 1/4 teaspoons
1/2 cup	**Golden or dark raisins**	2/3 cup

*Use the same amount for either size loaf.

GARNISHES

Powdered Sugar Glaze (page 205), slivered almonds and cherries

CYCLE SWEET OR RAISIN/NUT

CRUST SETTING LIGHT RECOMMENDED

1 Stir saffron into milk; heat mixture in microwave on HIGH power for 30 seconds (or heat in a saucepan for 1 minute to 80°F). Add to the bread pan with remaining ingredients (except raisins and garnishes) according to the manufacturer's directions for your machine. Measure raisins to add at the beep or when manufacturer directs. Set the CYCLE, LOAF SIZE, and CRUST SETTING. Press START.

2 After about 5 minutes of kneading, check the consistency of your dough. If dough is not in a smooth round ball, open lid and with machine ON, add liquid a tablespoon at a time if too dry, or add flour a tablespoon at a time if too wet.

3 Remove the bread promptly from the pan when the machine beeps or on completing the cycle. Cool on rack. Garnish with *Powdered Sugar Glaze,* slivered almonds, and cherries.

Scotch Oatmeal Bannock

This traditional Scottish bread is served on many holidays throughout the Scottish calendar. It has a nice molasses flavor.

1 1/2-POUND	INGREDIENTS	2-POUND
1 cup	**Warm water (80°F)**	1 1/4 cups
1/4 cup	**Molasses**	1/3 cup
1 1/2 tablespoons	**Vegetable oil**	2 tablespoons
1 1/2 tablespoons	**Nonfat dry milk**	2 tablespoons
1 1/2 teaspoons	**Salt**	2 teaspoons
1/2 cup	**Oatmeal, dry**	2/3 cup
2 3/4 cups	**Bread flour, unsifted**	3 1/3 cups
2 1/4 teaspoons	**Active dry yeast or bread machine yeast**	2 1/2 teaspoons
1/2 cup	**Currants or raisins**	3/4 cup

CYCLE SWEET OR RAISIN/NUT
(DELAY-BAKE CAN BE USED)
CRUST SETTING AS DESIRED

1. Measure ingredients into the bread pan (except currants or raisins) according to the manufacturer's directions for your machine. Measure currants and raisins to add at the beep or when manufacturer directs. Set the CYCLE, LOAF SIZE, and CRUST SETTING. Press START.

2. After about 5 minutes of kneading, check the consistency of your dough. If dough is not in a smooth round ball, open lid and with machine ON, add liquid a tablespoon at a time if too dry, or add flour a tablespoon at a time if too wet.

3. Remove the bread promptly from the pan when the machine beeps or on completing the cycle. Cool on rack before slicing.

CHAPTER

9

Glazes, Butters, and Spreads for Breads

QUICK AND EASY BREAD GLAZES

POWDERED SUGAR GLAZE

CHOCOLATE GLAZE

CINNAMON SUGAR

BUTTER SHAPES

HONEY-ORANGE BUTTER

CINNAMON HONEY BUTTER

ROSEMARY-DIJON BUTTER

BASIL-LEMON BUTTER

SUN-DRIED TOMATO BUTTER

GARLIC-ANCHOVY BUTTER

BLUE CHEESE AND CHIVE BUTTER

ANCHO CHILE-CHIPOTLE BUTTER

SPANISH OLIVE TAPENADE

ROASTED GARLIC SPREAD

CURRIED EGGPLANT SPREAD

Quick and Easy Bread Glazes

These simple glazes work best on breads that have just been removed from your bread machine.

Butter Glaze: Brush loaf with 1 tablespoon softened or melted *butter* or *margarine*.

Seasoned Butter Glaze: Brush with Butter Glaze, then lightly sprinkle on *garlic salt, grated Parmesan* or *Romano cheese, kosher* or *coarse salt,* minced *fresh parsley,* or your favorite crushed *dried herb*.

Sweet Butter Glaze: Brush with Butter Glaze, then sprinkle on a mixture of 1 tablespoon *sugar* and ½ teaspoon *ground cinnamon*.

Milk Glaze: Brush loaf with 1 tablespoon *milk* (any type) or *light cream*.

Shiny Egg Glaze: Brush loaf with a mixture of 1 beaten *egg* or *egg yolk* and 1 tablespoon *water*. Sprinkle with *sesame, poppy seed,* or *caraway seed,* if desired.

Shiny Salt Glaze: Brush loaf with a mixture of 1 tablespoon *water* and a dash of *salt* (especially good for French or sourdough breads).

Shiny Sweet Glaze: Brush loaf with a mixture of 1 tablespoon each *sugar* and *water*.

Baking Tips

Decorating with Seeds

Embellish your glazed breads with a generous sprinkling of seeds. There are many types to choose from, and they can all lend a special character to your loaf. Sesame seed, caraway seed, and poppy seed are the most popular choices used by bakers, but try these seeds for a change of pace: roasted or black sesame seed (available in Asian markets); sunflower seeds, plain or toasted; fennel seed (great for pizza crusts, focaccia, or anise-flavored dark breads); or anise seed for a flash of licorice flavor on whole grain breads.

Powdered Sugar Glaze

Once you've decorated your bread or coffeecake with this sweet icing, you can add a variety of decors, including toasted sliced or chopped nuts, candied fruits, maraschino cherries, or shredded citrus peel.

INGREDIENTS

1 cup	**Sifted confectioners' sugar**
2 tablespoons	**Butter or margarine, melted**
½ teaspoon	**Vanilla or almond extract**
2½ tablespoons	**Milk**

VARIATIONS

For Lemon Glaze, substitute ¼ teaspoon lemon extract for the vanilla; add a few drops yellow food coloring if desired. For Orange Glaze, substitute orange juice for the milk; add a few drops yellow and red food coloring, if desired.

Combine all ingredients until smooth and of a glazing consistency. Add a few drops more milk to thin, if necessary. Use immediately. Makes about ⅔ cup.

Chocolate Glaze

This shiny chocolate glaze is ideal for the chocolate breads you'll find in Chapter 4.

INGREDIENTS

1½ cups	**Sifted confectioners' sugar**
2 squares (2 ounces)	**Semisweet chocolate, melted**
1 tablespoon	**Butter or margarine, melted**
1 teaspoon	**Vanilla extract**
2 to 2½ tablespoons	**Hot tap water**

Combine ingredients until smooth and of a glazing consistency. Add a few more drops hot water to thin, if necessary. Use immediately. Makes about 1 cup.

Cinnamon Sugar

It's the ultimate comfort food–spread toast generously with butter and sprinkled heavily with this sweet concoction. The Variation is a bit spicier but just as wonderful. Keep either combination in a shaker jar near the toaster.

INGREDIENTS

1 cup	**Sugar**
4 teaspoons	**Ground cinnamon**

VARIATION

For Five-Spice Sugar, substitute 2½ teaspoons *Asian five-spice powder* for the cinnamon, and add 1 tablespoon finely grated *lemon* or *orange peel,* if desired.

Mix well. Store in a tightly covered container. Makes 1 cup.

Butter Shapes

These festive butter shapes are so simple you'll be surprised at how easy it is to add their elegance to your table. Note: For each of these butter shapes, start with 1 cup (2 sticks) butter or margarine. Follow one of the variations below for shaping the butter.

Butter Cut-Outs: In a food processor or on medium speed of electric mixer, blend softened butter until creamy. Spread butter between 2 sheets of waxed paper or plastic wrap on a baking sheet. Using a rolling pin, roll butter to ¼-inch thickness. Refrigerate about 1 hour or until firm. Using small cookie cutters, cut out simple shapes, such as diamonds, hearts, or scalloped rounds. Transfer them with a metal spatula to another waxed paper-lined baking sheet. Sprinkle shapes with minced parsley, gently pressing it into the butter. Cover and refrigerate shapes until needed.

Butter Curls: Start with well-chilled butter; let stand at room temperature for 15 minutes. Use a butter curler (found at gourmet and kitchen shops). Dip the blade in hot water, then slowly draw the butter curler across the surface of the butter. Transfer each curl to a bowl of ice water to firm. (If the curls crack as you are making them, the butter is too firm; allow it to stand 15 minutes more and try again.) Cover and refrigerate curls until firm.

Butter Stars: In a food processor or on medium speed of electric mixer, blend softened butter until creamy. Spoon butter into a piping bag fitted with a star or fluted tip. Pipe star shapes onto a waxed paper-lined baking sheet. Sprinkle with paprika if desired. Cover and refrigerate stars until firm.

Herbed Butter Pats: Slice firm butter into ¼-inch-thick slices. (Dip knife in hot water occasionally.) Arrange on a waxed paper-lined baking sheet. Press small leaves of fresh herbs, such as rosemary, basil, dill, or oregano, into each butter pat. Cover and refrigerate until firm.

Honey-Orange Butter

Perfect for sweet breads or just regular toasted bread.

INGREDIENTS

1 cup (2 sticks)	**Butter or margarine, softened**
3 tablespoons	**Orange marmalade**
1 tablespoon	**Honey**

In a food processor or on medium speed of electric mixer, blend butter or margarine until creamy. Add marmalade and honey; mix until blended. Cover and refrigerate to store. Makes 1¼ cups.

Cinnamon Honey Butter

This is nice on whole wheat breads.

INGREDIENTS

1 cup (2 sticks)	**Butter or margarine, softened**
¼ cup	**Honey or real maple syrup**
½ teaspoon	**Ground cinnamon**

In a food processor or on medium speed of electric mixer, blend butter or margarine until creamy. Add honey and cinnamon; mix until blended. Cover and refrigerate to store. Makes 1¼ cups.

Baking Tips

Storing Flavored Butters

You can refrigerate flavored butters like those in this chapter for up to several weeks. Or turn butter into a freezer container and freeze for up to 1 month. Defrost butter in the refrigerator overnight.

Rosemary-Dijon Butter

Slather this on warm French or sourdough breads, and while you're at it, spread some over your grilled fish. Add the mustard to taste.

INGREDIENTS

1 cup (2 sticks)	**Butter or margarine, softened**
2 to 3 tablespoons	**Dijon mustard**
2 tablespoons	**Chopped fresh parsley**
1 tablespoon	**Dry white wine (or 2 teaspoons lemon juice)**
1 tablespoon	**Chopped fresh rosemary**

In a food processor or on medium speed of electric mixer, blend butter or margarine until creamy. Add remaining ingredients; mix until nearly smooth. Cover and refrigerate to store. Makes 1 1/4 cups.

Basil-Lemon Butter

Try this on cheese-flavored breads.

INGREDIENTS

1/2 cup (1 stick)	**Butter or margarine, softened**
1/3 cup	**Chopped fresh basil**
1/2 teaspoon	**Grated lemon peel**
1/4 teaspoon	**Cracked black peppercorns**

In a small food processor or on medium speed of electric mixer, beat butter or margarine until creamy. Add remaining ingredients; mix until nearly smooth. Cover and refrigerate to store. Makes 1/2 cup.

Sun-Dried Tomato Butter

Try this superb butter on cheese or herb breads, cornbread, sourdoughs, and onion breads.

INGREDIENTS

1 cup (2 sticks)	**Butter or margarine, softened**
½ cup	**Drained and chopped oil-packed sun-dried tomatoes**
2 teaspoons	**Chopped fresh oregano, marjoram or rosemary**
¼ teaspoon	**Cracked black pepper**
1	**Garlic clove, minced**

In a food processor or on medium speed of electric mixer, blend butter until creamy. Add remaining ingredients; mix until smooth. Cover and refrigerate to store. Makes 1⅓ cups.

Garlic-Anchovy Butter

Keep anchovy paste on hand for butters like this one. Try it on toasted triangles of cheese or onion breads for an appetizer.

INGREDIENTS

1 cup (2 sticks)	**Butter or margarine, softened**
1 tablespoon	**Chopped fresh parsley**
1 tablespoon	**Drained capers**
1 to 2 teaspoons	**Anchovy paste**
2	**Garlic cloves, minced**

In a small food processor or on medium speed of electric mixer, beat butter or margarine until creamy. Add remaining ingredients; mix until smooth. Cover and refrigerate to store. Makes 1¼ cups.

Blue Cheese and Chive Butter

If you want to enhance the flavor of any fresh bread, plain or seasoned with herbs, onions, or cheese, this butter will be perfect. It's also great over steamed asparagus, grilled steaks, and baked potatoes.

INGREDIENTS

½ cup (1 stick)	**Butter or margarine, softened**
½ cup (2 ounces)	**Crumbled blue, Stilton, Roquefort, or gorgonzola cheese**
1 tablespoon	**Chopped fresh chives**
¼ teaspoon	**Cracked black pepper**

In a food processor or on medium speed of electric mixer, beat butter or margarine until creamy. Add remaining ingredients; mix until nearly smooth. Cover and refrigerate to store. Makes 1 cup.

Baking Tips

Using Flavored Butters

You can use flavored butters for more than just a spread–try them for cooking scrambled eggs, sautéing vegetables, or on a hot baked potato. You can also use them as flavorful toppings for grilled fish, such as halibut or salmon, or to mix with shrimp or scallops for a sophisticated sauté.

Ancho Chile-Chipotle Butter

You'll find dried ancho and chipotle chiles in the Mexican food section or in bags in the produce section of larger markets or specialty food markets. The dried chiles must first be soaked to use the flavorful, spicy pulp. This sweet and smoky-spicy butter is great for cheese breads and corn bread. Add the higher level of cumin for extra flavor.

INGREDIENTS

3 large	**Dried ancho chile peppers**
3 medium	**Dried chipotle chile peppers (dried jalapeños)**
1 cup	**Water**
1 cup (2 sticks)	**Butter or margarine, softened**
2 tablespoons	**Tomato paste**
1 tablespoon	**Chopped fresh parsley**
½ to 1 teaspoon	**Ground cumin**

In a saucepan, combine the chiles and water; bring mixture to boiling. Reduce heat; simmer 5 minutes. Drain chiles; cool slightly. Slit chiles and remove seeds and veins. (**Warning:** Hot chiles exude oils that can give you skin burns. Be sure to keep your hands away from your eyes and face while handling chiles, and wash your hands thoroughly with hot soapy water after handling.) Scrape the pulp from the skin; discard skins and stems. In a food processor or on medium speed of electric mixer, beat butter or margarine until creamy. Mix in chile pulp and remaining ingredients until smooth. Cover and refrigerate to store. Makes 1¼ cups.

Spanish Olive Tapenade

Tapenade is a Spanish-style olive spread or paste that is served with toasted bread or crackers. This makes a great appetizer. Add anchovy paste to taste.

INGREDIENTS

1 cup	**Chopped pitted cured black olives (such as Kalamata, or Provençal olives)**
2 tablespoons	**Olive or vegetable oil**
1 tablespoon	**Lemon juice**
2 teaspoons	**Drained capers**
1 to 2 teaspoons	**Anchovy paste**
2 large	**Garlic cloves, minced**
1/4 teaspoon	**Dried thyme**
1/4 teaspoon	**Cracked black peppercorns**

In a food processor or blender, place all ingredients. Cover and process until mixture is nearly smooth. Serve at room temperature. Cover and refrigerate to store. Makes 1 cup.

Roasted Garlic Spread

An aromatic garlic spread made with roasted garlic, cream cheese, and herbs. It promises to be a hit!

INGREDIENTS

10 large	**Garlic cloves (or 2 cloves elephant garlic), peeled**
¼ cup	**Olive or vegetable oil**
1 (8-ounce) package	**Cream cheese, softened**
½ cup	**Dairy sour cream**
1 teaspoon	**Worcestershire sauce**
1½ teaspoons	**Chopped fresh thyme (or ½ teaspoon dried thyme)**
¼ teaspoon	**Dry mustard**
¼ teaspoon	**Salt**
¼ teaspoon	**Cracked black peppercorns**
2 tablespoons	**Sliced green onion**
2 tablespoons	**Chopped fresh parsley**

Preheat oven to 350°F. Place garlic in a small baking dish; pour oil over cloves. Bake, covered, about 30 minutes or until tender. Remove from oven; cool 15 minutes. A new "skin" that is tough forms on the cloves when the garlic is baked, so split cloves in half and spoon softened garlic from inside cloves into a food processor bowl or blender container. Add oil; cover and process until smooth. Scrape down sides of container with a spatula, if necessary. Add remaining ingredients except green onion and parsley; cover and process until blended. Stir in green onion and parsley. To store, cover and refrigerate up to 2 days ahead. Let stand at room temperature 30 minutes before serving with bread, breadsticks, or toast triangles. Makes 1⅔ cups.

Curried Eggplant Spread

This aromatic eggplant spread has a somewhat spicy flavor. Serve it spread on French bread, sourdough bread, or with breadsticks or toasted bread cut-outs.

INGREDIENTS

1 (1-pound)	**Eggplant, peeled and finely chopped**
2 tablespoons	**Olive oil or vegetable oil**
1 small	**Onion, chopped**
1 cup	**Grated carrots**
¼ cup	**Well-drained sliced pimiento**
1	**Garlic clove, finely chopped**
¼ cup	**Tomato sauce**
2 tablespoons	**Red wine vinegar**
2 tablespoons	**Curry powder**
1 tablespoon	**Chopped fresh cilantro or parsley**
½ teaspoon	**Salt**
Garnish	**Lettuce leaves**

In a large skillet, sauté chopped eggplant in hot oil with onion, carrots, pimiento, and garlic over high heat for 5 minutes, or until eggplant is tender. Reduce heat. Stir in remaining ingredients except Garnish. Simmer, uncovered, for 20 minutes, stirring occasionally. In a food processor or blender, process mixture until vegetables are coarsely chopped. To store, cover and refrigerate for up to 2 days before serving. To serve, let stand at room temperature for 30 minutes. Turn mixture into a lettuce-lined bowl to serve with breads. Makes 1 cup.

CHAPTER

10

Quick Breads, Jams, and Easy Treats

APRICOT PECAN BREAD

CAPPUCCINO BANANA BREAD

ESTHER'S BRANDIED APPLESAUCE BREAD

QUICK BRAN-RAISIN BREAD

RHUBARB-CINNAMON TEA BREAD

GRANOLA DATE BREAD

GINGERED CRANBERRY LOAF

PEAR TEA BREAD

SPICED PERSIMMON LOAF

PINEAPPLE CARROT BREAD

EASY-MIX QUICK BREADS

SANTA FE CORN BREAD

HEATHER'S HEAVENLY CHOCOLATE CAKE

SOUR CREAM GINGERBREAD

TWO-BERRY JAM

STRAWBERRY-BANANA JAM

LOW-SUGAR PEACH JAM

MICHIGAN BLUEBERRY JAM

LORRAINE'S DRIED APRICOT JAM

SPICED RHUBARB BUTTER

GINGER PEAR BUTTER

EASY WINTER FRUIT JAM

CHRISTMAS FRUIT JAM

DRIED PEACH CHUTNEY

HOLIDAY CRANBERRY-RASPBERRY SAUCE

Apricot Pecan Bread

If your bread machine has a "Quick Bread" or "Cake" setting, make sure the baking portion of the cycle is at least 75 minutes long, to produce a well-baked quick bread.

INGREDIENTS

(For 1½- or 2-pound Bread Machines)

½ cup	**Orange juice**
⅓ cup	**Butter or margarine, softened and cut up**
2	**Eggs**
⅔ cup	**Brown sugar, packed**
2 teaspoons	**Grated lemon peel**
1 teaspoon	**Salt**
2 cups	**All-purpose flour, unsifted**
2 teaspoons	**Baking powder**
¾ teaspoon	**Baking soda**
1 cup	**Chopped dried apricots**
½ cup	**Chopped pecans (or walnuts)**

CYCLE QUICK BREAD OR CAKE

1. Measure all ingredients into the bread pan according to the manufacturer's directions for your machine. Set the CYCLE and press START.

2. After about 5 minutes of mixing, open the lid and with machine ON, scrape any flour residue from the sides of the bread pan with a rubber spatula. If your bread machine requires it, press START again to resume the cycle.

3. At the end of the cycle, cool the bread in the pan for 10 minutes, then carefully remove the loaf to a cooling rack. Cool completely before slicing.

Cappuccino Banana Bread

Quick breads are very tender, cakelike breads, so after you've removed the bread pan at the end of the cycle, allow the bread to cool in the pan for 10 minutes for easier removal.

INGREDIENTS
(For 1½- or 2-pound Bread Machines)

⅔ cup	**Mashed ripe bananas**
½ cup	**Cappuccino or coffee-flavored yogurt**
⅓ cup	**Vegetable oil**
1	**Egg**
1½ teaspoons	**Vanilla extract**
½ cup	**Sugar**
½ teaspoon	**Salt**
1¾ cups	**All-purpose flour, unsifted**
1 teaspoon	**Baking powder**
½ teaspoon	**Baking soda**

CYCLE QUICK BREAD OR CAKE

1. Measure ingredients into the bread pan according to the manufacturer's directions for your machine. Set the CYCLE and press START.

2. After about 5 minutes of mixing, open the lid and with machine ON, scrape any flour residue from the sides of the bread pan with a rubber spatula. If your bread machine requires it, press START again to resume the cycle.

3. At the end of the cycle, cool the bread in the pan for 10 minutes, then carefully remove the loaf to a cooling rack. Cool completely before slicing.

Esther's Brandied Applesauce Bread

A friend of my parents, Esther Babiracki, was kind enough to contribute her marvelous recipe, in hopes it could be made in the bread machine. It can!

INGREDIENTS

(For 1½- or 2-pound Bread Machines)

1 cup	**Applesauce**
⅓ cup	**Brandy or apple juice**
½ cup	**Butter or margarine, softened and cut up**
1	**Egg**
1 cup	**Sugar**
1 teaspoon	**Ground cinnamon**
½ teaspoon	**Salt**
½ teaspoon	**Ground nutmeg**
¼ teaspoon	**Ground allspice**
¼ teaspoon	**Ground cloves**
1¾ cups	**All-purpose flour, unsifted**
1 teaspoon	**Baking soda**
1 cup	**Raisins**

CYCLE QUICK BREAD OR CAKE

1. Measure all ingredients into the bread pan according to the manufacturer's directions for your machine. Set the CYCLE and press START.

2. After about 5 minutes of mixing, open the lid and with machine ON, scrape any flour residue from the sides of the bread pan with a rubber spatula. If your bread machine requires it, press START again to resume the cycle.

3. At the end of the cycle, cool the bread in the pan for 10 minutes, then carefully remove the loaf to a cooling rack. Cool completely before slicing.

Quick Bran-Raisin Bread

Serve this wonderful breakfast bread warm or toasted.

INGREDIENTS
(For 1½- or 2-pound Bread Machines)

¾ cup	**Milk**
½ cup	**Butter or margarine, softened and cut up**
1	**Egg**
½ cup	**Sugar**
1 teaspoon	**Vanilla extract**
⅓ cup	**Whole wheat flour, unsifted**
½ cup	**Bran cereal**
1 cup	**All-purpose flour, unsifted**
1 teaspoon	**Baking soda**
½ cup	**Raisins**

CYCLE QUICK BREAD OR CAKE

1 Measure all ingredients into the bread pan according to the manufacturer's directions for your machine. Set the CYCLE and press START.

2 After about 5 minutes of mixing, open the lid and with machine ON, scrape any flour residue from the sides of the bread pan with a rubber spatula. If your bread machine requires it, press START again to resume the cycle.

3 At the end of the cycle, cool the bread in the pan for 10 minutes, then carefully remove the loaf to a cooling rack. Cool completely before slicing.

Rhubarb-Cinnamon Tea Bread

This bread is like a rich, spicy cake.

INGREDIENTS

(For 1½- or 2-pound Bread Machines)

½ cup	**Vegetable oil**
1	**Egg**
1	**Egg yolk**
1¼ cups	**Well-drained, diced fresh or frozen, thawed rhubarb**
¾ cup	**Brown sugar, packed**
1 teaspoon	**Ground cinnamon**
1 teaspoon	**Vanilla extract**
½ teaspoon	**Salt**
¼ teaspoon	**Ground nutmeg**
1½ cups	**All-purpose flour, unsifted**
1 teaspoon	**Baking soda**
¼ teaspoon	**Baking powder**
⅓ cup	**Chopped nuts (any type)**

CYCLE QUICK BREAD OR CAKE

1 Measure all ingredients into the bread pan according to the manufacturer's directions for your machine. Set the CYCLE and press START.

2 After about 5 minutes of mixing, open the lid and with machine ON, scrape any flour residue from the sides of the bread pan with a rubber spatula. If your bread machine requires it, press START again to resume the cycle.

3 At the end of the cycle, cool the bread in the pan for 10 minutes, then carefully remove the loaf to a cooling rack. Cool completely before slicing.

Granola Date Bread

Never use bread flour in quick bread recipes; the protein level is too high for these cakelike breads.

INGREDIENTS

(For 1 1/2- or 2-pound Bread Machines)

2/3 cup	**Hot tap water**
2/3 cup	**Chopped dates or dried figs**
1/2 cup	**Granola**
1 cup	**Buttermilk**
1/4 cup	**Vegetable oil**
1	**Egg**
1/2 cup	**Sugar**
1/2 teaspoon	**Salt**
1 3/4 cups	**All-purpose flour, unsifted**
1 1/2 teaspoons	**Baking soda**

CYCLE QUICK BREAD OR CAKE

1 Pour hot water over dates and granola in a bowl; let stand 5 minutes.

Measure all ingredients into the bread pan with the granola mixture according to the manufacturer's directions for your machine. Set the CYCLE and press START.

3 After about 5 minutes of mixing, open the lid and with machine ON, scrape any flour residue from the sides of the bread pan with a rubber spatula. If your bread machine requires it, press START again to resume the cycle.

4 At the end of the cycle, cool the bread in the pan for 10 minutes, then carefully remove the loaf to a cooling rack. Cool completely before slicing.

Gingered Cranberry Loaf

You can find cranberries all year long, packed in freezer bags at your market.

INGREDIENTS

(For 1½- or 2-pound Bread Machines)

¾ cup	**Orange juice**
2 tablespoons	**Butter or margarine, softened and cut up**
1	**Egg**
¾ cup	**Sugar**
1 cup	**Halved fresh or frozen, thawed cranberries**
2 teaspoons	**Grated orange peel**
2 teaspoons	**Grated fresh ginger**
1 teaspoon	**Salt**
2 cups	**All-purpose flour, unsifted**
1½ teaspoons	**Baking powder**
½ teaspoon	**Baking soda**

CYCLE QUICK BREAD OR CAKE

1 Measure all ingredients into the bread pan according to the manufacturer's directions for your machine. Set the CYCLE and press START.

2 After about 5 minutes of mixing, open the lid and with machine ON, scrape any flour residue from the sides of the bread pan with a rubber spatula. If your bread machine requires it, press START again to resume the cycle.

3 At the end of the cycle, cool the bread in the pan for 10 minutes, then carefully remove the loaf to a cooling rack. Cool completely before slicing.

Pear Tea Bread

This loaf is a nice change from the standard banana bread.

INGREDIENTS

(For 1½- or 2-pound Bread Machines)

⅔ cup or 1 (6-ounce) jar	**Pureed ripe pear, or baby food pears**
½ cup	**Dairy sour cream**
⅓ cup	**Vegetable oil**
1	**Egg**
1 teaspoon	**Vanilla extract**
½ cup	**Sugar**
1 teaspoon	**Ground cardamom**
½ teaspoon	**Salt**
1¾ cups	**All-purpose flour, unsifted**
1 teaspoon	**Baking powder**
½ teaspoon	**Baking soda**
½ cup	**Chopped walnuts or pecans**

CYCLE QUICK BREAD OR CAKE

1 Measure all ingredients into the bread pan according to the manufacturer's directions for your machine. Set the CYCLE and press START.

2 After about 5 minutes of mixing, open the lid and with machine ON, scrape any flour residue from the sides of the bread pan with a rubber spatula. If your bread machine requires it, press START again to resume the cycle.

3 At the end of the cycle, cool the bread in the pan for 10 minutes, then carefully remove the loaf to a cooling rack. Cool completely before slicing.

Spiced Persimmon Loaf

It takes about two small Hachiya persimmons to make 3/4 cup puree. Wait until the fruit is very ripe to puree it.

INGREDIENTS

(For 1 1/2- or 2-pound Bread Machines)

3/4 cup	**Persimmon puree**
1/3 cup	**Vegetable oil**
1	**Egg**
3/4 cup	**Sugar**
1/2 teaspoon	**Salt**
1/2 teaspoon	**Ground cinnamon**
1/4 teaspoon	**Ground nutmeg**
2 1/3 cups	**All-purpose flour, unsifted**
1 tablespoon	**Baking powder**
1 cup	**Chopped pecans**

CYCLE QUICK BREAD OR CAKE

1. Measure all ingredients into the bread pan according to the manufacturer's directions for your machine. Set the CYCLE and press START.

2. After about 5 minutes of mixing, open the lid and with machine ON, scrape any flour residue from the sides of the bread pan with a rubber spatula. If your bread machine requires it, press START again to resume the cycle.

3. At the end of the cycle, cool the bread in the pan for 10 minutes, then carefully remove the loaf to a cooling rack. Cool completely before slicing.

Pineapple Carrot Bread

This bread is very moist; wrap and refrigerate it after it has cooled and it will keep very well.

INGREDIENTS
(For 1½- and 2-pound Bread Machines)

½ cup	**Well-drained crushed pineapple**
⅓ cup	**Milk**
2 tablespoons	**Butter or margarine, softened and cut up**
1	**Egg**
½ cup	**Finely shredded carrot**
½ cup	**Sugar**
½ teaspoon	**Salt**
½ teaspoon	**Ground cinnamon**
2 cups	**All-purpose flour, unsifted**
1½ teaspoons	**Baking powder**
½ cup	**Chopped walnuts or pecans**

CYCLE QUICK BREAD OR CAKE

1 Measure all ingredients into the bread pan according to the manufacturer's directions for your machine. Set the CYCLE and press START.

2 After about 5 minutes of mixing, open the lid and with machine ON, scrape any flour residue from the sides of the bread pan with a rubber spatula. If your bread machine requires it, press START again to resume the cycle.

3 At the end of the cycle, cool the bread in the pan for 10 minutes, then carefully remove the loaf to a cooling rack. Cool completely before slicing.

Easy-Mix Quick Breads

This method converts any quick bread mix into a bread machine quick bread mix. You'll find these mixes in numerous flavors in the dessert mix aisle of your market.

INGREDIENTS
(For 1½- or 2-pound Bread Machines)

1 (14-ounce) package	**Quick Bread mix, any flavor**
As directed	**Water**
As directed	**Vegetable oil**
As directed	**Egg(s)**

CYCLE QUICK BREAD OR CAKE

1 Measure all ingredients (as specified on the bread mix) into the bread pan according to the manufacturer's directions for your machine. Set the CYCLE and press START.

2 After about 5 minutes of mixing, open the lid and with machine ON, scrape any flour residue from the sides of the bread pan with a rubber spatula. If your bread machine requires it, press START again to resume the cycle.

3 At the end of the cycle, cool the bread in the pan for 10 minutes, then carefully remove the loaf to a cooling rack. Cool completely before slicing.

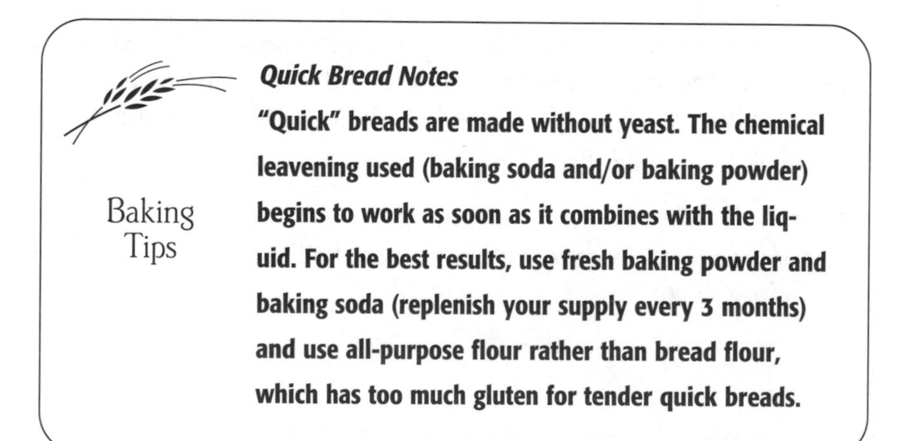

Baking Tips

Quick Bread Notes

"Quick" breads are made without yeast. The chemical leavening used (baking soda and/or baking powder) begins to work as soon as it combines with the liquid. For the best results, use fresh baking powder and baking soda (replenish your supply every 3 months) and use all-purpose flour rather than bread flour, which has too much gluten for tender quick breads.

Santa Fe Corn Bread

Hearty and spicy, this cornbread is a southwestern treat with nothing but a pat of butter!

INGREDIENTS

(For 1½- or 2-pound Bread Machines)

1 cup	**Milk**
3 tablespoons	**Vegetable oil**
1	**Egg**
½ cup	**Drained and diced red bell pepper or pimiento**
¼ cup	**Minced green onions**
1 to 2	**Fresh hot chiles, such as jalapeños, serranos, or banana chiles, seeded and minced**
1	**Fresh or drained canned mild green or Anaheim chile, seeded and minced**
3 tablespoons	**Sugar**
½ teaspoon	**Salt**
1 cup	**Yellow or blue cornmeal**
1 cup	**All-purpose flour, unsifted**
4 teaspoons	**Baking powder**

CYCLE QUICK BREAD OR CAKE

1. Measure all ingredients into the bread pan according to the manufacturer's directions for your machine. Set the CYCLE and press START.

2. After about 5 minutes of mixing, open the lid and with machine ON, scrape any flour residue from the sides of the bread pan with a rubber spatula. If your bread machine requires it, press START again to resume the cycle.

3. At the end of the cycle, cool the bread in the pan for 10 minutes, then carefully remove the loaf to a cooling rack. Serve warm.

Heather's Heavenly Chocolate Cake

This cake is so good, all it needs is a sprinkling of confectioners' sugar to top it off.

INGREDIENTS
(For 1½- or 2-Pound Bread Machines)

1¼ cups	**Buttermilk**
½ cup	**Solid vegetable shortening, cut up**
3	**Eggs**
1¼ cups	**Brown sugar, packed**
½ cup	**Unsweetened cocoa powder**
1 teaspoon	**Vanilla extract**
½ teaspoon	**Salt**
¾ cup	**Instant mashed potato flakes**
1½ cups	**All-purpose flour, unsifted**
1½ teaspoons	**Baking soda**
1 cup	**Raisins or chopped walnuts or pecans**

CYCLE QUICK BREAD OR CAKE

1 Measure all ingredients into the bread pan according to the manufacturer's directions for your machine. Set the CYCLE and press START.

2 After about 5 minutes of mixing, open the lid and with machine ON, scrape any flour residue from the sides of the bread pan with a rubber spatula. If your bread machine requires it, press START again to resume the cycle.

3 At the end of the cycle, cool the bread in the pan for 10 minutes, then carefully remove the loaf to a cooling rack. Cool completely before slicing.

Sour Cream Gingerbread

Serve this warm, wonderful gingerbread with a dollop of lemon yogurt.

INGREDIENTS
(For 1½- or 2-Pound Bread Machines)

¾ cup	**Dairy sour cream**
¾ cup	**Molasses**
⅓ cup	**Butter or margarine, softened and cut up**
1	**Egg**
¼ cup	**Brown sugar, packed**
1 tablespoon	**Minced fresh ginger**
1 teaspoon	**Ground allspice**
½ teaspoon	**Salt**
1¾ cups	**All-purpose flour, unsifted**
1 teaspoon	**Baking soda**

CYCLE QUICK BREAD OR CAKE

1. Measure all ingredients into the bread pan according to the manufacturer's directions for your machine. Set the CYCLE and press START.

2. After about 5 minutes of mixing, open the lid and with machine ON, scrape any flour residue from the sides of the bread pan with a rubber spatula. If your bread machine requires it, press START again to resume the cycle.

3. At the end of the cycle, cool the bread in the pan for 10 minutes, then carefully remove the loaf to a cooling rack. Cool completely before slicing.

Two-Berry Jam

For an ice cream topping, omit the pectin.

INGREDIENTS
(For 1½- and 2-Pound Bread Machines)

1 cup	**Sliced fresh or frozen, thawed strawberries**
1 cup	**Fresh or frozen, thawed boysenberries or raspberries**
1 cup	**Sugar**
1 tablespoon	**Lemon juice**
Half of a (1¾-ounce) package (3 tablespoons)	**Dry fruit pectin**

CYCLE JAM

1 Spray your bread pan with aerosol cooking spray. Measure ingredients into the bread pan according to the manufacturer's directions for your machine. Set the CYCLE and press START.

2 When the cycle is complete, remove bread pan. Allow mixture to cool in pan at least 15 minutes. Transfer mixture to a covered container. Refrigerate for up to several weeks, or freeze for up to 6 months. Makes 1 cup.

Strawberry-Banana Jam

Try other combinations such as raspberries with raspberry gelatin or peaches with peach gelatin—you get the idea!

INGREDIENTS
(For 1½- and 2-Pound Bread Machines)

2 cups or 1 (16-ounce) package	**Sliced fresh or frozen, thawed strawberries**
2 tablespoons	**Lemon juice**
1 (3-ounce) package	**Strawberry-banana flavor gelatin (not sugar-free)**

CYCLE JAM

1. Spray your bread pan with aerosol cooking spray. Measure ingredients into the bread pan according to the manufacturer's directions for your machine. Set the CYCLE and press START.

2. When the cycle is complete, remove bread pan. Allow mixture to cool in pan at least 15 minutes. Transfer mixture to a covered container. Refrigerate for up to several weeks, or freeze for up to 6 months. Makes 1½ cups.

Low-Sugar Peach Jam

If you don't want to skimp on sugar, double the amount here. This low-sugar version is a thin jam, so it can also be used as a low-calorie dessert sauce.

INGREDIENTS

(For 1½- and 2-Pound Bread Machines)

3 cups	**Peeled, chopped fresh or frozen, thawed peaches**
½ cup	**Sugar**
2 tablespoons	**Lemon juice**
1 (1¾-ounce) package	**Dry fruit pectin**

CYCLE JAM

1. Spray your bread pan with aerosol cooking spray. Measure ingredients into the bread pan according to the manufacturer's directions for your machine. Set the CYCLE and press START.

2. When the cycle is complete, remove bread pan. Allow mixture to cool in pan at least 15 minutes. Transfer mixture to a covered container. Refrigerate for up to several weeks, or freeze for up to 6 months. Makes 1½ cups.

Michigan Blueberry Jam

This blueberry jam reminds me of the beautiful blueberries my Aunt Tillie used to send my family every summer from Michigan. We had great fun using up the berries in recipes like this one. With the convenience of frozen berries, you can make this any time of year. Try it also served warm as a sauce over ice cream.

INGREDIENTS

(For 1½- and 2-Pound Bread Machines)

2 cups or 1 (16-ounce) package	**Well-drained fresh or frozen, thawed blueberries**
½ cup	**Water, or juice from thawed berries**
1 cup	**Sugar**
1 tablespoon	**Lemon juice**
Half of a (1¾-ounce) package (3 tablespoons)	**Dry fruit pectin**

CYCLE JAM

1 Spray your bread pan with aerosol cooking spray. Measure ingredients into the bread pan according to the manufacturer's directions for your machine. Set the CYCLE and press START.

2 When the cycle is complete, remove bread pan. Allow mixture to cool in pan at least 15 minutes. Transfer mixture to a covered container. Refrigerate for up to several weeks, or freeze for up to 6 months. Makes 1¼ cups.

Baking Tips

If you like to bake with fresh berries, pick (or buy) them when they are at their peak. Wash the berries and dry them. Then place them on a baking sheet and freeze. Bag them and return to the freezer to use as needed.

Lorraine's Dried Apricot Jam

I adapted this recipe from the one my mother Lorraine Brown used to make on the rangetop. It's superb for peanut butter and jelly sandwiches—or just slathered on toast.

INGREDIENTS

(For 1½- and 2-Pound Bread Machines)

2 cups	**Chopped dried apricots**
1 cup	**Boiling water**
1 tablespoon	**Lemon juice**
½ cup	**Sugar**

CYCLE JAM

1 Spray your bread pan with aerosol cooking spray. Measure ingredients into the bread pan according to the manufacturer's directions for your machine. Set the CYCLE and press START.

2 When the cycle is complete, remove bread pan. Allow mixture to cool in pan at least 15 minutes. Transfer mixture to a covered container. Refrigerate for up to several weeks, or freeze for up to 6 months. Makes 2 cups.

Spiced Rhubarb Butter

This is not a "butter" at all, but a smooth fruit spread. If you use thawed frozen rhubarb, press out all of the liquid from the fruit before using it.

INGREDIENTS

(For 1½- and 2-Pound Bread Machines)

4 cups	**Well-drained diced fresh or frozen, thawed rhubarb**
2 tablespoons	**Water**
2½ cups	**Sugar**
1 teaspoon	**Ground cinnamon**
⅛ to ¼ teaspoon	**Ground cloves**

CYCLE JAM

1 Spray your bread pan with aerosol cooking spray. Measure ingredients into the bread pan according to the manufacturer's directions for your machine. Set the CYCLE and press START.

2 When the cycle is complete, remove bread pan. Allow mixture to cool completely in the pan. Transfer butter to a food processor or blender; cover and puree until smooth. Cover and refrigerate to store (mixture thickens when chilled). Refrigerate for up to several weeks, or freeze for up to 6 months. Makes 3 cups.

Ginger Pear Butter

This is scrumptious on toast, fruit breads, or as a condiment for roast pork or poultry.

INGREDIENTS

(For 1½- and 2-Pound Bread Machines)

1 pound	**Ripe peeled chopped pears**
2 tablespoons	**Apple juice**
3 tablespoons	**Sugar**
3 tablespoons	**Honey**
1 tablespoon	**Lemon juice**
2 teaspoons	**Grated lemon peel**
2 teaspoons	**Minced fresh ginger**
1 teaspoon	**Ground cinnamon**
¼ teaspoon	**Ground nutmeg**

CYCLE JAM

1 Spray your bread pan with aerosol cooking spray. Measure ingredients into the bread pan according to the manufacturer's directions for your machine. Set the CYCLE and press START.

2 When the cycle is complete, remove bread pan. Allow mixture to cool completely in the bread pan. Transfer butter to a food processor or blender; cover and puree until smooth. Cover and refrigerate to store (mixture thickens when chilled). Refrigerate for up to several weeks, or freeze for up to 6 months. Makes 2 cups.

Easy Winter Fruit Jam

If you have canned fruit and fruit pectin on hand, you can always make jam.

INGREDIENTS

(For 1½- and 2-Pound Bread Machines)

1½ cups	**Well-drained chopped canned pears**
1½ cups	**Well-drained chopped canned apricots or peaches**
1 (8-ounce) can	**Well-drained crushed pineapple**
¼ cup	**Sugar**
1 tablespoon	**Lemon juice**
¼ teaspoon	**Ground cinnamon**
⅛ teaspoon	**Ground nutmeg**
1 (1¾-ounce) box	**Dry fruit pectin**

CYCLE JAM

1 Spray your bread pan with aerosol cooking spray. Measure ingredients into the bread pan according to the manufacturer's directions for your machine. Set the CYCLE and press START.

2 When the cycle is complete, remove bread pan. Allow mixture to cool in pan at least 15 minutes. Transfer mixture to a covered container. (Mixture thickens when chilled.) Refrigerate for up to several weeks, or freeze for up to 6 months. Makes 2¾ cups.

Christmas Fruit Jam

This jam makes any bread or toast a holiday treat.

INGREDIENTS

(For 1½- and 2-Pound Bread Machines)

1 (8¼-ounce) can	**Well-drained crushed pineapple with ¼ cup juice reserved**
1 cup	**Peeled, finely chopped fresh ripe pear**
½ cup	**Chopped mixed candied fruit or candied cherries**
2 tablespoons	**Sugar**
Half of a (1¾-ounce) package (3 tablespoons)	**Dry fruit pectin**

CYCLE JAM

1 Spray your bread pan with aerosol cooking spray. Measure ingredients (including reserved pineapple juice) into the bread pan according to the manufacturer's directions for your machine. Set the CYCLE and press START.

2 When the cycle is complete, remove bread pan. Allow mixture to cool in pan at least 15 minutes. Transfer mixture to a covered container. Refrigerate for up to several weeks, or freeze for up to 6 months. Makes 1¼ cups.

Baking Tips

It's important to use the exact proportions of sugar and pectin given in the jam recipes in this chapter. The combination of both pectin and sugar, along with the sugars present in the fruit, are the ingredients that create a soft-set jam.

Dried Peach Chutney

This chunky fruit condiment with an exotic spicy flavor is delightful spread on meat or poultry sandwiches, or served alongside grilled fish, meat, or poultry. Or thin a few tablespoons of it with balsamic vinegar and use it as a salad dressing.

INGREDIENTS

(For 1½- and 2-Pound Bread Machines)

½ cup	**Orange juice**
¼ cup	**White wine vinegar or cider vinegar**
1 tablespoon	**Lime or lemon juice**
1⅓ cups	**Finely chopped dried peaches, pears, or apricots**
½ cup	**Brown sugar, packed**
½ cup	**Minced onion**
⅓ cup	**Raisins**
1 tablespoon	**Minced fresh ginger**
1	**Garlic clove, finely minced**
¼ teaspoon	**Dry mustard**
¼ teaspoon	**Ground nutmeg**

CYCLE JAM

1. Spray your bread pan with aerosol cooking spray. Measure ingredients into the bread pan according to the manufacturer's directions for your machine. Set the CYCLE and press START.

2. When the cycle is complete, remove bread pan. Allow mixture to cool in pan at least 15 minutes. Transfer mixture to a covered container. Refrigerate for up to several weeks or freeze for up to 6 months. Makes 1½ cups.

Holiday Cranberry-Raspberry Sauce

There's one less thing to worry about when you can make this in your bread machine at the holidays! Increase the sugar to 1 1/4 cups, and it becomes a dessert sauce for bread pudding, ice cream, custards, or baked fruit.

INGREDIENTS

(For 1 1/2- and 2-Pound Bread Machines)

2 cups	**Chopped fresh or frozen, thawed cranberries**
1/2 cup	**Water**
1/2 cup	**Prepared raspberry jam**
3/4 cup	**Sugar**
1 1/2 teaspoons	**Grated lemon peel**

CYCLE JAM

1 Spray your bread pan with aerosol cooking spray. Measure ingredients into the bread pan according to the manufacturer's directions for your machine. Set the CYCLE and press START.

2 When the cycle is complete, remove bread pan. Allow mixture to cool in pan at least 15 minutes. Transfer mixture to a covered container. Refrigerate for up to several weeks, or freeze for up to 6 months. Makes 1 3/4 cups.

CHAPTER

11

Delectable Uses for Day-Old Bread

HOMEMADE BREAD CRUMBS

HOMEMADE CROUTONS

ITALIAN-STYLE CROUTONS

GARLIC BREADSTICKS

ELAINE'S BLUE-RIBBON POULTRY STUFFING

APPETIZER MUSHROOM TOASTS

BRIE CROSTINI

ASPARAGUS PÂTÉ RAFTS

APRICOT-NUT STUFFING

TOASTED BAGUETTE NIÇOISE

ORANGE FRENCH TOAST

CHOCOLATE FRENCH TOAST

SHRIMP AND ASPARAGUS BRUNCH STRATA

CANADIAN BACON AND BROCCOLI-CHEESE STRATA

STRATA MEXICANA

CHOCOLATE BREAD PUDDING

Homemade Bread Crumbs

Bread crumbs are handy to keep around for such uses as coating a chicken breast, turkey fillet, or fish fillet, or for making a meatloaf, burgers, meatballs, or stuffed mushrooms. You can refrigerate fresh bread crumbs for several days, or better yet, freeze them in self-sealing bags for use any time.

Soft Bread Crumbs: Remove crusts from bread; crumble bread with fingers or process in a food processor or blender until crumbly. One slice of bread makes about 3/4 cup soft bread crumbs.

Fine Dry Bread Crumbs: Prepare Soft Bread Crumbs; place on a baking sheet. Toast crumbs in a 325°F oven for about 5 minutes, or until crisp and dry. Crush dried crumbs with a rolling pin or process in a blender or food processor until fine.

Buttered Bread Crumbs: Prepare Fine Dry Bread Crumbs as above. Add 1 tablespoon melted *butter* or *margarine;* toss to moisten crumbs.

Herb-Seasoned Dry Bread Crumbs: Prepare Fine Dry Bread Crumbs. For each 3/4 cup (1 slice bread) prepared bread crumbs, add 1 tablespoon melted *butter* or *margarine,* 1 to 2 tablespoons finely grated *Parmesan cheese,* 1/2 teaspoon crushed *dried herbs* (such as *basil, dill, oregano, fines herbes,* or *Italian herbs*) and a dash of *salt* and *pepper,* or to taste.

Homemade Croutons

Use croutons for stuffings, to toss into salads, in bread puddings, or atop baked fruit crisps. You can also sprinkle croutons over hot soups or stews.

INGREDIENTS

As needed	**Butter or margarine, softened**
2 slices	**Stale bread**

Lightly butter stale bread (2 to 3 days old) on both sides. Cut bread into 1/2- or 1-inch cubes. Arrange cubes on an ungreased baking sheet; toast in a 375°F oven for 7 to 9 minutes, stirring once halfway through the baking time. Store in a tightly covered container or freeze for up to several months. Makes 3 cups.

Italian-Style Croutons

These are perfect for simple salads or as preseasoned stuffing cubes.

INGREDIENTS

2 cups	**Cubed stale bread (about 1½ slices bread)**
3 tablespoons	**Olive oil or flavored vegetable oil**
2	**Garlic cloves, minced**
2 to 3 tablespoons	**Finely grated Parmesan or Romano cheese**
1 tablespoon	**Chopped fresh parsley**
1 teaspoon	**Dried Italian herbs**
½ teaspoon	**Salt**

VARIATION

For Herb and Onion Croutons, prepare Italian-Style Croutons as above, but omit garlic, parsley, and Italian herbs. Add 1 finely chopped, green onion to the sauté mixture. Stir in 1 tablespoon chopped fresh herbs, such as basil, dill, rosemary, sage, or marjoram, and ¼ teaspoon paprika.

1 In a skillet, sauté the bread cubes in olive oil with garlic for 5 to 7 minutes, stirring frequently. Add cheese, parsley, and seasonings; toss well to coat.

2 Use at once in a salad or soup, or wrap tightly and freeze for up to several months. Recipe can be halved. Makes 2 cups.

Garlic Breadsticks

Here's a wonderful way to recycle French or sourdough bread, or even dark rye. You can also make them with any day-old bread.

INGREDIENTS

1/4 loaf	**Any leftover bread, nonsweet type**
2 tablespoons	**Melted butter or margarine, or vegetable oil**
2 to 3 teaspoons	**Garlic salt**

VARIATION

For Garlic Croutons, slice bread and brush on both sides with the melted butter or oil. Cut bread into 1/2-inch cubes. Toss cubes with the garlic salt and bake in a 375°F oven for 5 to 8 minutes or until golden brown, stirring once halfway through the baking time.

1 Slice loaf lengthwise into 6 x 1-inch sticks. Brush breadsticks on all sides with melted butter or oil.

2 Sprinkle liberally with the garlic salt. Place on an ungreased baking sheet.

3 Bake in a 375°F oven for 8 to 10 minutes or until lightly browned and crisp. Serve hot. Makes about 12 breadsticks.

Baking Tips

Garlic in Bread

If you like the flavor of garlic in bread, beware: garlic itself acts as a yeast inhibitor in bread doughs. There are safer ways to enjoy the flavor of garlic in bread: spread your bread with garlic butter, or use the delectable Roasted Garlic Spread recipe on page 214.

Elaine's Blue-Ribbon Poultry Stuffing

When it's time to stuff the turkey, we always turn to my Godmother's recipe. For the dried bread cubes, let cubed leftover bread sit out uncovered for a day or overnight.

INGREDIENTS

¼ cup	**Butter or margarine**
1½ cups	**Chopped onions**
1½ cups	**Chopped celery**
1	**Turkey or chicken liver, finely chopped (optional)**
10 cups	**Dried bread cubes (7-8 slices bread)**
2	**Eggs, lightly beaten**
2 teaspoons	**Dried sage leaves, crushed**
1 teaspoon	**Salt**
1 teaspoon	**Poultry seasoning**
½ teaspoon	**Ground sage**
¾ to 1 cup	**Chicken broth**

VARIATION

For Shortcut Poultry Stuffing, use Turkey Stuffing Bread (page 189) for your bread cubes; omit the sage leaves, ground sage, and poultry seasoning.

1. In a large skillet, melt the butter; sauté onions, celery, and chopped liver, if desired, for 10 minutes over medium-low heat, stirring occasionally.

2. Place bread cubes in a large bowl; add sautéed vegetables. Pour beaten eggs over bread and add seasonings. Toss well to coat. Add chicken broth (use less for a drier stuffing, more for a moister stuffing) and toss well.

3. Use mixture to stuff a 12- to 20-pound turkey. Or bake stuffing in a greased shallow baking pan, covered, at 325°F for 1 hour. Makes 12 to14 servings. Recipe can be halved.

Appetizer Mushroom Toasts

Make this quick hot appetizer in 15 minutes.

INGREDIENTS

4 slices	**Day-old bread, nonsweet type**
1½ tablespoons	**Olive or vegetable oil**
2 cups	**Chopped fresh mushrooms, any type**
¼ cup	**Finely chopped onion**
1 tablespoon	**Chopped fresh chives**
2	**Garlic cloves, minced**
½ teaspoon	**Crushed dried thyme or basil**
3 to 4 tablespoons	**Grated Parmesan or Romano cheese, or crumbled blue cheese**

1 Remove crusts from bread. Cut bread diagonally into quarters. Toast bread pieces on a baking sheet in a 350°F oven for 7 to 10 minutes or until golden brown, turning once halfway through the baking time. Set aside.

2 In a skillet, heat oil; sauté mushrooms with onion, chives, garlic, and thyme over medium-low heat for 5 minutes, or until liquid has cooked away. Mound mushroom mixture onto toast triangles; sprinkle with grated cheese. Return to the oven and bake for 7 to 9 minutes more, or until cheese is melted. Serve immediately. Makes 16 appetizers.

Brie Crostini

Crostini is an Italian gourmet treat.

INGREDIENTS

2 slices	**French or sourdough bread, quartered**
1 (2-ounce) wedge	**Brie or Camembert cheese**
4	**Strawberries, halved, or 8 walnut halves**

1. Remove crusts from bread, if desired. Cut bread diagonally into quarters. Toast bread pieces on a baking sheet in a 350°F oven for 7 to 10 minutes, or until golden brown, turning once halfway through the baking time.
2. Top each bread piece with a thin slice of cheese, and return to the oven for 3 to 4 minutes, until melted.
3. Garnish each crostini with a strawberry half or a whole walnut. Serve immediately. Makes 8 crostini.

Asparagus Pâté Rafts

These are easy and quite elegant looking. Keep a can of good-quality pâté on hand, or buy some at your supermarket deli.

INGREDIENTS

1 pound	**Fresh asparagus spears**
5 slices	**Day-old bread, nonsweet type**
2 tablespoons	**Butter or margarine, softened**
1 (4-4.5-ounce) can	**Pâté, any type**

1. Break off the bottom inch of each asparagus spear and discard. Cut spears into 2-inch pieces. Steam asparagus over simmering water for 5 minutes; drain.
2. Remove crusts from bread. Toast bread slices until golden; cut diagonally into quarters. Spread bread pieces with butter or margarine; arrange on a serving tray.
3. Spread pâté on each bread piece; arrange 2 pieces of asparagus on each piece. Serve immediately. Makes 20 appetizers.

Apricot-Nut Stuffing

This stuffing is nice with pork or Cornish hens.

INGREDIENTS

3 tablespoons	**Butter or margarine**
1½ cups	**Chopped dried apricots**
½ cup	**Chopped walnuts or pecans**
½ cup	**Diced celery**
⅓ cup	**Sliced green onions**
6 cups	**Dry bread cubes or Homemade Croutons (page 244)**
¼ cup	**Raisins**
½ teaspoon	**Salt**
½ teaspoon	**Ground allspice**
¼ cup	**Orange juice**
¼ to ½ cup	**Chicken or vegetable broth**

1 In a large skillet, melt butter; sauté apricots with nuts, celery, and green onions for 5 minutes over medium-low heat, stirring frequently.

2 Place croutons in a large bowl. Add sautéed apricot mixture, raisins, and seasonings; toss well. Drizzle orange juice and enough broth to moisten mixture as desired, tossing well.

3 Use to stuff poultry, or bake, covered, in a greased shallow baking dish in a 325°F oven for 30 to 35 minutes. Serves 6 to 8.

Toasted Baguette Niçoise

Here's a nifty French-style pizza or a spur-of-the-moment snack or hors d'oeuvre.

INGREDIENTS

Half loaf	**French baguette bread, or 6 slices leftover white or whole-grain bread, nonsweet type**
1 tablespoon	**Olive or vegetable oil**
1	**Red, yellow, or green bell pepper, seeded and cut into julienne strips**
3	**Shallots, peeled and sliced, or 3/4 cup sliced onion**
1	**Garlic clove, finely chopped**
1/2 cup	**Sliced ripe olives**
1 (2-ounce) can	**Anchovies, well drained and cut up (optional)**
1/2 to 3/4 cup	**Shredded mozzarella cheese**

1 Cut baguette crosswise into 1-inch pieces; place cut side down on an ungreased baking sheet. (If using regular bread, halve bread slices diagonally.) Toast bread pieces in a 350°F oven for 7 to 10 minutes or until golden brown, turning once halfway through the baking time. Remove from oven and preheat broiler.

2 Heat oil in a large skillet; sauté bell pepper with shallots and garlic for 3 minutes, stirring frequently, until vegetables are tender but not brown. Spoon mixture onto toast pieces; sprinkle with sliced olives, anchovies if desired, and cheese.

3 Place pan under broiler about 4 inches from heat, and broil just until cheese is melted. Serve immediately. Makes about 16 slices.

Orange French Toast

Serve this easy breakfast toast topped with fresh berries or slices of peeled orange.

INGREDIENTS

2	**Eggs**
2 tablespoons	**Milk**
2 tablespoons	**Orange juice**
1 teaspoon	**Grated orange peel**
Dash	**Ground nutmeg**
1 to 2 tablespoons	**Butter or margarine**
4 slices	**Sourdough, French, or sweet bread**

GARNISH

Sliced fresh strawberries, or fresh blueberries or raspberries, or peeled orange slices

1. In a shallow bowl, whisk together eggs, milk, orange juice, orange peel, and nutmeg until blended.

2. Melt butter in a large skillet. With a fork, dip each bread slice into egg mixture to coat well on both sides, allowing excess batter to drip off. Transfer to skillet. Sauté bread slices about 2 minutes on each side over medium heat, until golden brown. Serve hot with fresh fruit. Makes 2 servings.

Baking Tips

Sautéed Fruit Toppers

Sautéed fruit makes a lovely, sophisticated topper for French toast. Melt a tablespoon or two of butter in a skillet, and sauté sliced apples, pears, peaches, or bananas for 3 to 5 minutes, or just until tender. You can also sauté sliced oranges or strawberries, but use medium-low heat, for just 2 minutes, tops. Sprinkle cooked fruit with a bit of Cinnamon Sugar (page 206).

Chocolate French Toast

If you've tried one of the chocolate sweet breads in Chapter 4, save a few slices to make this French toast for chocoholics!

INGREDIENTS

2	**Eggs**
¼ cup	**Milk**
1 teaspoon	**Vanilla extract**
Dash	**Ground cinnamon**
1 to 2 tablespoons	**Butter or margarine**
4 slices	**Chocolate sweet bread**

GARNISH

Sifted confectioners' sugar
Sliced strawberries or sliced bananas

1 In a shallow bowl, whisk together eggs, milk, vanilla, and cinnamon until blended.

2 Melt butter in a large skillet. With a fork, dip each bread slice into egg mixture to coat well on both sides, allowing excess batter to drip off. Transfer to skillet. Sauté bread slices about 2 minutes on each side over medium heat, until golden brown. Serve hot topped with confectioners' sugar and fresh fruit. Makes 2 servings.

Baking Tips

Egg Substitutes

Pasteurized egg substitutes, such as EggBeaters, can be substituted for the eggs called for in recipes in this book. One egg is equivalent to ¼ cup of the egg product. For example, you could substitute ½ cup of the egg product for the 2 eggs called for in the recipe above. There won't be any noticeable difference.

Shrimp and Asparagus Brunch Strata

I adapted this recipe from one that my friend Pam Scott shared with me. Start this the night before.

INGREDIENTS	
1½ tablespoons	**Butter or margarine**
1 cup	**Sliced yellow onion**
1 (9-ounce) package	**Frozen cut asparagus, thawed and well drained**
6 slices	**Sourdough, white, herb, or cheese bread**
½ pound	**Small cooked (bay) shrimp**
1½ cups	**Shredded Swiss cheese**
1 tablespoon	**Chopped fresh dill**
4	**Eggs**
1½ cups	**Milk**
1 teaspoon	**Salt**
¼ teaspoon	**Cracked black peppercorns**

1 Begin this dish about 4½ hours ahead or the night before you plan to serve it. Spray a 9x9x2-inch or a 12x8x2-inch baking dish with aerosol cooking spray. In a large skillet, melt the butter; sauté the onion and asparagus over medium heat for 3 to 5 minutes, or until vegetables are tender but not brown. Remove from heat.

2 Remove crusts from bread; halve bread slices diagonally. Arrange half the bread slices in prepared baking dish. Spoon half the asparagus mixture over bread, spreading evenly. Top with half the shrimp, cheese, and dill. Repeat layers.

3 Whisk together eggs, milk, salt, and pepper until blended. Pour mixture over bread, saturating it. Cover baking dish and refrigerate 4 hours or overnight.

4 Uncover and bake in a preheated 350°F oven for 50 to 60 minutes or until set. Let stand 5 minutes; cut into squares. Makes 6 servings.

Canadian Bacon and Broccoli-Cheese Strata

Once you make this strata, you'll find it not only a good use for day-old bread but also a great brunch or lunch dish.

INGREDIENTS	
4 cups	**Cubed bread, any nonsweet type (3 to 4 slices bread)**
1 (10-ounce) package	**Frozen chopped broccoli, thawed and well drained**
1 cup	**Diced Canadian bacon, ham, or cooked chicken or turkey**
1 cup	**Shredded cheddar or mozzarella cheese**
3	**Eggs**
1⅔ cups	**Milk**
1 tablespoon	**Dijon mustard**
½ teaspoon	**Salt**
½ teaspoon	**Paprika**
3 tablespoons	**Grated Parmesan or Romano cheese**

1. Begin this dish about 4½ hours ahead or the night before you plan to serve it. Spray a 9x9x2-inch or 8x8x2-inch baking pan with aerosol cooking spray. Sprinkle bread cubes in bottom of pan. Sprinkle broccoli, Canadian bacon, and cheddar cheese evenly over bread cubes.

2. Whisk together eggs, milk, mustard, salt, and paprika until well blended. Pour evenly over ingredients in pan. Cover pan and refrigerate 4 hours or overnight.

3. To bake, uncover and sprinkle Parmesan cheese over the top. Bake in a preheated 350°F oven for 35 to 40 minutes, or until set. Let stand 5 minutes; cut into squares. Makes 6 servings.

Strata Mexicana

If you like spicy food, add bottled hot pepper sauce to taste or one or two finely chopped jalapeños to the mild green chiles. This recipe is mildly spicy. Olé!

INGREDIENTS

6 slices	**Cheese, sourdough, or onion bread**
1 ½ cups	**Shredded Monterey jack or cheddar cheese, or a combination**
½ cup	**Drained sliced ripe olives**
¼ cup or to taste	**Drained canned diced green chiles**
¼ cup	**Chopped green onions**
4	**Eggs**
1⅔ cups	**Milk**
½ teaspoon	**Salt**
¼ to ½ teaspoon	**Bottled hot pepper sauce**

GARNISH

Prepared salsa, avocado slices, dollops of dairy sour cream

1. Begin this dish about 4½ hours ahead or the night before you plan to serve it. Spray a 9-inch round pie pan with aerosol cooking spray. Remove crusts from bread; halve bread slices diagonally. Arrange half the slices in the pan, cutting to fit, if necessary.

2. Sprinkle the cheese, olives, chiles, and green onions evenly over bread. Arrange remaining bread slices over filling, cutting to fit, if necessary.

3. Whisk together the eggs, milk, salt, and hot pepper sauce. Pour egg mixture evenly over bread in pan to saturate it. Cover and refrigerate 4 hours or overnight.

4. Uncover and bake in a preheated 350°F oven for 50 to 60 minutes, or until set. Let stand 5 minutes; cut into squares. Serve with garnishes. Makes 6 servings.

Chocolate Bread Pudding

Make this with leftover chocolate bread, sweet, nut, or French. See chocolate bread recipes (pages 89-94).

INGREDIENTS

5 cups	**Cubed dry bread, such as chocolate, any sweet bread, French, sourdough, or white bread**
1/4 cup	**Butter or margarine, melted**
1 cup	**Semisweet chocolate chips**
3	**Eggs**
2 cups	**Milk**
1/4 cup	**Sugar**
2 teaspoons	**Vanilla extract**
1/3 cup	**Slivered almonds or chopped walnuts or pecans**
	Kahlua Custard Sauce (recipe below)

KAHLUA CUSTARD SAUCE

In a heavy saucepan, whisk together 1 egg, 1 3/4 cups milk, 1/4 cup sugar, and a dash of salt. Cook over medium heat, whisking constantly, until mixture forms bubbles around sides of pan. Remove from heat. In a small bowl, stir together 1/4 cup milk and 2 tablespoons cornstarch; whisk into hot mixture. Return pan to heat; cook and stir over medium heat until mixture thickens and bubbles. Remove from heat; stir in 2 to 3 tablespoons Kahlua to taste, or substitute 1 teaspoon vanilla. Serve warm or cool. Cover and refrigerate leftovers. Makes about 2 cups.

1. Preheat oven to 350°F. Spray an 8x8x2-inch baking dish with aerosol cooking spray. Sprinkle bread cubes in the bottom of the baking dish. Drizzle melted butter over bread. Sprinkle chocolate chips over bread.

2. Whisk together eggs, milk, sugar, and vanilla until sugar is dissolved. Pour mixture evenly over bread cubes. Sprinkle the almonds over the top. Let stand 10 minutes to absorb egg mixture.

3. Bake pudding, uncovered, for 35 to 40 minutes or until set. Serve warm or cool with Kahlua Custard Sauce. Cover and refrigerate any leftovers. Makes 6 servings.

Index